THE MAPS
THEY GAVE US

THE MAPS THEY GAVE US

ONE MARRIAGE REIMAGINED

WAYNE SCOTT

BLACK LAWRENCE PRESS

Black Lawrence Press

Executive Editor: Diane Goettel

Interior Design: Zoe Norvell

Cover Artwork: "Lovers Asleep" by Jelena Djokic

Copyright © Wayne Scott

2025

ISBN: 978-1-62557-154-0

Published 2025 by Black Lawrence Press.

Printed in the United States.

The rules break like a thermometer,
quicksilver spills across the charted systems,
we're out in a country that has no language
no laws, we're chasing the raven and the wren
through gorges unexplored since dawn
whatever we do together is pure invention
the maps they gave us were out of date
by years...

ADRIENNE RICH,
"Twenty-One Love Poems"

TABLE OF CONTENTS

AUTHOR'S NOTE

—

To write this memoir, I drew from journals, emails, photo albums, social media posts, and recollections of friends and family, even my children as they grew older. I researched the plants, trees, rivers, lakes, forests, and mountains, revisiting them many times. I changed the names of most people unless I had permission to use their real names. A few characters are composites.

All story-telling draws on imagination and emotions, which have their own kind of truth and their own kind of imperfection, and I drew on both freely to recreate episodes in my life where memory alone would not have been enough.

NOT HOLDING HANDS ON SOUTHEAST DIVISION STREET

It is odd that to get a divorce you tread together down the same path: you walk next to each other as usual, you negotiate the details. (Who will drive? Will we grab coffees beforehand? Will we be on time?) You sit in the car and then in the beige-white-cream waiting room, as you have waited for so many things in your lives, sometimes holding hands, but not today, no hand-holding today, not on your way to get a divorce.

It is odd that to get a divorce you walk side by side to a common destination. The weight of memory colors the trek with flashes of other tandem journeys (first visit to the pediatrician, new infant in tow; mountain hikes through fields of yellow balsam roots and purple lupines, toddler in backpack, baby in sling; a wait in line to see the Indigo Girls for the tenth time). The heaviness of it presses down, overwhelms you, make you breathless, because today there is a jaggedness to your emotions; wisps of conversation that don't feel ordinary despite their ordinariness. (Did you tell the babysitter when we'd be home? Was there enough bread for the kids' lunches?) The silences in between, loaded with sentences too painful to speak, foreshadow an apartness, when you will be just yourself, and all the memories of the ordinary things of your togetherness will be tucked into albums, dusty, in a shadowy part of some place where you will live that you cannot yet imagine; the past and not the present and not the future.

The documents of the thing that failed.

It is odd that to get a divorce you ask each other questions, similar to other times you've figured out things together. (How many blankets do you put over an infant for a walk in December? What's the best way to part with a panicky kindergartner? Is it time to get a vasectomy?) But the questions today are about things you never imagined doing. (Did the mediator say the appointment was for nine o'clock? How many meetings will it take until we're done?)

It is odd.

Derived from Old Norse, *odde*, the word originally referred to any number, like three, that follows an even number. (We have an odd number of children. We will be an odd number of people sitting in the mediator's office.) In the late Renaissance, it shifted to mean strange or peculiar, lacking the symmetry of an even-numbered pair: "the odd man out."

After the divorce I will be odd.

Of course, that Saturday morning we arrive insanely early for our meeting with the mediator. (You don't want to be late to get divorced.) We have to decide what to do with ourselves for half an hour. It is February, the grayest month in Portland, Oregon, when warmth and sunlight are the stuff of bitter nostalgia, and everyone is plodding and suffering and waiting for the season to change, but it won't anytime soon.

I park the dirty blue minivan on Southeast Division Street, glancing back at the three car seats, a tattered copy of *Harry Potter and the Half-Blood Prince* splayed on the floor. I don't know whether Rosie or Louis is reading it. The food carts are shuttered and the restaurants are closed.

Here and there someone peeks out of a coffeeshop to flip the OPEN/ CLOSED sign or to arrange chairs and café tables on the sidewalk. In the distant haze, bathed in the pink light of morning, Mount Hood looms, a pastel smudge on a blue canvas, barely believable.

Eva has those high cheekbones, that tilted nose, green eyes that crinkle when she smiles. But she is not smiling. The scooped neck of her cream-colored peasant blouse shows her strong collarbone. Like me, she is forty-three. She looks away when she asks, "Linné does both marital counseling and mediation, right?"

"Yes."

"But the fees are different?"

"It's $220 for mediation and $150 for couple's therapy—"

"Oh my god, that's expensive."

"Mediation means more work for her," I say. "There are agreements she has to draft."

"But we *are* doing mediation," she interjects. She stares hard at the dashboard.

"We need to clarify that with Linné," I say, heart pounding, timpani-like, against my chest.

Maybe she notices my hurt look. "We are doing mediation," she says, more gently. Even when she is furious, she attends to me. "And it'll be OK."

I am mostly silent during this journey. I have been exposed as a bad husband. I have accepted a new identity as the father-in-exile living at a dingy studio—no furniture, no heat—seven blocks from the family home in northeast Portland.

I used to be a more interesting person.

How did I become this cliché? The philandering husband kicked out of the house by his wife. How is it when the man is kicked out, he does as he is told? I could have refused to go. I could have slept on the couch. But that awful night I did not question anything. The words repeat, an endless loop in my mind:

Get.

Out.

Now.

In the conventions of marriage, there are good husbands and bad husbands; keepers and exiles; mensches and schmucks. I have been pretending to be a good husband. But because I accept the dark anti-order of things, the way things unravel; because we are married, and I have strayed: I left and now we must divorce.

Because I am a deadbeat.

Because I am nobody.

I am supposed to leave.

A few days after I moved out of the house in the dead of night, I push myself, pale and shaking, to attend a work conference, and I run into Linné. We are both social workers in a small town, and we distantly know each other. The pressure behind my eyes is a dam holding back a flood. I know she is a family therapist, I have heard she is magic, and I am suggestible, especially when miserable. We are desperate for help, but I don't know how to bring it up in this stiff environment.

Linné has long, thick, gray hair; a compact build that moves efficiently; elite degrees from Smith, Stanford, and Berkeley; a huge heart that's evident to anyone who comes within five feet of her; and a frankness and softness in the way she meets my eyes.

After some professional banter, I ask, "Do you still do mediation and couples therapy—"

"I do."

"—because my wife and I are separated."

Then everything shifts. Her face falls. Her eyes become moist. "Oh, honey, I'm so sorry."

Suddenly I am "honey." I feel hugged. I want to tell her more, but I don't know the words to say it. I wish there was a label, an identity shorthand that feels right, that would ease this coming out, save me from telling the shameful truth. But there is no simple label for me. Finally, I ask, "Have you seen the show 'Will and Grace'?"

She smiles, a well of joy in her face. "Oh sure, I love that show!"

"Well, we're 'Will and Grace' with kids and cats and a mortgage."

"I understand," she says. "I work with many unconventional couples."

Later, I share her information with Eva, and we agree to get help from her.

When Linné sends a first email to both of us, with materials orienting us to how she works, the message begins "Hi Wayne, hi Eva," and I realize—the first sting of new language—that we are no longer "Wayne and Eva."

We go to a coffeeshop on Southeast Division Street. Eva sits down at an antique table with a graffiti-covered surface and pages through a newspaper, but I can tell she isn't reading.

I wait at the counter, then take our cups to the oak buffet with sugar, honey, and so many types of milk: almond, coconut, hemp, oat, and cow's. I know exactly how she likes her coffee: the dark color of a too-crisp chocolate chip cookie.

When I hand her the cup, she is staring out the window, at the sputter of traffic on wet black streets. These days we speak mostly in strained sentences that break off into sighs.

Out of nowhere, Eva says, "I thought we had fixed it, that we were better, when we saw John, after you had that affair five years ago."

"It wasn't really an affair. More of a hookup." I regret this response as soon as the word *hookup* slips out.

She bristles. She has not touched her coffee, even though it is perfect. "It was the same guy, over and over."

"He was just like me. He loved his wife. He was never going to leave her."

There is so much unsettled between us, remnants of the past where we've never seen eye-to-eye, left to simmer. We stare at the rain streaking the windowpanes.

"John did help us, at the time," I offer.

"Not enough."

"He never seemed comfortable talking about sexuality."

"Why didn't you bring it up then?"

"I don't know. You got so upset every time it came up. John seemed awkward. The kids were so young. They needed both of us. I just wanted us to get stable again for everyone's sake."

"That's no excuse."

The rain and wind are unrelenting. I don't know what to say. We fall into the same defeated silence. I am exhausted being myself.

I had had a sleepless night.

The first time I wake up it is two in the morning. My mind is buzzing, mulling over sex scandals, the kind that happen to married politicians and television evangelists and sports celebrities. They follow a formula. There is an affair, often conducted via the internet, that dark highway of the collective unconscious. Maybe there is an ugly dick pic. The news spills out, often because of sloppy computer use or misunderstanding about the public record of the exchanges. At first the man responds defensively, shocked, testing to see if he can still hide. When facts emerge, he shifts to a more contrite stance. He apologizes. He admits he is human. He asks for forgiveness. A minister stands nearby.

Another important part of the formula is the wife's promise to stick by him. At the news conference, she stands in the background, symbolically in the place she needs to be, to buffer her husband from the third element of a sex scandal.

The third part is contempt. Condemnation; never-ending criticism; jokes. How can well-spoken men in pin-striped suits, starched, blindingly white shirts, and perfectly knotted ties be undone by sexual desire? Why can't they control themselves? In the public chatter that is an essential element of the formula, no one mentions longing, loneliness, desperation, the invisible truths pulsing in the body.

I flop around on the mattress. It is losing air again. By dawn, I will be sleeping on the hard floor. At three, my mind wanders to old memories.

After the ceremony almost fifteen years ago, my mother, Grace, makes a toast. She wears a mint-green dress with a broad-brimmed sun hat, her hair is a bright blond, and her glasses have burgundy frames with jewels in the corners. ("Oh honey, that outfit *pops*," my friend Todd gushes, giving her an embrace.) She has never been afraid of color.

We are in the spacious windowed downstairs of Bishop Brent House on the South Side of Chicago. As undergraduates we nicknamed it "Bent House." There is not enough room for the ninety guests in the living room even though it sprawls over half the first floor of the Georgian mansion. Other guests, listening in, fill the kitchen and the sunroom and the front porch where a cool breeze blows on the hot July afternoon. Some sit on the stairwell that curls up to the second floor where my bedroom used to be. Guests separate into cohorts, cliques of people who knew each other from disconnected parts of our lives. (College, social work jobs, newspaper colleagues, fellow writers, my East coast family, Eva's family from northern Illinois and Texas.) My father is not here. My grandmother, his mother, boycotts in solidarity.

Eva wears a simple, straight, sleeveless lace sheath; a single strand of pearls with matching earrings; little make up; no veil; no bouquet. Everyone who sees her that day marvels that she, so conflicted about marriage, found a dress without any frills; appropriate to the occasion without really admitting to be an actual wedding dress. My suit, made of an ivory linen, matches.

Smiling mischievously, my mother begins with a gush, "When Wayne was in college, he hand-stitched the most gorgeous piece of embroidery."

There is a howl from the sunroom where some of my gay friends and former boyfriends cluster, then some giggling murmurings about embroidery. Other rooms are quiet, unaware of the irony. Eva's father and his wife shift in their seats. Had they missed a joke? They have already grudgingly accepted that I am an odd man who knows nothing about basketball or car parts or beer.

Grace's gaze moves around the room, beyond the hallway where others gather. "I still have it hanging above my mantel at home," she continues. "It has a passage from the writer Audre Lorde..."

There is a whispered rustling on the stairs where some of Eva's lesbian friends collect. "Audre!" "Oh, I love her!"

No one else knows who Audre Lorde is, and they are quiet.

> *I give the most strength to my children by being willing to look within myself, and by being honest with them about what I find there...*

"So I have to be honest, Wayne," my mother continues, looking down at me sitting on a chair. "I really didn't think you'd *ever* get married."

The sunroom erupts in hoots and laughter. Eva's father looks confused, as if he missed another joke. My grandmother, eighty-five, wrinkles her nose. She generally thinks the world lacks decorum. But it is a day for tolerance.

Grace shares warm words about me and Eva and how much she admires our relationship. We work together well. It is an egalitarian partnership. There is an implicit reference that only the women her age and older, my aunts and Eva's aunts, my grandmother and Eva's mother, nodding around the room, disappointed with their own husbands and ex-husbands, understand: *You are not your father or your uncle or your grandfather.*

She raises her glass of wine, and we all take a sip. I hug her.

It is a perfect toast, reflecting who we are together, an unconventional pairing between a straight, feminist woman and the queer man who fell in love with her.

Lying in my squishy bed the night before we begin the conversation about divorce, I realize with a pang that Grace could only reflect the whole of me by leaning on ironies and implied meanings that not everyone in the room grasped. This was the beginning of a kind of compartmentalization that protected Eva and me from judgment in the various worlds we frequented, around people we loved who we presumed would never understand our unique bond. It would get more rigid as the years passed.

We were taking a risk at the time, I know. But we had surmounted so many challenges in our first five years together. We understood each other better than anyone else. There was no one else but her for me—I had won a relationship lottery—but I also didn't know what lay ahead. No bride or groom did. But somehow everyone leapt into the future, unknown and uncertain, hoping. Even then, in the back of my head, I wondered: Would this compartmentalization be our undoing?

Linné's office is tucked in the back of a home on Southeast Division Street that's been converted into offices for therapists. The entrance is in the back, so we enter the side gate, feeling like intruders, walk back, plug the code into the door, and enter a waiting room. Linné emerges and leads us to her tiny office.

Eva sits in one upholstered chair and I face her in another just like it. Our knees are so close. I didn't know it was possible to be together comfortably in such a tight space, let alone divorce. Can this really be a space for couples who are furious at each other? It feels like we hold something in this three-legged stool of an arrangement: the spirit of our battered marriage, suspended over our three heads.

Linné squats between us, on a blue bouncy ball, and leans in close. She has intense focus. She looks almost like she might cry, and I wonder if this is what compassion looks like. "What brings you to me today?"

Eva sighs. "Wayne is gay. I've had enough. I want out."

Linné's gaze does not flinch although I am flinching as Eva's story, which is not mine, comes out.

"He had an affair. I found the email."

Affair. I don't say anything. Unknown to anyone except my friend Scott, I had sent an email to a man I found on a gay men's hookup site. He didn't respond which I thought was because of my age and lack of attractiveness. Really it doesn't matter. Everything comes across as defensiveness and that doesn't help. The bigger truth remains: for years I was straining within the definition of our marriage, hiding my unhappiness, unable to talk about revision. There had been other hook-ups.

The space between us is so close. I must be intentional, when I want to shift my leg, not to brush against Eva's. The air between us feels like an electrical field: all the untapped, inarticulate pain of our failure crashing down on the heads of me, her, and the three children who didn't ask for any of this; the charged anti-words, pockets of shame, if shame could come in a pure, heart-stopping, tribe-robbing form. Shame vibrates between us but in my imagination it absorbs into my body, encircling my lungs, squeezing me to death: an electric boa constrictor. Does she feel any piece of it? It is my shame, I tell myself.

I stare hard at the window, stray drops zig zag on the pane. I cannot look at Eva, afraid of the hardness and certainty that I will see in her expression. If I look at her, her rage will knock me over. But in this desperate moment, it is her I need. I need to look past the charged field of failure, to see her, maybe only to confirm that she really is, still, that furious.

So I steal a glance. She is not Medusa. Her hands are folded in her lap. Her tousled blond hair frames her face. Her green eyes become brighter when she is sad. She looks hurt, on the verge of tears. I sigh. She is still capable of surprising me.

Linné tells me that it's my turn to share. She coaches Eva—"listen to understand, not to respond"—and be prepared to summarize what she heard. Eva looks at her earnestly, avoiding my gaze.

"It's true I don't fit in this marriage," I say. I hate how the words sound. I am a man who is a traitor to his vows. "I wish I did. For Eva and the kids. For years I tried. In the beginning it was OK. We joked with friends about my past as a queer man, how amazing our love for each other must be if I had fallen for her. Then we moved twice—to Washington, DC, then Oregon—and then the kids—and we got farther and farther away from ourselves. I stopped telling people who I am, who I was. It seemed odd, displaced, a legacy that wasn't part of us anymore."

Linné stops me and asks Eva to say back what she heard, to check for understanding. Eva looks at me as if she might cry and shares what she heard. "Did I get that right?" she asks. She was always an A student. "Is there more?"

"When you tell people the story of what happened, you tell people I am 'gay.' It ignores my desire for you. That's real for me."

"You were hooking up with a man," she interrupts. The pang of rejection—her rejecting me, her feeling rejected—rises again. "You're confused. You need to decide what you are."

Linné puts her hand on Eva's arm. "For now, focus on listening to understand his story."

"It's true I was doing that," I say. "But all the people you've talked to—people in the neighborhood, our doctor, or relatives who never knew the whole story—assume that I came out late in life. I hate the looks of misplaced pity. Some people even congratulate me on coming out like it took bravery at my age."

How did I lose the story of who I was?

The funny joke we used to make about the queer man who fell in love with a woman became less funny over time. Questions hung uncomfortably in the background: What kind of odd marriage do you have? Well, what do you do with the gay part of yourself? Are you faithful? Are you honest? There were some gay men who interpreted the joke as a kind of implicit advertisement, a desperate reaching out that could only lead to trouble.

We are near the end of the session. We forget to clarify the fee. I will not raise the issue, because I do not want to hear the words "divorce" or "mediation." Outside the window the sky is an unrelenting swirl of grays. Linné shifts on the blue bouncy ball. "Any couple going through a transition will have different perspectives about their marriage," she tells us. Her voice is warm and matter-of-fact. "But it's important to find elements of the shared narrative. If you are going to tell your family and friends—and your children—what happened, it will go more smoothly if you have a common story. Otherwise people latch onto one or the other person's polarized version. They take sides, which isn't helpful."

Our challenge, she tells us, is to create a common story.

PART ONE

—

SHIFTING TECTONIC PLATES

*It was a while before we came to realize that our place was
the very house of difference rather the security
of any one particular difference.*
AUDRE LORDE, *Zami: A New Spelling of My Name*

1
—

THE DOOR WITH THE CROSS

Chicago, 1987

"Why is it called 'Bent House'?" I had asked on my first tour.

"Oh, you know," Todd said, flipping his wrist in a way that made me cringe. "*Bent.*" Like many gay men I knew, Todd's goal was to communicate gayness in every chatty sentence that escaped his mouth. Tall, with short brown hair and perfect teeth, he was a graduate student at the Art Institute. In exchange for a free room, he was House Manager.

A formidable four stories, with blood-red bricks, angles softened by harsh Midwestern seasons, and several chimneys, the Georgian mansion sat thirty feet back from Woodlawn Avenue, a tree-lined artery that ran through Chicago's South Side, in the same neighborhood where I attended college.

"Nasty British word for queer," he added.

"I get it."

"We're re-appropriating the epithet."

"I've heard of that."

Officially, it was called Bishop Brent House, the university's

Episcopal Center. In the well-lit basement there was a chapel; on the first floor a parlor, dining area, and industrial-sized kitchen; and on the upper floors, the priest's window-lined office and bedrooms for half a dozen students who enjoyed the big rooms and the low rent and the Friday afternoon Sherry Hours.

Todd's room was across the hall from mine. During the day, as he dusted with a red feather mop, Barbra Streisand echoed through the stairwells. He considered himself a radical political artist, like Keith Haring, drawing simple, dancing ink figures on the white-painted wainscoting.

Another resident, Larissa, a high-strung soprano, a graduate student in Music Performance, practiced by the grand piano in the parlor every evening, her voice trailing up the stairs. Twenty-year old Calhoun, lone, shy straight boy, Economics major, lived there because his parents knew Father Sam and they wanted their son to feel at home with another Southerner. They didn't grasp that Sam was gay and Calhoun, who neither liked to say the word *homosexual* nor to make eye contact with any of the eccentric residents, had never felt at home. Whether it was Larissa singing Puccini, Streisand screaming "Enough is Enough," or Todd belting out "It's Raining Men" in the shower, Calhoun cringed at the ubiquity of divas.

It was a very gay house.

Father Sam was short, dignified, and often churlish when he wasn't ridiculing either my lack of employment or Todd's post-modern graffiti. There was always a sermon due on Sunday, always funds to be raised to keep the ministry alive, always undergraduates to counsel. With the trace of a North Carolina drawl, he spoke in wise, looping sentences with impeccable diction. When he talked, he wove in epigrams from Oscar Wilde and Quentin Crisp and Dorothy Parker. He had strong opinions about how to brew afternoon tea.

Often, to tease him, I called him "Dad." He was constant and predictable. He was always in the house, in his office, walking the stairs and thinking about a sermon, sorting the mail, or receiving visitors. He didn't mind if I wandered into his office, across the hallway from my room, to chat or ask a question. When he greeted me or said goodbye, he kissed and hugged me.

Father Sam didn't judge. He was one of the only people who knew that, although publicly I was gay, I had a furtive interest in girls. I belonged to the campus Gay and Lesbian Association, GALA, an acronym that rolled off the tongue without any mention of bisexuals, about whom nearly everyone was skeptical. I wrote book and theater reviews for the city's gay and lesbian newspaper, *The Windy City Times*, a free weekly. The work paid almost nothing, but I loved the intimacy of writing within a tightknit community, where I knew so many of the readers. I craved bylines—sometimes two or three a week. Six months earlier I had graduated with a multidisciplinary degree in literature, history, and critical theory, and I suffered, ill-matched to a more practical world. On the monthly checks she sent to pay my rent, Grace wrote on sticky notes, "How's the job search?"

So everyone had a role. I was the resident frustrated writer and drifter and mostly closeted bisexual who passed as gay before the word queer was used in polite company. I wasn't Episcopalian either, but I liked visiting with Father Sam and going to Bent House's Friday afternoon Sherry Hours. "I'm Episcopalian in a cultural sense," I announced to him, sipping a glass of Amontillado.

"That's a load of horseshit," Sam said.

That January there was a rumor that fit perfectly with the tone of that time, just a few years into the crisis: Cass—the boyfriend I had broken up with three years earlier; my first real boyfriend, a museum docent ten years older than me; a man with whom I lived for a year, although I was overwhelmed by his intensity—had AIDS. From his history of sleeping around, even during our time as a couple, I had no reason to doubt this news.

Pressing a stethoscope to my heart and lungs, Dr. White said, "I'd be surprised if you have AIDS." An openly gay man, the go-to doctor for all the sexual minority men on campus, he was thin-shouldered, in his fifties, with thick glasses and a twitchy moustache. "This disease happens to men who are hard on their bodies, who have been sleeping around and doing drugs for years. That's not like you at all, is it?"

I was dressed in the nondescript uniform of the American college man: wrinkled khakis, a button-down blue oxford shirt, worn boat shoes, no socks. People always told me I looked "boyish." I hadn't brought him the chart I was making diagramming all my sexual liaisons. *That's not like you at all, is it?*

"I still want to get tested."

"Well, it won't be here. That wouldn't be a good idea."

"Why?"

"Here it would go in your medical chart," he said. "Even if it's negative—which I'm sure it will be—the fact that you requested a test would mean to insurers that you engage in high-risk behaviors. They'd discontinue your coverage."

"Where will I get tested?"

"I'm giving you the number of a free clinic that does anonymous testing. It takes three weeks."

"What?!?" I covered my mouth to cough. My throat was raw.

"There are a lot of people who want this test done. It's a new technology. There are false positives. If you have a positive test, they have to do another test to confirm."

"Why can't I get rid of this cough?"

"It's winter. People get sick. I'll give you an antibiotic." He walked me to the door, a fatherly hand on my shoulder. "Go to the free clinic and get tested and you'll feel better. You'll see I'm right."

I wondered if he was consciously lying or if he believed what he was saying.

Outside the sidewalks were slick and shiny. Dirty snow was piled high on the edges of the street. I coughed: an aggressive, involuntary drumbeat in my chest.

For the past six months, I had a boyfriend, Ivan, a first-generation Cuban-American with a square forehead, short, curly black hair, alert brown eyes, and high cheekbones. A rower, he was lean and strong; beautiful to look at and charming in cocktail banter; yet another art historian. After he and I found the free clinic and got our blood drawn, we walked home in the snow. We weren't saying anything, lost in our separate orbits of concern. Then I asked him, "Are you angry at me?"

"For what?"

"For making you that kind of man," I said.

"What kind of man?"

A man and woman, around our ages, holding hands, passed us. I felt like I needed to whisper. "You know, a pariah."

When Ivan and I first met, we bonded over our shared experience of being chronic teachers' pets, obsessively dutiful best-little-boy-in-the-world types who didn't care if other boys snickered, as long as our mothers gazed at us adoringly.

"That wouldn't make any sense," Ivan said. He took my hand, but I pulled away. Cass, the in-your-face activist, used to compel public displays of affection, often in situations where men jeered and harassed us, to press the point that he belonged wherever he went and that he would fight anyone. He would chastise me for cowardice if I pulled away. I still hated holding hands in public. "You didn't purposefully do anything."

"I guess I didn't." I didn't believe him.

The days passed with a gray numbness. I immersed myself in the mindless routine of sending off resumes, trying to imagine myself into the future, a job with steady pay. Hiding in my room at Bent House, I wrote in my journal, sometimes panicked, touched by the painful aliveness of one who believes he might be on the edge of his prematurely ended life. I gazed out the window, at the snow falling steadily, silently. Searching for some mooring, I read and re-read Audre Lorde's *The Cancer Journals*: "I was forced to look upon myself and my living with a harsh and urgent clarity." What would I do when I found out I was terminally ill? Would I still need to find a job? Would I return to my mother's place? I had only just started to be an adult.

Dr. White's prescription didn't help. During the day, I tried to suppress my cough. It was a deep, ominous rattling in my chest. I hadn't told anyone what was happening, but I was convinced they could see the truth on my pale face, hear it in my hacking cough. One afternoon Larissa rushed by me to practice in the parlor, no eye contact, with only a clipped hello. Todd seemed to avert his eyes, too busy even to exchange sarcastic barbs.

I couldn't wait for three weeks to know what was true.

Cass and I met at The Medici, a dark campus hang-out on 57th Street with wooden booths carved with decades of student graffiti. It had been three years since I saw him. I was struck by the tightness in his expression, the controlled way he forced a grin when I saw him through the restaurant window. His hair, always loaded with some new product, stood up like straw. He seemed thin. We had broken up because he needed to be with another formidable intellectual, like a professor, which I wanted so badly to become, and he needed to be with another Jewish man, but

I couldn't honestly say I wanted to convert. He was disappointed that I wasn't a gold star gay.

I was no longer the kid in need of cultural guidance, no longer a mind to be molded. I made a secret commitment to myself: *Do not cough.*

Cass smiled when I sat down. "You still look like such a teenager."

It's starting, I thought.

"I'm twenty-two now," I said. "Not a teenager. How have you been?"

"The dissertation's a bitch." He took a sip of his water, looking away and smiling, distracted by a raucous group of handsome undergraduate jocks sitting nearby. Cass assumed every man was potentially gay. "I've had three advisors, if you can believe it. No one wants to work with these topics. I have a radical way of seeing homoeroticism in Johns' work. The old guard isn't ready. Even in academia, there's virulent homophobia."

His familiar David and Goliath story, transported to the Ivory Tower. He was always worried about pushing the boundary too far and losing his funding.

The first time I met him, he lured me back to his apartment to show me some street art he collected. I had no idea it was a date—he was so much older than me—until he put his hand on my thigh. "Can I invite you to my bedroom?" he whispered in my ear, and I followed him, curious. "Can I fuck you?" he asked after we had been making out on the bed. "I've never done that before," I admitted. "I'm very good with virgins," he said, and I consented, and he was right. For the whole year our relationship lasted, I believed he was the one who was right about everything because I had so much to learn.

We placed our order for deep dish spinach pizza and root beer. I hid my face in my arm, coughing hard. *Shit.* My lungs ached.

"How've you been feeling," I asked, hoping he might stop talking about art. "Like, physically?"

He looked at me hard. "It's wearing me down," he said. "I expect real academics to be able to take in new ideas."

We made banter, but I was restless. He kept glancing at the raucous athletes and smiling. I couldn't eat my salad. "I heard something—"

"You heard what?"

The Medici was packed with young people eating and talking and laughing. The wait staff were running around frantically. "I heard you were sick. I heard"—I lowered my voice—"I heard you have AIDS."

"Who the hell told you that?"

"Ivan heard it from someone on campus. It isn't true?"

"That's a fucking load of shit!" he said. The jocks sitting at the next table were suddenly quiet, looking at him. "So *that's* why you wanted to get together?"

"I heard the news," I said, still whispering, "about the AIDS. I was scared."

"For God's sake, you didn't care about seeing *me*. You only cared about your own fucking self."

"When did you get it?"

"Whatever I have is my business. It's not something I'm broadcasting to you and all your little college buddies. For God's sake now I can remember exactly why we broke up. You haven't matured a bit, have you? Now you've fallen prey to conservative hysteria."

"I'm worried about people I've been with since you. Do I need to warn them? Should we all get tested?"

He looked at the ceiling furiously. "That test is a ploy to get gay men to self-identify so that insurance corporations can mark us for life, discontinue our insurance, and quarantine us onto some deserted island."

"Are you serious?"

"I'm outta here." He pulled out his wallet. "Wayne, when are you going to get hip to the fact that there's oppression? That not everyone is a privileged straight-passing white boy?" He slammed a few dollars down on the table.

Bewildered, I tried to apologize, unsure what I had done, but embarrassed at the spectacle. "But the pizza's not even here yet."

"You should be ashamed," Cass said. "If you pass on this nasty rumor, I swear to God you'll regret it."

I watched him walk away, saw the stiffness in his shoulders. And I knew the unspoken truths ensnaring him, choking him. The one I came for; the one I didn't think was possible for one so madly bold.

He had AIDS.

He was terrified.

"When will you be home?" I wrote on thin blue airmail paper later that night. Naomi had been my best friend since our first year of college when we were both cursed with classes that met at eight in the morning. Bleary-eyed, we noticed each other across a basement coffeeshop and started sitting together. We told friends she was the sister I never had. "I miss you," I scribbled. It wasn't the first time I'd asked about her plans, which kept changing. I was afraid she would think I was needy.

She had been working in a pub in London for five months. She didn't know what was happening with me because it wouldn't fit on a postcard, or even in a letter. It seemed like it should be kept secret, a despicable ugliness. She had never judged me. But what would she do when she found out I was the kind of man who got AIDS?

"Maybe summer," she wrote back eventually, unaware. It was a postcard of Buckingham Castle. "The tips are great, and I love the guys' accents!" I couldn't bring myself to tell her I was in a kind of crisis. I couldn't find the words to tell anyone, even my mother.

I waited. I fretted over the chart I had created of everyone I had slept with since Cass. It was a map of my undergraduate life, a journey through parties and dates and late nights trapped, bored and horny, in the library that stayed open and crowded until one in the morning. *How had the number gotten so high?* I listed all the old boyfriends and one-night stands, then all the boyfriends of boyfriends and their casual encounters. I winced when I wrote in Todd's name. He had a habit, late at night, if he knew I was alone in my room, of knocking on the door and asking, "Do you want to have sex?" I didn't have a word for what he was, but when he left less than thirty minutes later he was just the House Manager again. I charted a web of sexual relationships, annotated with as much gossip as I could recall: with whom I had had sex and with whom they had had sex, if I knew, and what I knew about each person's sexual practices. Did he have anal sex? Did he take poppers? Had he had other diseases?

Even on this private chart I noted the three women with initials, not names.

There was so much grief surrounding me, so many cut-offs, so many disappointed parents, so many outcast sons.

Jeff worked three part-time jobs to earn tuition money that his parents refused to pay after he came out. Tim's family had cut off all communication when they discovered he was dating a man, except to write pleading letters about all the girls back home. "You're an attractive, smart, young man," they wrote. "You could have any woman you wanted. Please don't throw it all away." Disowned by his family, Joseph was determined to finish college and paired up with a much older gay professor. They lived in an elegant high-rise by the lake—a nicer place than any of the rest of us inhabited—but no one knew what to say to him because his boyfriend was so old.

Jeff and Tim and Joseph believed that I was gay like them. Everyone else in GALA, except Father Sam, believed the same thing. To say one slept with women and men was to give ammunition to a prejudiced world. I did not want to betray my friends.

After calling half of the men and women on my list, to suggest they get tested for HIV as well, I let out a deep sigh and took a break. I looked at my reflection in the mirror: the dark circles under my eyes, the wrinkled brow, an itchy outbreak of acne, my blond hair unruly and unwashed. In the hallway, I checked mail. One unstamped envelope was addressed to "The Great White Brotherhood of the Iron Fist" with my name and address listed as the return address. I recognized the group's name. They had sent inflammatory letters to the campus newspaper, resenting what they saw as liberal coverage of South African apartheid. The anonymous members had also attached their group's name to posters on campus. "Death to Fags and Fag Lovers!" Inside the envelope the card pictured a skull and crossbones. At the bottom, someone had handwritten: *Happy Death!*

My hand started shaking. I tried to suppress the cough agitating in my chest. Only Ivan, the doctor, and the men and women I had called had any knowledge. How did anyone else know? "Todd!"

"I'm painting!"

"I need you."

In the parlor Todd was painting a canvas of dancing black figures, their bodies simple triangles. He looked at the card and winced. "Fuck," he said. "You need to tell Sam."

"Did you tell anyone about Cass?"

"Well, I certainly didn't tell the Great White Brotherhood!" he said, adding flippantly, "We hang out at different bars."

The disease was contagious on so many levels; its stigma traveled, multiplied, like out-of-control cancer cells. "I asked you not to tell *anyone.* Cass will be furious."

"Who gives a shit about Cass? He's an asshole."

"You're not the one he'll yell at!"

"What's going on?" Father Sam came down the stairs, holding a pencil, manuscript in his hand. "Boys, why are you arguing?"

"Wayne got a death threat."

Father Sam looked at the note, expression pained, then put a hand on my shoulder. He was of a generation when gay men spoke in codes and subtle cues, in a church that churned with controversy about its gay members. He was strong in who he was, but also discreet. "Pre-Stonewall" was the catty phrase my undergraduate friends whispered about older men like him. "Cowards who send a note like this aren't the kind who act on their threats," he offered. "They're scared, immature people."

"Why are they focusing on me?"

He put his arm around me, but I pulled away. I didn't want him to feel my body shaking. "You haven't done anything, son," he said. It was an ugly card; a scribbled piece of child's artwork; harmless as name-calling on the playground. Why couldn't I stop trembling? I still hadn't told Sam that I was waiting for my HIV test results—worried it would change how he saw me—although I longed for him, for anyone, to tell me it would be alright. "I'll ask campus security to keep an eye on the house."

Even before the card arrived, I had retreated from the world, withdrawing into my room, worrying. Now I withdrew even more deeply. I stopped writing for the newspaper. I didn't want anyone to see my name. I told *The Windy City Times* editor I was sick and needed a break. When I talked to him, I had a coughing fit and he grew quiet and didn't ask any questions. When I walked outside, on streets that once seemed friendly, I looked over my shoulder, wondering who had sent the card. I tried to smother the ache-burst of my cough, so no one could see me, the AIDS outcast. *Death to Fags and Fag Lovers.* I wanted to disappear. I did not understand how they could hate me so much.

In my hiding I had Audre Lorde. Under the covers I re-read *The Cancer Journals*, her diary of her struggle with breast cancer. I had a fantasy that she was the sole friend who understood. We were both sick together, although she was much sicker. She didn't mind my hacking cough just like I didn't mind that she refused to wear a prosthesis. We were queer together, we loved words, and the world, well, say it: the world despised us. The world who did not know us, who'd never even honestly talked with us, sent us hate mail. The world wanted us dead.

It was not just the men—stealth, stupid undergraduate bullies— who sent the death threats. It was all the fag- and dyke-hating people, all the name-calling middle school boys who grew up and became people with power. Leaders, politicians, presidents. *Fucking Reagan.* Men who could turn a blind eye toward AIDS victims, who could pretend there wasn't a higher incidence of lethal cancers in Black women, who could refuse to listen when we showed up for doctors' appointments. They could convince themselves we deserved to be ill and hated and ignored and forgotten.

But this was the marvel about Audre, friend in exile, who cuddled in bed with me—I even convinced myself the book was warm to the touch—while I waited for test results to confirm I too was ill with a fatal disease. Her words illuminated the darkness. "If I can look directly at my life and my death without flinching," she whispers to me, "I know there is nothing they can ever do to me again." Her words blazed across the night sky. She sang about the communities of women who came to her when she needed them, surrounded her with love, and I wondered, as always, about the inadequacies of men. Put a sensitive poet in an impossibly painful predicament, where she doubted she would live, except in words and poems and essay-bursts, and you'd get a survival genius. You'd get a stab of adrenalized brilliance that made you think you too could keep going.

I pulled out my journal and scribbled her words to hold onto them. Then I wondered, if I still hadn't told anyone except Ivan and Todd, who might also be infected, who would make a quilt panel for me.

A few days later, on a bitterly cold January morning, I went outside to fetch the snow-covered newspaper. When I turned back to the front door of Bent House, I caught sight of a marking. Something had been burned onto the honey-colored oak. At first I couldn't make sense of what it was.

The jagged sign, like blades on a destructive windmill, filled the width and height of the church door. The dark blue spray-paint was dry, indelible. It was a swastika. The door, original to the hundred-year-old house, was ruined.

Upstairs Todd was taking a shower. His tape deck was blasting Gloria Gaynor and he was singing. Normally I wouldn't intrude on him in the bathroom. I clicked the tape recorder off.

"Who's there?"

"It's me." I told him about the swastika.

"Oh, God." He turned the shower off. His hand reached out from behind the shower curtain for his towel.

"It's dark blue. Almost black." I don't know why the color mattered.

"Why is this happening?"

Father Sam alerted the police and campus security. He sent copies of the death threat to the Dean of Students, asking for assistance. Over the next week a half dozen gay and lesbian students received more death threats and someone plastered the signposts on campus with fliers declaring, "GAY = Got AIDS Yet?" and "Fight AIDS, Castrate All Gays." The University President published a letter in the newspaper, condemning the acts as "outrageous and cowardly." The story of the swastika made it into *The New York Times*, in a feature on the growing incidence of hate crimes on college campuses.

Father Sam wrote a letter to the university newspaper:

> *Inasmuch as this symbol has come to us without interpretation, we feel free to interpret it as we will...While the cross imposed may well have been intended as a swastika, the artist actually rendered a Cross Cramponee, being similar in design to the swastika, except that the returned arms are shorter. This shape derived from the Cross Potent, also known as the Jerusalem Cross, is so called because of its resemblance to an ancient crutch. It is, according to scholarly sources, 'a very fine form, and symbolic of the Savior's power to heal the diseases of...bodies and souls.'...*
>
> *The sign with which our doorpost has been smeared is ours now, and we accept it. We accept it and invite all who share our life and pass through our door to ponder it...We do not know for whom it was intended. Whether this sign be intended for one individual, it was placed on the door of a Christian house and thus belongs to us all. Even as some of our own ancestors bore innocently the yellow Star of David and the pink triangle, so we together bear this sign that those for whom it may have been intended may know they do not bear it alone.*

So there were crosses that looked like swastikas that were actually shaped more like crutches? And they represented the Christian power to heal the body? Neither convinced nor reassured, I stayed in bed under the covers as much as I could, reading and re-reading Audre Lorde. The sign on the door made me want to hide from the world even more, but now there was no place to hide, because my home was marked.

I waited and waited and waited.

To cope with the heaviness of it all, Ivan did the only thing he knew in situations ripe with misfortune: he threw a lively soiree for his art historian friends. No one was supposed to know we were waiting for our HIV results. "It'll bring the party down," he said, attaching Art Nouveau ornaments, dangling from silver rings, to wine goblets so that guests could distinguish their drinks.

The party talk was confined to art, books, and opinionated professors. I wandered through the group, occasionally taking up part of a conversation. Would I ever get passionately argumentative about Barthes? Did I care about the materiality of the frame? As some guests prepared to leave, I realized that I hadn't seen Ivan in almost half an hour. I made my way through the kitchen, through the hallway, to the living room and the sunroom. Had he stepped out to the liquor store?

When Todd announced that he couldn't wait any longer, I offered to fetch his coat. I opened the walk-in closet door and found Ivan with a red-faced undergraduate named Irv, their half-naked bodies intertwined.

"Wow," I said.

Irv pulled on his shirt and made a beeline for the door.

I didn't know what else to say. My face burned red. I could feel party-goers looking at me.

"Sorry about this," mumbled Ivan to the group of guests, mostly gay men, standing near the closet and smirking. He zipped his pants. "I should use the bathroom. My apologies, folks."

Not noticing who heard, I called after him, "I thought you weren't angry at me."

"I didn't think you'd care," he muttered.

"*You're* not being responsible," I said.

Ivan and I were young men caught in a liminal era, the sexual rules shifting too rapidly to comprehend. Talking about monogamy had never occurred to us as something people in relationships did. Four years into the pandemic, we were beginning to wonder about taking safe sex seriously—maybe it applied to us?—with different degrees of ambivalence. But the misery of waiting for my HIV test results had crystalized my feelings: I didn't want to take any chances anymore.

That night, I tried sleeping at his apartment, pretending nothing had happened, hurt and confused, but I couldn't. Was he putting me at risk? Was he another dangerous, lying man? Any lust between us seemed to have died. My back to him, I pressed myself to the wall, trying to get distance, so my coughing wouldn't shake him. But my cough worsened. He thrashed back and forth. It was as if we didn't fit together in the bed anymore.

Finally, I stood. "I should go. I'm keeping you awake."

"Come back," he said from the darkness. "I don't care about your cough."

"Now you really are lying."

Walking through the deserted streets after midnight, I rehearsed the litany of his faults. He didn't share his feelings, he didn't see my feelings, he was superficial, he avoided conflict, he was passive-aggressive. Without saying anything, while we waited for our test results, we had stopped having sex. The truth was, even though Ivan wanted to spend every free moment we had together, when I was with him, sometimes even when we were close, I felt empty and alone. Like he would never be enough.

I was marked with the sense of abandonment. I was done with him.

It was one o'clock when I finally arrived at Bent House. The lights were out and the building was shuttered and dark. The wind swept across my face like an icy comb. The sky was bright with stars. In the glow of the surrounding snow, I had an image of the angry, ignorant men (they must have been men) who crept up to the house after dark to mark it with their clumsy, poorly-researched swastika and in the same moment the voice of the doctor with his reassurances, so far above the ragged uncertainties of the time, and the noise of rampant gossip, and the unheroic acts of people I knew and from whom I wanted more. No one really knew what was happening. There was a terrified constriction of the common soul to which we all belonged—like we couldn't breathe, like there wasn't enough oxygen for everyone, all of us gasping to get air in our lungs, and we were scrambling to survive—that gave a hard meanness to everything.

Even though Bent House was my home, more my home than my mother's place, I was afraid, because I was coughing so hard, to go inside. I would ruin everyone's sleep. I would bring in the ugly taint of mortality.

A light snow was falling. As I trudged up the walkway, I noticed that the door with the swastika had been removed. Father Sam may have momentarily embraced the symbol, but he also hated ugly things. The new oak door had the same turn-of-the-century style, with carved panels and squares of leaded glass near the top. The surface had none of the blemishes that marked its predecessor. It appeared, to my weary mind, as if healed, insistent, risen above the hatred that had damaged it.

It was Sunday morning. In a few hours the believers would arrive. It was Lent, season of atonement and preparation. On the side of the house, a light flicked on. A yellow glow from his second-floor office spilled onto the snow. *Damn, his sermon's not done yet,* I thought, smiling.

> *We together bear this sign that those for whom it may have been intended may know they do not bear it alone.*

Then, for the first time, it occurred to me, a consolation that had been there all along: he must have been writing those words to me.

Not knowing what I would be told at the clinic a few days later, I walked through the unmarked drifts of snow toward that new door, the pariah returning home, each footstep a blue shadow on a white winter canvas.

2

THE SCENT OF HER

"Why does someone always bring a boom box?" I asked. On a bench spattered with bird droppings, three high schoolers were blasting "I Eat Cannibals" and watching undergraduate women in bathing suits focused on books. "I hate this song."

"It's not so bad," Naomi said and smiled, waving to a friend. She liked the noisy, rollicking scene at The Point: runners in nylon shorts whipping like flags, yellow Walkmans clipped to their waists; a group of cyclists in neon tights paused on the bike path, drinking water and comparing notes; couples cuddling on hidden-away rocks or eating croissants from the bakery on 57th Street. Three men in tank tops with skinny arms—to the relief of men with bodies like mine, the "fit waif" look was in—were tossing an orange frisbee on the grass. I remembered them from a class on Plato's *Republic*. Hot gusts interfered and it kept landing in the lake and one of them had to dive into the water by the NO SWIMMING sign.

That summer, Naomi and I spent most weekend afternoons on a man-made peninsula jutting into Lake Michigan, white-gray granite blocks stepping down to the waves. A mile from the center of campus, Promontory Point was vast. We could see The Shoreland, our old yellow brick dormitory, behind us.

Even in a crowded city it was possible to find a solitary perch, on the north-facing rocks, with a view of the Chicago skyline, mecca of ambition and industry far away, to lie on my towel, surrounded by books, and to gaze at the lapping of waves against the boulders, sun warm on my shoulders. Just twenty-three, I wanted to be alone with my books and my journal and the lake and soft guitar music, and I didn't want to be with anyone who reminded me that I needed to be somebody else.

Only weeks earlier the nurse at the free clinic, without looking at me, reported, "Your results are negative," as if it were the most ordinary sentence. Breathless in front of her, I never saw her eyes. As I exited the office, the next nervous young man filed in.

Everywhere gay men were disfigured by illness, bodies covered in purple bruises, racked by coughing.

Ivan was also HIV negative. Within days of getting the news, I officially broke up with him. For once I didn't have a boyfriend or a girlfriend or even a date scheduled. I was lonely but I didn't want to be with anyone. I was still rattled by what it meant to be alive. The future stretched out—the lake fading into the distant foggy horizon—impossible to see.

That afternoon Naomi and I both brought our books to the Point. I was lying on my stomach on a threadbare towel. Distantly, behind us, students chattered. Before us, swimmers sliced languid strokes through the water. I rotated tapes of k.d. lang, Tracy Chapman, and Suzanne Vega through my Walkman and pored over the "Twenty-one Love Poems" (which are actually twenty-two poems) in Adrienne Rich's *The Dream of a Common Language*. I wanted to understand their mysterious rhythms, to become the third intimate in this fiery, sexual, political partnership, the start of her lifelong relationship with writer Michelle Cliff.

After Naomi returned from her post-graduate backpacking trip in Europe, it seemed natural that she would share my room at Bent House. Her mattress was on the floor of the walk-in closet. Her mother worried she would be tainted and never find a good Jewish man. Naomi and I shared a common fascination with our classmates from New York City, the volume and lightning-like interruptions of their intellectual sparring—a marvel to witness, that quickened the breath, that made no room for anyone—while she and I spoke slowly, quietly. We wished we could keep up. We comforted each other when we could not.

Naomi had set up her towel and books a few feet away. She was sitting on a boulder, dangling her feet in the water, reading *The Golden Notebook*. Her thick brown hair was cut asymmetrically, so that it touched her shoulder on one side. She wore a black swimsuit with a generous skirt that covered her thighs. At her mother's cajoling, she was always trying a new diet. With her perfect heart-shaped face and wide, curious, brown eyes, I thought she was beautiful, although she was self-conscious about her size.

On my towel I could feel the roughness of the boulder through the cloth. The sun warmed my body. The breeze off the lake was soft on my shoulders. The page glowed. I wanted to inhabit the world of the poems, to live in their love story, cocooned in this Manhattan apartment away from the men who controlled the world.

> *...that the planetary nights are growing cold for those*
> *on the same journey, who want to touch*
> *one creature-traveler clear to the end;*
> *that without tenderness, we are in hell.*

It had never occurred to me that the gentleness of two humans touching could be an antidote to the too-rough realities of the world (in truth, at twenty-three, the brutality of the world was only just hitting me); that the endurance of a bond could be part of that comfort; that I wanted this thing called tenderness, which was so lacking with my boyfriends; that it was possible to see a woman's body without cruelty. I flipped in a new cassette and listened to Tracy Chapman sing "The Promise." Naomi moved back to her towel and her Walkman. "I might be ready to leave soon," she said. "Uh huh," I murmured, without looking up.

> *Did I ever walk the morning streets at twenty,*
> *My limbs streaming with a purer joy?*

It had never occurred to me that a relationship could be a source of buoyancy, sustaining against rocky tides and harsher realities. I gazed at the slate-gray lake, the fine wrinkles of waves touching the horizon.

There is that love poem she calls "floating poem, unnumbered," an outlier, without a roman numeral to signify its place, which I read and re-read, mesmerized, memorized, then re-read again.

> *Your traveled, generous thighs,*
> *Between which my face has come and come—*
> *The innocence and wisdom of the place my tongue has*
> *found there—*

It had never occurred to me that something as ordinary and animal as a tongue could discover something profound, that the body could be an instrument of knowing.

I gazed at the lake, turning the words over in my head. I wanted this tender joy. As long as I read the poems, there was this mysterious uncontrollable bodily response. Naomi was packing up her things. "Can we get going?" she asked. We had made plans to go to The Medici for pizza. "It's getting chilly."

Maybe it was the rough boulder against my body, or the sun on my naked shoulders, but really I think it was the poems. I couldn't get up from the towel, even to turn over on my back, because my dick was hard. I couldn't get it to go down.

"Can I join you later?"

"But we said we would go together. I'm getting hungry."

"Can I join you in half an hour?"

She was annoyed. "What difference will half an hour make?"

My dick was unbearably stiff. I wanted to shout: *Because my boner won't go away!* "Please just go, Naomi. I'll join you soon," I said.

Friends teased us that we were like an old married couple, always together, platonic confidantes. I was devoted to her but today I had no choice. Pursing her lips, she packed her books into her backpack, put on her jeans and blouse, and walked toward Hyde Park without me. I knew she was pissed.

In the moral universe of these beautiful almost-sonnets, I was pretty sure my boner was wrong, wrong, wrong. But it was also my secret, between my torso and the towel, only the rough granite palpable and judging. I tried to get myself to calm down. It's alright, I told myself, I didn't do anything wrong. It's just life in my body. The sun was low on the horizon, it was getting cold, and I was hungry.

Naomi and I moved to Chicago's North Side, to a small dark basement apartment with two real bedrooms. The plan was to go dancing. Earlier that week Naomi had seen her new friend Eva at the bus stop at the end of the street where we lived. They were both waiting for the #53 Sheridan to go downtown. I didn't know Eva well, but I knew of her from college dances and parties and classes. Naomi and I had taken "Feminist Theory and Practice," the first class of its kind at The University of Chicago, and Eva took the same class the next year. We all read Adrienne Rich, Hélène

Cixous, Alice Walker, Judith Herman, and Catherine MacIntosh. I was one of two men in the class.

Naomi was in the bathroom when the doorbell buzzed. "Will you let her in? I'm not ready yet."

Technically I wasn't dressed to go out either, in a white t-shirt and dirty jeans, but I thought I could get away with changing to a short-sleeve black button-down shirt. (Same dirty jeans, but the club would be dark and I would be sweaty anyway. Who notices pants?) I opened the door. An honest man, even the feminist sort, would admit he has a type, and mine was some amalgam of Bernadette Peters, Laura Dern, and glamorous old photos of my mother, from the years before she had a husband or children, wearing a luminous green bathing suit and tossing her sandy hair. Eva was wearing a polka dot black and pink tank-top and a short black skirt that clung to her lean frame. She had a canvas bag slung over her shoulder, a boxy pager clipped to the strap. She was tan, shoulder-length hair sun-streaked blond from a back-packing trip to Europe. She had high cheekbones, a bright smile, and wide green eyes. "Aren't you ready?" she asked.

I stared at her. The air left my lungs. My mind went dark. I leaned against the door to support myself.

"Don't you remember me?" she asked. "Seriously, Wayne?"

Looking sideways I pushed out the words, "Oh, yeah."

Was this what fainting felt like?

"I'm Eva," she said, smiling, tilting her head.

"I know, I know," I said. "Naomi's getting ready." I stole a glance at her again, to see if I could get back to normal, but the sight of her (those cheekbones, the strong collarbone, that narrow waist)... I knew that the polite thing to do was to look at her like a friend might, eye to eye, but I couldn't bring myself to do it, as if that first sight of her had weakened me enough.

"Can I come in then?"

"Oh yeah."

By the time we got back to the apartment, Naomi was dressed and they started talking. I retreated to my bedroom, to breathe and change my shirt. (*Fuck,* I thought, *am I getting sick? But I want to go dancing!*) Naomi was in the market for a best friend and Eva was a good candidate: smart, politically active, an earthy, warm look, the effect of frequent trips to the Goodwills in the trendy neighborhoods; so cool. Eva was a Board member at a non-profit called Rape Victim Advocates which required her, when she was on duty, to carry a pager clipped to her backpack. Everyone who knew Eva hated the pager.

When I emerged, they were talking about Adrienne Rich. As a member of the Women's Union in college, Eva had written, asking Rich to deliver a lecture on campus. The poet sent a typed postcard, apologizing that she couldn't make it without more notice. There was a signature in ink.

My heart thrilled. "I kind of worship her," I said. "I've read every book of her poetry. All of her essays."

"I read some of the essays, in that class we all took, but not much poetry," Eva said. "But I want to."

"I would buy that postcard from you," I offered.

"I am never parting with it." The crisp edge of her certainty: it startled me, pulled at me.

"You sure you won't consider?" I said. "I'd pay."

"No fucking way," she said and laughed. "You can come and visit it at my place."

All night, as we drank and danced in the dark, crowded club, Berlin, vibrating with Prince, Madonna, and The Pet Shop Boys, I couldn't look at Eva, not comfortably. Neither dancing nor drinking lessened it. Every glance brought up the same light-headedness. At first, I thought it was terror, but that didn't make any sense. She was just a girl from college. She was just someone Naomi was courting for friendship. She had nothing to do with me.

Later that night, lying in bed, hand on my balls, I felt the electricity humming in my center. The music still echoed in my body. My ability to reduce everything to language evaded me. Was it fear? Was it desire? The punched feeling had happened before with other girls, but not this scary and out-of-control. I had no answer to the questions, other than another question: had they, fear and desire, really been the same thing all along? What is the line between the things that frighten us, and curiosity, or adventure? Alone in my dark bedroom, stripped of my usual contingencies, allegiances, and rebellions, I let myself sit with the indecipherable feelings. My penis was so hard it hurt. I needed to beat off if I was ever going to sleep.

When I was a child, my family—mom and dad; Dean, Bruce and I, so close in age—lived in a short, narrow, brick townhouse at the top of a hill in a town called Toby Farms outside Philadelphia. There were two bathrooms for five people. One morning when I was ten years old, taking a break from Saturday morning cartoons, squeezing my crotch, having waited too long as I often did, I stormed up the stairs to find my younger brother Dean locked in the hallway bathroom. I dashed into my parents' room. My father was getting ready for the day. He was a handsome thirty-five-year-old man: blue eyes, perfect straight nose, muscular build, the easy confidence of someone accustomed to having the world handed to him. At his bureau with the beveled mirror, he was carefully combing the crest of his pompadour. About to explode, I barged into their bathroom. My mother, naked, was leaning over the tub. I had never seen her nude. Unaware of me, she stirred steamy bath water with her palm.

Closing the door, praying not to be seen, I turned, heart thumping like a trapped rabbit. My father noticed my shocked expression. "Did *you* see your mother's *heinie?*" he asked, smiling mischievously.

There were no words for my shock. It was one thing to accidentally intrude on her, but then to be mocked for it.

He loved to tease. "Did you see your mother's *heinie?*" he asked, louder, beaming at his joke, hoping she might hear. "Grace!" he shouted. He couldn't stop laughing. Was it my shocked expression or the violation of my mother's privacy? Was I the joke or was she the joke? *"Wayne just saw your heinie!"*

I don't know what my mother did, I couldn't wait to bolt from their bedroom, but she was used to him making remarks about her body, the weight she had gained after my brother was born. Sometimes he pinched her butt in front of us, to get us to laugh at her, the only woman in a family of men. Outnumbered. And now somehow, I felt complicit, as if he and I were together against her.

I ran to my bedroom and hid under the covers and tried to forget that I needed to pee. The pain in my bladder was punishing. A dribble of urine escaped on the sheets, but I didn't care. Humiliation was everywhere. I did not know if it was mine or hers or ours. It was all wrapped up in something I wanted nothing to do with: my father's mean-spirited gaze. Hiding under the sheets, as if the darkness might erase what had happened, I felt like I had betrayed her—I loved her so much, more than anything—even though I knew it was an accident. *If he thinks I'm on his side just because I'm a boy*, I thought, *he's wrong*. And I swore I would never betray her again.

Every week in the free newspaper called *The Chicago Reader* there was a cartoon called "Sylvia" by Nicole Hollander. A recurring character was "The Woman Who Blames Herself for Everything." Naomi and Eva's other friends agreed that this was Eva with her energetic volunteerism; her plunging into social justice work all hours of the day and night; a quickness to say "I'm sorry" when things went wrong, even things beyond her influence; her conviction that she wasn't doing enough, even though by the common estimate she was doing more than anyone else. It was hard not to feel lazy. The standard was merciless.

We both had crushes on her. Naomi saw her as her own brand of cool, mysterious and distant; even more cool, because she was not a New Yorker, but from the Midwest.

Eva was stuck in my head, an enigmatic song. I thought that she was more than "The Woman Who Blames Herself for Everything," bigger than a cartoon. In spite of the faintness of heart that came over me, I wanted to know her better. I couldn't parse all the centripetal forces sweeping us into each other's paths: my best friend wanted to be her best friend; she and I had both graduated from the same college, studying English literature and the Humanities, and we were looking to go into social work school at the same university; and we both loved our single mothers, who struggled against our fathers' bullying and angry entitlement. There was an irresistible pull to be near her body.

Naomi confided that Eva had asked her, "Why is he wanting to get together...?" and she had answered, "I think he's interested in you," and Eva replied, "But I thought he was gay?" and Naomi said, "Not all the time." I wanted to ask Eva on a date, it seemed like it should be a simple thing, but I was so naïve and undeserving and out of her league.

I did not understand women's bodies, all the hidden parts. At the age of twenty-four, my knowledge about sex was a checklist of accomplishments.

Blow job (get): *Check!*

Blow job (give): *Check!*

Heterosexual intercourse (fuck): *Check!*

Homosexual intercourse (get fucked): *Check!*

Cunnilingus:

I felt like I really should know more about women. I had only had two girlfriends, for short periods, and two one-night stands. I was behind most straight men my age. I knew there was an act called "going down." I liked the word "cunnilingus" better. It sounded more refined, like something you might do at a wine tasting. But I thought the Latinate word would make me sound affected before I even knew what it entailed, so I just used it in my head.

I knew that I loved getting blow jobs; all my gay male friends loved getting blow jobs; the majority of gay men I knew loved giving oral sex. But all of my girlfriends had only been interested in blow jobs out of what appeared to be a dragging sense of duty, like cleaning the toilet bowl.

And then there was how they felt about the business of going down. Natalie liked the formula of warm bodies pressing and cuddling and hugging and kissing, culminating in intercourse, mouths locked, eyes always closed. When one day I mentioned going down, since I assumed that that's what everyone wanted, she bit her lip and whispered, "OK," piously looking up and away like a saint about to be burned at the stake. As my mouth got closer to the mystery of it all she let out a sound. Was it disgust? Or panic? It wasn't anything good in this world. I gave up.

With Lisa, I didn't get that close. When my kisses traveled downwards, past her breasts and her belly, curiosity building, I could feel her body tighten.

"Please," she said. "Not that."

That fall I moved back to the university on the South Side, six miles away, to go back to graduate school. I invited Eva, just by herself, to come for dinner at The Medici. No alumni could resist the lure of their signature dessert, Never on a Sundae (French vanilla ice cream, brandy sauce, and chocolate shavings). I told her we could watch a movie back at my studio afterwards.

Inviting someone without a car who lived on the North Side of the city to come to South Side on a weekend evening had a subtext. In 1988, the city was dangerous, assaults were frequent, late-night travel was especially fraught, and the #6 Jeffrey, the safest route running north and south, following a path along the lake to downtown, stopped running after six o'clock. Every other person I knew had a story about being mugged or assaulted and it felt like we were all just waiting for our turn. Anyone stranded on the South Side on a Saturday evening would have to pay exorbitant cab fair or spend the night with a friend.

Neither of us mentioned this complication.

We met at the restaurant, bustling with Saturday evening revelry. Eva had her backpack with the pager attached. She wore a sun dress with a yellow geometric pattern and a light crocheted green sweater. "What movie did you get?" she asked.

"Have you seen *Cabaret*?"

"That's a ... musical?" I could see her suppressing a sour expression.

"With Liza Minelli," I said. We were splitting a deep-dish spinach pizza. "Based on the Christopher Isherwood novel. About Nazi Germany leading up to the war."

"Oh," she said. The sound hung hollow in the air.

"There's no violence or war scenes," I reassured her. "It's more metaphoric."

"It's not that," she said, taking another bite. "Generally I don't like musicals."

"Really." My "really" had the same vacant echo as her "oh." It had never occurred to me that someone could be apathetic about musicals.

"I'm sorry," she offered smiling. "I'll try. Maybe I'm wrong about this one."

During dinner I resisted mentioning the postcard again, even though I still wanted it.

We returned to the studio. "Oh wow," Eva said, then corrected herself. "I mean, this is cozy!" There was no couch, not even a love seat, only a double bed in front of a television with a videocassette player. The window had a view of the moon over The Point. "I guess I'll just sit on the bed?"

"That's the only option," I said, feeling sheepish. "I'm sorry."

"I'll be fine," she said smiling.

I had seen *Cabaret* many times. In spite of herself she might have enjoyed Liza Minelli singing "Maybe This Time." But by the time Joel Grey sang "If You Could See Her" to the gorilla in a dress, she was trying to conceal her yawning. Eva leaned her body into mine. My arm draped around her. My favorite line is close to the film's end. There is a wealthy playboy named Max who latches onto both Sally Bowles and the waspy Brian Roberts early in their flirtation. At one point a jealous Brian yells at Sally, "Screw Maximillian!" and she confesses, "I do," and Brian smirks and, without missing a beat, says, "So do I."

Eva put her hand on my chest. It was clear we weren't going to make it that far in the film. I turned off the video. My breath quickened, but this time I knew it wasn't fear. Her hand moved gently to my thigh and she knew I was hard.

That night, in the semi-darkness, Eva and I kissed and held each other, mammals cuddled in a forest den, and my kisses moved down her body, and she made soft noises. For a long time, I lay with my head on her thigh, breathing in the salty sweet smell, considering. She did not flinch. The scent of her traveled into my body, filled my brain, overwhelmed my senses, awakening some unknown force, a kind of remembering, although there was no memory. It wasn't fear anymore. It was an urgency sweeping through my body. I wanted to kiss her in that place that I didn't understand.

My mouth moved closer. Innocence. Wisdom. The scent grew stronger. It scrambled any sense of who I was. I was not an identity. I was a body tensed with an untamed current.

At first it was a soft kiss, then a deeper one, then when no one asked me to stop, I heard a murmuring like quiet joy, my tongue swept along fleshy, warm folds, and I knew it was her desire I was touching, more real than anything she could ever say about who she was. I reached up and held her hand. She made the soft sound again. I touched my mouth to the place, the pearl-center of her, small, hidden, like a secret that I might never have discovered if I had been rushed, but I didn't rush.

"Is it OK?"

"Yes," she said on the edge of a breath.

I stayed there. Any sense of time was erased. I did not want to leave, ever. Then I said, "Wow," and she giggled. "What?"

I didn't say anything. I didn't want to kill the delicious scrambling sense of awe. This wasn't an item on a checklist. Suddenly I felt a deep shame that there had ever been a checklist. The checklist evaporated into embarrassed memory.

Between my overnight dates with Eva, I didn't wash my left hand, the non-dominant one, so it could hold the secret. That December, wandering the campus, studying in the library, and going to classes, I discovered I could get through the day without using my left hand, without picking up a pen or extending it to anyone. Mostly I kept it in my pocket. When no one was looking, I put my fingers to my nose. Like recollecting a beach vacation, I breathed in the memory of her, it filled my lungs, the scent traveled straight to my dick. The press of her embrace would come back, as if it were real, and I would harden.

The scent of her infused me. It overwhelmed and erased me. When it filled my nose and lungs and heart, I became some force outside of culture, outside of society, pure, a momentum rising in my body, from parts I didn't understand, with nothing to do with conscious, rational thought or ideology. I wasn't who I thought I was. I was an animal driven by smell. The secret surprise of it astonished me.

When I held my left hand to my nose, like I was about to sneeze, the world narrowed, any sense of time disappeared, and my whole being was swept back into that bedroom memory when my body was next to hers, our mouths touching, the press of her breasts against my chest, my mouth wandering. I was in an Adrienne Rich love poem.

> *Your traveled, generous thighs*
> *Between which my whole face has come and come—*

It became a ritual. Throughout the day I could steal a moment from whomever I was talking to or whatever task was deadening my consciousness, put my fingers to my nose, and I would be there, in bed with her, my head between her legs, my tongue on the soft, moist folds of her. The scent was overpowering—a private ocean of unknown depth, a coming together of her depths, my depths, all those parts of myself that I didn't know she could enliven.

The thing I loved most about the scent of her, so carefully hidden in my pocket for midday dream-breaks, was its power to humble me: You do not know who you are. *You have no fucking idea.* There is no identity inscribed in your cells. You are no received definition, no fixed idea of a human being, some capitalized adjective. Your tribe is not your tribe. You are deep and unknowable.

There is no politics which can stand in this mysterious place of dissembling.

It was a phone call, simple, short, and pointed. It happened three weeks after we started sleeping together. My mind was still whisked away in the heady rush of her. I was alone in my studio at The Shoreland, lying on the bed, reading a text book about reflective listening, and listening to Nina Simone. My eyes frequently strayed to the window and the view of The Point in the distance. But that evening Eva had been thinking, she said, an urgency took over, and she called.

"What's up?" I asked. I was going to see her in two days.

"I need to know something," she said. "I need to know what we are to each other."

"It's just been a few weeks," I said, stumbling. "Isn't that...too soon to know?"

"Not if we're sleeping together," she said. "I need to know what you're thinking."

"I guess I don't understand why we have to decide so quickly," I said. "Three weeks."

She took a deep breath. "If we're going to sleep together, I need you to be monogamous."

"Oh," I said. I didn't know what to think. In previous relationships, the topic had never come up. Definitely not with gay men. I thought back to my last night in Ivan's bed, before I knew my HIV results, when I had that cough, and I couldn't shake the image of him tumbling out of the closet with a naked, red-faced undergraduate. *We can't keep doing this,* I thought. *We're going to kill ourselves.* But I couldn't quite articulate the alternative.

Monogamy. What an idea.

"I'm not comfortable sleeping together anymore unless I know it's just the two of us."

Her assertion didn't seem demanding or rushed. It felt safe. It felt protected. It felt like the beginning of some kind of love. I wished it had occurred to me to say something to Ivan about why I was so uncomfortable with the way we did things. I gazed out the window. The moon glowed yellow in the indigo sky. A few streetlamps marked the path that led to The Point. It was deserted.

My body shivered with the thought of her. I put my hand to my nose but the scent of her was faint. "I guess...yes," I said.

Later that year we moved in together. We lived in a first-floor, one-bedroom apartment on the North Side of the city, on a street jammed with cabs and buses and pedestrian traffic. Halsey Street, teeming with gay bars and a noisy night life, bustled two blocks away. She placed the Adrienne Rich postcard in a pink porcelain frame on the fireplace mantel.

"Moving in together," she said one of our first nights in the apartment. She sat on the polished wood floor unpacking boxes of books. "It was really just about the postcard, right?"

"Well..."

"Now you can look at it every day."

I was reviewing Madonna's new book *Sex* for *The Windy City Times*. The book was ridiculously huge with an indestructible aluminum cover. It could not be hidden anywhere. Left on the floor it might slice open your toe. Even on a table under magazines and books it gleamed like Las Vegas. Everybody knew about it. It was filled with black-and-white photos of the rock star in various stages of undress, accompanied by porn actors and rap celebrities.

"I don't want that book in here," she said.

"Well, I didn't *buy* it. I'm just reviewing it!"

"I don't want to look at it. I don't want my friends to see it. This is my place too."

"But she's a gay icon," I said, paging through the book. I thought the pictures were shocking in a dumb, predictable way. "She's naked, yes, but it's stylized, like Mapplethorpe. Not oppressive."

"My father always kept pornography in his shop, hanging on the walls," Eva said. "It made me so uncomfortable as a teenager. When I asked him to get rid of it, he refused. Said it was *his* shop, *his* house. I never went down there again. Sometimes I would feel sick when I was in his house."

"It's not like that old gross *Playboy* porn. It's not meant to be taken literally."

When she was angry, she clenched her jaw and her eyes glared. "I don't give a fuck." It made my heart bang in my chest like a boy in trouble.

We called Naomi to arbitrate. We both agreed to let her decide. "I don't think I'd want it in my apartment either," Naomi said. "Sorry, Wayne."

I didn't know what to do anymore because I was right and they were wrong and Madonna had a pretty body. But I didn't want to be like Eva's father. I didn't want to be like my father. I wanted to be the best boyfriend in the world. I still published a review of the book—though I didn't bring a copy of that issue to the apartment—then I gave *Sex* to Ivan and his new lover. They kept it on the coffee table in their living room.

The following summer Eva and I were in the kitchen getting ready for a party. She was washing cremini mushrooms then slicing them on the wood cutting board, a hand-made gift from her father. At the stove I was stirring the roux, sweeping the butter and flour from side to side, then adding the hot milk, stirring and stirring. I loved the friends who were coming to this potluck: Sarah and Cassandra; Mary and Christa; Meg and Deb: all couples like us. All social workers or teachers or graduate students. All lesbians; not like us. Naomi had sent regrets. She had been dating a guy for several months—the perfect Jewish man, really; a lawyer who had gone to Yale—and he had broken it off, and she was devastated.

Eva wore a form-fitting pink top with a black skirt with generous folds that reached below her knees. Everything about her flowed. I kept looking for reasons to brush against her body, but she was concentrating on the recipe. Was I embarrassed that I, the special feminist boyfriend, loved having a partner who loved to cook? This was a small secret. I wondered if she was what Clarissa Dalloway would have been like, before the war, if Virginia Woolf had been writing about a twenty-three-year-old woman, not a woman of middle years. Eva was always hosting dinner parties, elaborate meals that required days of planning and preparation, with folksy women's music and more people than could comfortably fit the space, because it was too painful to think that anyone should feel left out. Just like the women in a Woolf novel, she expanded herself so far into the universe of people who needed her, sometimes I wondered what was left at her core, if it was there: small and hidden and embattled.

At one point after the guests arrived, outside Eva's hearing, Christa whispered in my ear, "You're *perfect* for her."

My face reddened. "Really?"

"She could never be with a typical straight man," Mary added.

Christa nodded. "Never. The last guy sometimes wore a dress for fun."

"Are you serious?"

"Campiest straight man ever."

"She really should have been a lesbian," Mary said, looking at Christa, who nodded. "She's a lesbian trapped in a straight woman's orientation."

"That makes you an honorary lesbian," Christa said.

"Is that a real thing?" I asked.

"Don't tell anyone I said it."

"Yeah, that doesn't sound right at all, Christa," Mary said.

Other friends arrived within a span of fifteen minutes and I circulated the long room that was both living and dining areas, filling wine glasses with Pouilly-Fuissé, the light lemony summer choice.

Sarah noticed Eva's pager on the counter and made a sour face. "Eva, are you really on call tonight? While we're having dinner?"

"I'm sorry," she answered, looking away as if embarrassed.

"Stop saying you're sorry!" Christa said exasperated.

"We're short on volunteers," Eva continued. She had been on call, it seemed, for weeks. A chorus of concerns followed, women's voices overlapping.

"You can't sustain this," Mary chimed in. "Not with graduate school as well. It's too much."

"I hate that pager. I can't think straight when it's in the room."

"Every time it goes off it means a woman got raped."

"I need a little bit of denial on the weekend."

"When do you sleep?"

I didn't want to participate in the conversation. The pager was a source of contention. Fiery loud like an ambulance, it often sounded at night, frightening both of us. "I don't know what else to do," she answered, taking a sip of wine. "We have a group of volunteers in training, so it'll get easier in a few weeks. There's been so much demand, especially this summer. Even though I'm the backup person, I've needed to go the ER a couple times a week."

"This fucking city," muttered Christa.

There were not enough chairs so guests sat on the floor leaning against the walls. In the background Melissa Etheridge was belting out:

> *Come to my window*
> *Crawl inside, wait by the light of the moon*

I worked in the kitchen, finishing the creamy pasta sauce with mushrooms and peas, a favorite from *The Moosewood Cookbook*, while Eva entertained her friends. Moving in and out of the common areas, I faded along the wall. I had become that man, the special boyfriend allowed at the all-female party, safe, comfortable to the point of being nearly invisible, in the background of a beehive bursting with conversation: women talking animatedly, finishing each other's sentences, laughing, interrupting.

The conversation turned to pelvic exams. Four out of the eight dinner guests earned money for their tuition or living expenses by acting as paid patient actors with various made-up ailments and complaints at the University's Obstetrics and Gynecology clinic. They worked for the benefit of medical students who would soon be performing these same exams on real patients coming from the worn-down neighborhoods on the South Side, women who might not speak up for themselves in the labyrinth-like university hospital with its authoritative doctors in white lab coats.

"He was actually doing fine for most of the exam," Meg said smiling, taking a bite of pasta. "He had almost finished, and I was starting to think, 'This guy did OK,' but he smiled at me and there was a hint of flirtation—"

"Are you *sure* about the flirting part?" Deb asked.

Meg stared at her. "And he said, *'I'm going to pull out now.'*"

Most of the women in the room groaned and a few laughed.

"I looked at him and said, 'Are you *serious*, Doctor Dude?'"

"You didn't!"

"I'm tired of being professional with these unconscious assholes!"

"They'll remember that lesson," Eva said, smiling.

Leaning over to Cassandra, the butchest of the friends, the closest I had to an ally in the room, I whispered, "I'm not actually sure what that guy did wrong."

Cassandra had once admitted to me that she thought doing real pelvic exams for fake ailments for the benefit of soon-to-be rich doctors was batshit crazy and you would never catch her in a hospital gown in that particular brand of feminist martyrdom. She whispered, "Well, I'm no expert on heterosexual relations, my man. But I think that might be what a lot of you boyfriend people say when you're, uh, finished with your business."

"Oh."

"It's got a little sexual ring to it," she said.

"But he really *was* taking the speculum out. What else could he have said?"

"Listen, this is not my thing either," Cassandra said. "These ladies are gluttons for punishment. But I've been listening to these stories for months. I think he's got to use language that very specific and professional."

"Like?"

"He could say, 'You're going to feel some discomfort when the speculum is removed now.'"

"That does sound different."

"Not sexy at all," she said, smiling. "That's the point. Believe me, it's *not* sexy."

After the pasta was finished and the last bottle of wine drunk, after long goodbyes and hugs and then more hugs, the guests drifted off into the night, taking platters and bowls, and we finished cleaning up, washing the dishes by hand and putting them on the rack. Melissa Etheridge was still singing in the background, the same throaty voice of longing and determination:

> *Nothing fills the blackness that has seeped into my chest*
> *I need you in my blood, I am forsaking all the rest*
> *Just to reach you*

Then Eva and I were on the futon, under the covers, kissing in that sleepy, comfortable way, holding onto each other in a place just on the edge of a dream. I might have fallen asleep but the scent of her rushed through me, worked its magic, took control of my body, filled me with energy I didn't know I had and, before I realized what was happening, my head was between her legs again, in the place where time disappears.

Crawl inside, wait by the light of the moon
Come to my window
I'll be home soon

I nestled my head between her legs, mind resting on the fantasy. I imagined my tongue at the opening of her body: arms of a swimmer, lapping through waves, moving away from the beach, at one with the depths. I am here, I am here, we are here, we are here.

Then the pager went off, loud. It was 1989 again. It was after midnight. Eva sat up and looked at the dining room table just a few feet away.

"Fuck."

"What would happen if you didn't go?"

"That's not an option."

I turned over on my back, my body still hungry for her. It was one in the morning. "This is getting difficult for me, Eva."

She was pulling on jeans and an old maroon sweatshirt with the words "The University of Chicago: Where Fun Comes to Die." She had a kit for rape survivors that she kept in her backpack. She had vouchers for a cab that would take her to the emergency room on the other side of the city. "I'm sorry," she said.

"Don't apologize anymore!" I snapped.

"It's got nothing to do with you."

"How long until you have a new batch of volunteers?"

She didn't answer. The door slammed. Was she angry? Was she mad at the pager, or the non-profit, or all the hours of the day when women are assaulted, or the doctors and nurses in the emergency room who couldn't be trusted to do the right thing without an advocate nearby to cajole them, or the other board members who weren't stepping up? Or was she mad at the never-ending work, and how the deck seemed stacked against her, and all women who struggled to the ER in the dead of night, and all the men who didn't listen when a woman said "Stop"? Or was she mad at me for not understanding? The last surprise of that season of beginnings, as we figured out how to live side by side in this small space that was becoming our home, was this:

Every relationship with a woman is haunted by the ghosts of brutal men.

Lying alone in the dark on the futon, my body was stranded somewhere between arousal and high alert. *And you are not in my arms...* The noise of the city, into which she had disappeared, was an unrelenting static in my ears.

3

—

SHANE

From my window on the eleventh floor of my building on North Michigan Avenue in Chicago, I had a view of the white boats that buzzed across the murky green river; the Chicago Tribune Tower looming, its façade studded with rocks and bricks carted back from sites across the globe; and the Michigan Avenue Bridge crowded with pedestrians gawking at skyscrapers. I was writing chart notes when Eva called to ask me when I was coming home—she was making *Beef Bourguignon*, her new obsession—and to tell me Dean and Bernadette Marie's wedding invitation had arrived.

"Wait," I said, putting down my pen. An orange sunset peeked through the skyscrapers. I was so tired of writing notes. "Don't I have to marry first if I'm the oldest brother?"

She laughed. "Is this some inept backdoor marriage proposal?"

"I just thought usually siblings were supposed to marry in our birth order."

I could hear pans clattering in the kitchen. "That's just daughters in a Jane Austen novel."

"I knew I read it somewhere."

"You're not even a man in possession of a good fortune," she reminded me. "Not yet at least. Finish up. I'll see you in half an hour."

We were entering a unique season. We were always going to and coming from weddings. In between trips, we were buying gifts and opening up more invitations. Again and again and again Eva was praying not to be asked to be bridesmaid. She needed a separate closet for all the poofy pink and lavender gowns. Bernadette Marie had told Dean who told me privately that she wouldn't ask Eva because we weren't engaged.

"Dodged that bullet," Eva said.

The invitation also meant I'd have to see my father after not seeing him for two years. That evening I picked up a tattered paperback copy of *Shane*, his all-time favorite book, to have a focus for my worrying. A nauseous dread started to build in my gut.

Dean was my father's favorite son. My whole life I had been convinced of it. Fifteen months younger than me, he was handsome and broad-shouldered and high-spirited and always smiling, a varsity soccer player in high school who excelled in the sciences and garnered first a computer engineering degree from Boston University and then a high-paying job in a major East Coast technology corporation. Whenever we reunited over family holiday gatherings, he casually asked me, "So how much are you earning these days?"

When I complained to her, Eva said, "Just don't answer the question!" An only daughter, she could not understand this verbal roughhousing, a constant among us brothers. "Why do this pissing match?"

"You have to answer the question."

"Why?"

"Because not answering makes you a wuss." How would I dodge the question? Just stare at him? "You have to play the game."

"I don't..." her voice trailed off. "Understand men."

Everybody knew the answer. Dean's salary was always higher. He was not a social worker. He did not write theater reviews for the local gay and lesbian newspaper at twenty-five dollars a pop. He had never brought a campy, wise-cracking boyfriend home to visit the family. With my father, whom everyone called Scotty, he talked about football or baseball over beers. By his side, Dean always seemed to have a smiling, quietly accommodating girlfriend. The girlfriends all had long dark hair, parted perfectly in the middle, as if it were a requirement to date him.

When Dean and his fiancée decided to get married, it was the pinnacle of his success as the uncomplicated, high-earning, indisputably heterosexual son. They planned the perfect wedding and invited over one hundred people to a hall in Alexandria, Virginia. Bernadette Marie resolved to hand-sew all the bridesmaid's dresses and her own veil. For months, a crafting chaos exploded in their apartment. Flowing over beds and couches and dining room tables were waves of floral pink and green fabrics and tangled masses of pressed green bows and rose-colored ribbons with shiny threads of gold flowing through them, and waterfalls of cream-colored lace. The sewing machine hummed, a panic in the background. A few days before the event she and Dean assembled, by hand, splashy rainbow-colored flower centerpieces. Wedding souvenirs—pink lollipops etched with their names and wedding date, wrapped in pink cellophane with emerald bows—adorned each place setting.

Just days before their wedding, Eva and I marveled at this spectacle. When no one was looking, I leaned in. "Wow," I said.

"Just to be clear," she whispered back, "I'm never going to do anything that looks like this. Ever."

At twenty-six years old, in spite of the office with the tall windows and my pressed oxford shirt with the silk tie, I was not a great therapist. The catalogue of flaws was building in my mind. With my clients, all men, so many of whom didn't want to be there, I had a looming irritation, a buzzing in my body, barely suppressed, when they arrived late. They claimed traffic, challenges pulling away from job demands, buses and trains breaking down. In my rational brain I knew these things happened—they happened to me too—but to my clients, the disappointing fathers, I lobbed the idea that they were not taking their therapy—*they were not taking me*—seriously. A late start as slim as ten minutes left me feeling churlish. It's doubtful my scowl was helpful to anyone.

I was angry all the time.

Just a few years into my career as a therapist I had carved out a niche: a caseload of men who mostly looked like me (white, educated, professional, middle-class) but older, who might be called "family men," most of whom worked downtown or near downtown. They also happened to have committed sex offenses. Even though they might be important men by their own estimation, they had a probation officer and an urgency to be done with this punishment—"conditions of supervision" included mandated therapy—and to return to lives of respectability. My office fit them. It was clean. It was well-located. The lobby announced a kind of grandness. There was no mention of sexual abuse or incest anywhere in the building, on any marquee, except my office where every session was a struggle over truth. These were not men who would see a counselor at a non-profit agency in an obscure, beaten-down place. Everyone paid out-of-pocket. There could be no paper trail.

My job was counseling the disappointing fathers of the world.

With men who commit sexual crimes, part of the work was addressing perverse manglings of the truth: outright falsehoods, denials, fancy rationalizations, minimizations, omissions, silences. Though this was a usual part of the work, my impatience flared, an outsized disgust. The feeling was impossible to hide from the client sitting opposite from me. "Why are you frowning at me?" one client complained. "What did I do?" I hated being lied to yet, for reasons I didn't fully understand, this was the work I had chosen. Men, if they wanted to be feminists, had to work to change other men, I told myself.

Sometimes I became so frustrated, I complained to their probation officers. Writing on official letterhead, I used words like "resistant," "defensive," and "ambivalent." A few times, I ended a man's counseling, used phrases like "unmotivated to change" and "failed to comply." Then he had to go back before his judge, often to return to jail, sometimes even to prison.

I was ruining lives. I had to do something, to change. If I did not do something, I would remain stuck: a terrible, cranky, flawed therapist; the disappointed son, forever.

Three years before the end of the Vietnam War, in 1972, though I was only eight, every night before sleeping I lay awake in bed, listening to war news on the radio and worrying about being drafted. The walls of our brick house were so thin, we could hear conversations and arguments and the blasting televisions of neighbors on either side. We knew which fathers drank and fought with their wives. We knew which children got spanked and which parents yelled and which parents cursed. We knew how broke everyone was.

One night after bedtime, my father shook me awake. "You have to see this," he said. His deep voice always startled me, seeming to draw a fearsome authority from an invisible bass chord. It was eleven o'clock. He jostled me in his arms as he rushed down the stairs. His favorite movie, *Shane*, was beginning on the late show. He propped me in front of the box television set, a bleary-eyed boy, wrapped in the orange and green afghan crocheted by my grandmother, to watch the story of a cowboy with a mysterious past. My two brothers, spared the required viewing, were asleep. Six-year-old Dean had a fiery temper and a passion for all sports, especially wrestling. Bruce was too young for anyone to worry if he would measure up. Having overheard their whispered conversations, I knew my parents had concerns about the type of boy I might become.

The story is simple enough. Shane arrives by horseback at a Wyoming homestead, befriends a family of three, and is persuaded to become their hired hand. Their son, Joey, about my age, idolizes him. But Shane's job involves more than just chores around the farm. A wealthy cattle baron, Rufus Ryker, is waging a war against the homesteaders. His hired men send herds to trample their farmlands. For all his even-tempered humility and kindness, when challenged, Shane is surprisingly adept with his fists and guns. He helps the father stand up to the bullies. In the end Shane shoots the cattle baron and the six men who work for him.

That night I was wide-eyed, panicked, at the spectacle, the war of cruelty and brute intimidation in this wilderness with sketchy law enforcement: endless, bloody bar fights; stool throwing and fists swinging; wooden tables overturned; chairs smashed on backs. Everyone was so quick to fire a gun. For a boy targeted by bullies at school, the film was sobering—terrifying, really—in its insistence that these were violent givens of a boy's life, and I felt sick.

"Now you run home to your mother and tell her everything's all right," Shane tells Joey after the last of Ryker's gang meets his bloody end. "There aren't any more guns in this valley."

So this was Shane: handsome in an angular kind of way; the determined cut of his jaw; the brim of his tan hat dropping a shadow on his face; gaze on the far-off horizon; low, unflappable voice. Throughout childhood I had watched my father, the performer, act out scenes from the movie with his friends, mostly my uncles and other dads from the neighborhood, all of them drinking, laughing at him, sometimes playing other characters in a scene. Seeing the movie for the first time, I had the uncanny sensation that Alan Ladd, who plays Shane, was doing a poor imitation of my father's version of the same character.

When he leaves the homesteading family, Shane, supposedly a decent man, still adored by the family, who has just killed seven men and must run from the law delivers a homily. It is one of many rules about being a man that Shane offers. "A man has to be what he is," he tells the boy. "Can't break the mold. I tried it and it didn't work for me."

The boy's last line, as his hero rides his horse toward purple mountains, is "Shane! Come back!"

As the credits scrolled, my father said "MOST. AMAZING. MOVIE. EVER." I wrapped the blanket around my shoulders, warm as my grandmother herself, and stared at him. I could not tell him that when I was not frightened, I was bored. He gathered me in his arms, a gesture worth the sacrifice of the viewing, and carried me back to bed.

> *Listen to me, son. Don't get to liking Shane too much...*
> *He's fiddle-footed...He'll be moving on one of these days*
> *and then you'll get upset if you get to liking him too much.*
> Jack Schaefer, *Shane (1949)*

At the wedding reception guests marveled that Dean and Bernadette Marie—well, mostly her—had made everything by hand, a testimony to their teamwork. My father arrived late to the reception. His pompadour was gray and thinning, his nose was rosy and chapped, his cheeks were gaunt. I was sure he was already drunk. He saw Eva and me, standing outside the hall, and walked over to us. Not only was this his first encounter with Eva, but it was his only time meeting any girlfriend I would bring home.

"Hi Dad—" I said. I extended my hand because we hadn't seen each other in a year but he pulled me into a hug.

Then he put his arm around Eva's waist. She stiffened. Her nose crinkled at the smell of cheap beer. "I love this girl," he gushed. "I just love her, you hear?"

"They're getting ready for the toasts, Dad," I lied, taking Eva's arm. "Let's head into the hall."

"He's just really affectionate with everyone, right?" Eva whispered in my ear. "He probably loved the boyfriends you brought home too?"

"Oh yeah," I said. We headed for the buffet. "Loved them."

During the reception my father had slipped out to get a cooler from the trunk of his gold Lincoln Continental. It contained Coors Light, his favorite. When he tried to bring it into the hall, a security guard blocked him. "Sir, you can't bring that in here."

Bruce and I heard the arguing outside and followed the sound. "Oh no," Bruce said. "Not today. Not here. He can't." On the spectrum of Scott boys, Bruce, the most unflappable of the three, was between Wayne and Dean: sensitive, soft-spoken, and studious, like me, but with a deeper voice and some skill on the baseball diamond, like Dean.

"But I'm the father of the groom!" he said, trying to move past the guard.

"It's the hall's rule," said the guard trying to be diplomatic. "Only the caterer can supply alcohol."

"It's not going to hurt anyone," Scotty said, raising his voice. His words mashed together.

Bruce tried to interject. "Come on, Dad…?" We didn't want Dean to hear. It would ruin the day.

"You'll have to take that back to your car, sir."

"You're not listening. I don't like the beer here."

The guard pursed his lips. "I have to ask you to leave your cooler outside the hall."

Scotty argued, louder and louder, garbled words competing with the music of the band. Other wedding guests stared, then moved awkwardly back into the hall. Who was this boorish drunk? Was he related to anyone? Wearing his black tuxedo with the red rose boutonniere that matched his wife's bouquet, Dean entered the fray, his best, smooth-talking, diplomatic self. If anyone could get my father to calm down, it would be Dean. Scotty was indignant. This was supposed to be a special day. He wanted his beer. He did not understand the rule. He did not notice the crowd of people watching him.

Confused about what to do, my mother, Bruce, Eva, and I watched from the sidelines. My face burned, as if the secret of my life was suddenly visible to the world. "This is futile," Eva whispered, taking my hand. Her father was in recovery. "There's no reasoning when they're this drunk."

Dean offered to help my father carry the cooler back to his car, but Scotty decided to leave the reception altogether. The guard had ruined the day—"Such a special day for a father!"—with his mean-spirited enforcement. "Stupid rules, stupid rules," he muttered. Rules were for ordinary people. When he drove out of the parking lot, his cooler in the back seat, I felt a familiar prick of moral panic: he was driving again.

At twenty-six years old, I had not learned to drive. This unmanly freakishness was a source of constant comment by friends, families, and colleagues, even people just meeting me who found out, and I could not explain myself to anyone. "The thing is," I confided in Jack, the steady, nodding, white-haired therapist whom I saw two times a week, two blocks down the street from my office, "every time I get behind the wheel, I'm convinced I'm going to die."

"Where do you think that feeling comes from?"

"I don't know," I said, even though I did.

It was many sessions later that I confessed it. "All during my childhood my father drove when he was drinking," I said, shifting under Jack's gaze, stealing a glance at the clock above his shoulder. My father had never felt any shame about this lapse, so I felt the feeling for him. "When he would take the three of us out for weekly visits. He never came into the house when he picked us up, so my mother didn't know."

Jack nodded gravely.

"As we got older, we realized—especially me—it was not safe to be in the car with him. I thought I needed to protect my brothers. But we were young then and we couldn't talk about his drinking. Later, after Dean got his license, my brothers and I argued about who would ask my father to take the passenger seat. He got angry at whomever said anything." Sometimes Dean drove and I sat with his fury at me for making him defy Scotty. Sometimes Scotty insisted on driving and I sat in the passenger seat, terrified of crashing, as if my vigilance could keep us alive if he careened off the road.

That night, with the noise from the band floating outside the hall, as my father drove away after the reception, I followed the car with a close, familiar scrutiny, heart pounding, alert to the way the long gold Lincoln Continental veered, just slightly outside the white traffic lines.

> *He was tall and terrible in the road, looming up gigantic in the mystic half-light. He was the man I saw that first day, a stranger, dark and forbidding, forging his lone way out of the unknown past in the utter loneliness of his own immovable and instinctive defiance.*

If you met him during the years he lived with us in Toby Farms, the first thing you'd notice were my father's biceps: bulging, hard, veined. The sleeves of his white T-shirts were tight. At home with the family, my father was often shirtless. The neighborhood dads, playing pinochle at the kitchen table with him, drinking beers and tossing horseshoes, or joining us around the fire on weekend camping trips, often commented on his impressive guns. (This was always odd for me, his oldest son, the quiet queer one, determined to pass.) After several beers, the men engaged in arm wrestling matches that lasted into the wee hours, and Scotty always won.

Every few months he challenged his three sons, one by one, to arm wrestle. At the kitchen table we faced off, our heads closer to each other than at any other time. "Your elbow can't leave the table," he reminded us, gripping our small hands too tightly, "or it's cheating." He allowed us to press his knuckles close to the table, almost winning. We glared at him. The unspoken lesson: You can have eyes-wide-open, staring-at-each-other intimacy with another man, if locked in mortal combat. My brothers and I cheered for each other, loving this moment of play, of grasping hands. I wanted to throw my whole body at him, to pin him with everything I had, but I had to keep my elbow on the table.

We were so fierce and sincere in our missions to prove ourselves: faces red, jaws clenched, arms exhausted. With a conqueror's determination, as if we were just like the neighborhood men, not his children, my father looked at us and smirked. Son by son, he pushed our arms to the table. Whoever wasn't arm wrestling groaned, "Aw, man," another part of the ritual. The fabrication of dashed hopes. But secretly we liked that he was strong. We liked that he was a charismatic man, never breaking a sweat, teasing us with the faint chance of triumph. We liked that he was interested in us, however briefly, even if we were losers. Only Dean, the athlete, seemed disheartened.

He was far off and unapproachable at times
even when he was right there with you.

If, as family therapists say, families are emotional mobiles, floating objects connected by a delicate balance of sticks and strings, the dip my father took that day of the wedding jostled the serene orbiting of our relationships.

My brothers and I had never agreed on the impact of his drinking. We accused each other of denial and exaggeration, of avoiding the problem and "hypersensitivity." Dean, the loyalist, hid how much my father's drinking bothered him. Bruce, sweet-tempered peacemaker, admitted the problem, saw the ways it ruined my father's work and family relationships, but denied he felt anger. Everyone's frustration and disappointment seemed to accumulate in my one body. I alternated between rage and guilt about my failings as a son. Had I done everything that I could? Or had I driven him to drink with my effeminate ways? As a young adult I had mostly cut off all contact. I called it our "gentlemen's estrangement." My mother alone had the luxury of a formal divorce. One of the great theorists of the field, the midcentury psychiatrist Murray Bowen, believed that cut-offs were psychologically unhealthy. Bowen called them a false independence, a cowardly avoidance. A cut-off meant you couldn't refashion your identity, on your own terms, within the troublesome relationship. You weren't tough. Maybe you weren't manly. After I began doing family therapy with adult survivors of abuse and their parents, I toed the party line. I encouraged truth-telling and unsettling disclosures in families more interested in armoring themselves with secrets and avoiding each other. Yet I wondered about cut-offs. Did Bowen ever know anyone who had an alcoholic parent?

After I became a therapist, whenever I mentioned the "gentleman's estrangement" to colleagues, I encountered disapproval. Once I asked my clinical supervisor, Mary Jo, whether cut-offs were ever acceptable. "Only if the parent is physically dangerous," she answered. "Severing ties like that disempowers the person who cuts off."

Damn, I thought to myself. I had to do something.

A family intervention is a therapeutic ritual when a relative has an addiction. With a therapist's help, everyone gets together and tells the addict about the impact of his behavior, ending silences and complicities, sometimes offering an ultimatum: Stop drinking or there will be consequences. After talking with Mary Jo and other colleagues, as a last-ditch effort to do better, I found a reputable family therapist near Scotty's home. Carol specialized in family therapy and addictions. The intervention took several months of planning: arguing with my brothers about being there and settling on an ultimatum we could all tolerate, cajoling Scotty to attend, and, together with my brothers, presenting a unified front about our desire for him to go into treatment.

A week before the intervention, Carol and I reviewed plans for our session. She asked if his second wife, whom I barely knew, was coming. While I had written her a letter and left a message on their answering machine, mysteriously she had not responded. I wondered if Scotty had blocked my efforts, or if his wife perceived me as some rogue meddler.

"I can almost guarantee," Carol said, "the intervention will fail if his second wife does not show up." I didn't think the intervention would work either. I wondered how to express what I wanted from our meeting—which had nothing to do with rehabilitation. She asked if I wanted to cancel the session. Helplessly, I told her no. We would meet in Baltimore, Scotty's hometown.

> *"I'll be riding out now.*
> *And there's not one of you that will follow."*

My mother told me that when she filed for divorce she listed "abandonment" as the reason. He had left the three-bedroom townhouse in Toby Farms. He had not told anyone where he was going. We did not hear from him for weeks. My grandparents helped with money for groceries and rent. "Abandonment" seemed like the right word.

His alcoholism had worsened. It was not uncommon for him to disappear for one or two days, but never this long. Exhausted by his surliness, his unsteady movements, his inability to attend to the simplest conversations, his scary driving, my mother had started to attend Al-Anon. No more rides home from the bars in the early morning hours. No more calls into his work for sick days when he was too hungover.

Months later when he resurfaced, finding out that she had used such a shameful word to describe his actions, he insisted she change it to "irreconcilable differences," which was also weirdly true. They differed in their beliefs about whether he had any responsibility to be present in the life of his family.

Abandonment is a thing you do. It's also a thing that happens to you. The loss settles in your gut like a mysterious knot. The word describes both sides of the coin: abandoner and abandoned. You can say "his abandonment" and "my abandonment," and the word flexes to include both of you, both experiences, leaving and being left. *It's a thing you do. It's a thing that happens to you.*

One morning, weeks after he had left, before anyone told us what was going on, I asked my mother, "Do you know where he is?"

She was sitting at the kitchen table with her coffee, gazing into space, looking soft and sad and worried. I never saw her eat in the morning. I was certain she wished that she didn't have to answer the question, but there was nowhere to look, no available distraction. "I don't know where he is," she said.

In the days and weeks after Scotty left, without explanation, and no word from him, there was a realization, a sick swirling in my body: *he is gone, he is gone, he is gone.* He had always been mysterious and secretive. Now it was locked in. Nothing would ever be revealed. We did not know if he would ever come back.

Week after week after week, when no one knew where he was, when my mother scrambled to find money for rent and food and school supplies, when she attended our school and sports events alone, the stable one who could be both mother and father, the words were still true, still a sick echo in my gut: *he is gone, he is gone, he is gone.* Like the final punctuation in a book, the ledge at which the story stopped and the void began. (What happened to the boy in the story when Shane headed for the mountains never to be seen again? All we know was that he wrote a book about his hero.)

The words lodged inside me, an urgent futility, settled like a kind of psychological sediment, an irregular heartbeat, persistent in its brokenness, that became a template for all relationships with men: friends, brothers, boyfriends. *He is gone, he is gone, he is gone.*

When, months later, on the advice of his divorce attorney, he called to speak with his three sons, he seemed to think it could be a simple chat. Whatever his life had become, we had no right to know. One by one, we passed the phone to each other, trying to keep our cool, and overheard each other's superficial conversations. Dean reviewed the scores of a football game he had watched the night before, which my father had also seen. When he handed the phone to me, I could not suppress my frustration. "Where are you, Dad?"

"I can't tell you," he said. When I demanded again, baffled that this response was acceptable in his mind, he repeated himself. "I can't tell you."

Why did it matter if we knew where he was? On what authority could this possibly be the right thing to do? *Who said he couldn't tell us?* I wondered furiously. His buddies at the bar? His divorce lawyer?

We hung up the phone and sat in silence.

Do people really do this? I wondered. Abandon their wives to raise the kids alone? Leave their children to be fatherless? Just exit, without explanation? At the core of my shock, I wondered if there was in me a germ, tucked into my heart, unopened like a fortune cookie, that I might someday be a father myself, one incapable of imagining that it would be OK to leave my children, to stop caring about whether they needed food, protection, or comfort; to forget who I was.

> *His past was fenced as tightly as our pasture...*
> *[H]e was reserved; courteous and soft spoken,*
> *yet withdrawn beyond a line of his own making.*

There was something about looking into the face of an alcoholic: the map of creases that testified to the soul's tension; the redness and puffiness expanding lines of worry, evidence of the flow of chemicals that soothed the body. Under the fluorescent lights of Carol's office, my father's face looked different to me: older, robbed of arrogance, broken down, terribly alone in the world. The symbolism of our family was reversed. It was he, finally, who was the subject of clinical inquiry; the patient; the family dilemma; the one who had "the problem."

Carol was tough. She had four men crowded in her office, closer to each other than we had ever been, without our mother, wives, or girlfriends to ease our connections. We were sweating with anticipation, wondering, after months of preparation, what we were doing here. Bruce was pretending to be calm. Dean, the anti-therapy problem-solving engineer, was glaring at me. His eyes said: *It's your fault I'm here.* We argued for months whether therapy helped anyone. "It's just talk!" A ceiling fan whirled above our heads, chopping up light and shadows, scattering them on the walls. Although rehabilitation was the intention of the session, I had no fantasies. I wondered, as perhaps my brothers did, why exactly we were here, if not to change him. What were we about to lose?

Carol had brown hair, cut pixie style, and simple pearl earrings. She was business-like and unruffled, a steadfast banker of emotion. Her legs crossed, she sat across from Scotty, confronting every rationalization.

"At what point in the morning do you have you first drink?" she asked.

Lunchtime.

"How many DUIs have you had?"

None.

Bruce countered that, since we were children, he has kept a cooler full of beer in the back seat of his car.

"I like my own beer," Scotty explained. "I'm taking it to wherever I'm going, that's all."

A fury surged through me. "Oh my God, Dad..."

"It's not that you're transporting the beer," Dean interrupted, voice shaky. "You drink while you drive. You've been driving drunk most of our lives, Dad."

His honestly startled me. Was Dean actually mad for once? I sighed, my body relaxing.

Scotty nodded helplessly. It was impossible to disagree with Dean. After a lifetime of silences, lies, and complicity, I was astounded by the uncomplicated way we were speaking—to him—about these ordinary facts of childhood.

As Carol's questions continued, Scotty became flustered. He was sober and dressed up in a suit. He was sweating. His hands were shaking. I reminded myself: it really is a disease. He had agreed to come to the session because his sons had presented an ultimatum: we would not see him under any other conditions over the winter holiday. Holidays were precious to him. He got something from having us nearby, but it had never been clear, through the haze of his drunkenness, what that something was.

Carol looked up from the notes she was taking. She asked how his drinking affected us growing up. This was the big moment. Because I was traditionally the ringleader, the son perceived as the "trouble maker," the angry one, we had agreed beforehand for Dean to speak first.

Dean sighed. He still hated therapy. He shared about his

embarrassment at the wedding. They had tried so hard to make it a perfect day. His voice broke. There would never be another wedding.

When it was my turn, I shared about the past, partly because, as the oldest son, I had the clearest memories. All our lives, our father had been a "good drunk," I said, a man who became more affable under the influence. Neighborhood kids who had alcoholic parents had been yelled at or even beaten. The Scott boys were considered lucky because, inebriated, our father was easy to ignore. It was his sobriety—when he was short-tempered, uneasy, withdrawn—that we all hated. Still I remembered calling him from college and, finding him drunk, endlessly repeating information to him because he neither retained nor understood what I said. "What's your major?" he asked again and again. "And you're living in the dorms, right?" He was famous for forgetting birthdays.

My father had been neither entirely absent from my life nor fully present. He had been, in the truest sense of the word, *vanishing*: in his own process of disappearing then reappearing, fading in and out of view; a mirage trembling on the sweating horizon. And I, like a weary traveler, saw the mirage and, hungering, continued to be tricked, imagining what I wanted to see.

Edmund White once wrote that "the unconscious...can't distinguish between abandoning someone and being abandoned...Even though I left you, it's come to seem as though you left me." Every friendship with a man, every romance, was riddled with the threat of this original disappearance: the subtle ways Scotty vanished, even though he was physically present. I forgot to return calls to friends, neglected my brother's birthdays, abruptly severed ties when I became disappointed with boyfriends, sabotaged friendships with men when they appeared to get too close, was always struggling with formless anger at work. I wondered: Was my cutting off my father keeping alive my own tendency to reject and abandon?

Eventually our Shane returned, to live out another cliched script: the seventies-style divorced father, visiting one night a week and the occasional, often canceled, weekend overnight sleepovers.

By my late teens, I had long since refused to arm-wrestle anymore, annoyed at the required humiliation, angry at my father, unable to put resentments aside, just tolerating his superficial conversations, withdrawn beyond a line of his own making, which seemed like such a smoke screen for his failings, the ways he had disappointed us, which we were not allowed to discuss. But Bruce and Dean still enjoyed the competition and gave it their best effort. It did give us something to do during those long, boring visits in which the main purpose—him keeping his secrets—was honored.

One day when he was sixteen, Dean, the strongest of the three, the one who physically resembled Scotty the most, offered to arm-wrestle again, as if it were the usual familiar game, sons against father, where we would cheer on Dean.

At this point he was the same height as Scotty. My father's strength, after years of drinking and smoking, had diminished. But he had no reason to think the game would be any different than hundreds of previous competitions. Elbows rooted on the table, Scotty and Dean gripped each other's hands, eyes locked on each other, bantering and teasing. But there was a difference. Dean was not smiling.

The match was interminable, as it was supposed to be. They gritted their teeth. The clock on the wall ticked. At the key moment when Scotty was supposed to push Dean's arm to the table, he could not budge it. Scotty's smile dimmed. His brow glowed with sweat. At sixteen, Dean stared back, not even breathing hard, not even red-faced, then pinned Scotty's arm to the table. When Scotty's knuckles hit, the dead thud ended something, as if a spell broke, the film reel stopped, and we found ourselves, not in the script, but in the quiet confusing darkness with our naked selves.

For years the three of us thought we wanted victory. But now there was no cheering, there was no "Aw, man." No one knew what to say or where the story would go, but there he was, our father, far off and unapproachable, an old man. And the three of us were right there, looking at him in a lost daze. Dean had his perfect, straight nose. Bruce had the square shape of his face. I had his angled jaw. None of us grasped that our childhood would never be the same. The visit ended. We never talked about it. We never arm wrestled again.

'A man is what he is...and there's no breaking the mold.
I tried that and I've lost.'

After we told him how his drinking hurt us over the years, we told him that we, his three sons, would not tolerate contact with him when he jeopardized his life. As Carol discussed ideas about treatment, Scotty's face reddened. His eyes looked moist—the first real emotion I had seen in him. Ever. Too quickly, he agreed to join the intensive outpatient addictions treatment program she described. *Yes, he will start the day after New Year's. Yes, he will come every night after work. Yes, he wants to be a better father to his sons.* All of these statements were true. They were wishes he had.

Without flinching, Carol added with stunning directness, "Of course, it's unlikely your sons will believe any of these assurances. They've been disappointed too many times. You'll need to rebuild trust." Her familiarity with people like us—anxious, sweating men who rarely name difficult truths like "our father is an alcoholic" and "we have rarely seen our father sober"—reminded me how clichéd we really were.

A week later, after I returned to Chicago, Carol called. In between sessions, I looked out my window on the eleventh floor. The yellow afternoon sun glimmered on the skyscrapers. "He didn't show up," she said in her brisk way. "Just as I anticipated. I don't have enough of a relationship with him to intervene further."

I thought: *Neither do I. Neither do any of us.*

Long before we orchestrated our intervention, I realized his illness had too strong a hold on him. But I arranged it anyway. I wanted to force the issue of his vanishing, to make him either clearly absent or clearly present. I wanted his pain to go away, so that my own might follow. I wanted to change our relationship before it became the template for my relationships with all men .

Once I had a dream that I was mourning at the grave site of my friend Roy's father, who died when Roy was twelve. I was mourning as if he were my father. The soil was fresh and brown, rich enough to grow flowers and grass. The tombstone was crisp and new in the sunlight. The letters of his father's name were sharp and bold. I was surrounded by mourners. Someone had a hand on my shoulder.

I awoke with a start, thinking, *But my father's not dead.*

What I wanted was a funeral, a separation ritual, a communal acknowledgment of my mourning. But my grief was stuck, bewitched, in my father's paradox: the simultaneity of his presence and absence; the chronicity of his particular illness in a world where other people changed, joined AA, showed remorse, and made amends to the people they loved.

After taking a day to digest Carol's pronouncement, I summoned my courage. I called in the early afternoon, hoping he'd be more alert. "What happened, Dad?" I asked. "What about your promise?"

He fumbled, offered some rationalizations. *It wasn't the right time. The cost was a concern. He wanted to look at other treatment programs.*

I reminded him about the ultimatum. "There will be weddings you won't be invited to," I said. "There might be grandchildren. I don't know what we'll do. You might not be welcome in their lives."

"I know, I know," he said, as if we were having a more routine exchange. I wondered how much he had drunk already.

In the spirit of Carol's brutal honesty, I swallowed hard. "Dad, you're saying the alcohol is more important than your relationship with me?"

There was a pause. I knew he was thinking about what I just said. Was he angry at me for being so forthright? He responded: "Yes. I guess so. The alcohol is more important than you."

Suddenly, after a lifetime of guessing, I had my answer.

Lost in my loneliness, I watched him go...

4

BOTCHING THE WEDDING

We were not supposed to get married.

For five years we lived in that dark, cramped, one-bedroom apartment on a traffic-congested street on the North Side of Chicago. We argued about the one true definition of cleanliness (germs vs. junk) and how frequently to clean the bathroom (once a week vs. once a month). We had a cat Eva had chosen for us from a shelter, a cross animal who hissed when anyone tried to pet him. When Oscar Wilde sensed we were leaving in the morning, he crouched behind a corner and sprung on our calves, claws bared. When we returned in the evening, he was poised to attack: punishment for these petty, daily abandonments. We kept a wicker basket of loaded water guns by the door and armed ourselves as soon as we arrived home and during any transition. We debated what to do with Oscar (suffer vs. adopt out).

Through all our squabbling, one mantra united us:

No marriage. No kids.

A convention that still banned sexual minorities in 1993, the word "marriage" had never been part of the story I told myself about who

I would be. Because I had seen so much tumult in the lives of married couples, I had doubts about marriage as anything useful.

No marriage. No kids.

Then, that spring, I had the option to go to graduate school on the East Coast. It offered an escape from an exhausting, bewildering job. In spite of the ups and downs of life in the tiny apartment with the fiercely neurotic cat, the idea of leaving town catalyzed a realization: I wanted Eva to go with me.

For Eva, our uncomplicated cohabitation became suddenly complicated. Her father George was a first-generation German who grew up in one of the city's white ethnic neighborhoods, in the long shadow of the Great Depression. He had wisps of white hair around the edges of his bald pate and he lumbered when he walked, like he was dragging bulky muscle. Gruff and curt, he was a printer who had landed a union job, a coup for a child of the 1930s, which brought him into home ownership and the middle class. He cared about financial stability. He worried about bad things happening again. In spite of his grouchiness, I never doubted what we had in common. We were devoted to his daughter.

One night, in his musty basement, under a flickering fluorescent light, he puttered at his work bench, making no eye contact as usual. I was supposed to be helping.

"Hand me the ratchet, will you?"

I looked in the toolbox in front of me, teeming with mysterious objects. While I considered whether I would make a wild guess or admit my ignorance, George muttered, "Jesus, never mind," and reached across the work bench for it.

I tried to tell him our plans.

He had a wide-eyed look of alarm. *Move? Leave a stable job? Take his unmarried daughter with me?*

I chickened out. "Well, it's just an idea," I lied.

Was she making a crazy decision? It would look that way to him. Move seven hundred miles away to be with a quirky, unemployed, thirty-year old dandy, a man with unprofitable, incomprehensible degrees: Humanities? Social Work? Add to the insanity the fact that the man with whom she had lived for half a decade—*with no mention of a ring*—would be getting another graduate degree in—What the hell is *that?*—Creative Writing.

Couldn't she have found better boyfriend material at that expensive university?

We had to throw the guy a bone. We had to render the terms of our commitment to each other into words and symbols he would grasp. It was like an act of translation, we rationalized. The quirky language of weddings wasn't our primary tongue, but the strange words—"bride," "groom," "maid of honor," "groomsman"—would mean something to the people we cared about, who needed to understand the strength of our bond.

Up until now Eva didn't want to get married, but she was his only child and she loved him. That spring before we needed to move east, Eva and I made a pact. Secretly, between ourselves, we would think of ourselves as "engaged," even though the word made us blanch. In the morning, as she slept, I cooed in her ear, "*Fiancée.*"

She shuddered and woke up. "Ugh," she said, burying her head in the pillow to hide from the day. "Why do you keep doing that?"

"Not romantic yet?"

"It's like waking from a bad dream."

If, after thirty days, we could still stand ourselves, we would go public. We would tell her father and relatives. We would really get married.

That June we took her father to dinner at a downtown German

bistro that heaped each plate with enough tender beef and creamed vegetables to feed three people—her father's criteria for excellent restaurant fare. We sprung the news before he became too lethargic from eating a mountain of scalloped potatoes.

"Are you sure?" he asked, looking only at Eva.

"We've been together five years, Dad."

He paused, as if considering the proper fatherly response at such a dramatic life juncture. "Well, OK then," he said and took a bite of his pumpernickel roll.

Smiling, Eva excused herself to go to the restroom and to breathe a sigh of relief. I looked at George and he looked at me.

"Is there a ring?"

"Like, an engagement ring?"

"Yeah, a ring."

"She doesn't want one. Really, I'd be happy to get her one, but she was clear. She didn't want one."

Pursing his lips, he looked away with what I thought was a *hmph*. *Cheap bastard.*

"You know how bossy she is," I tried to explain.

"Yeah, yeah," he said, looking away, and wiped the last of the mushroom sauce from his plate with half a roll.

That week, as we gradually told her relatives, others found more diplomatic ways to ask about the ring. In the Northern European neighborhoods of Chicago's West Side, a chunky diamond signaled the groom's intentions to do well by his future wife. The next weekend, I found myself in a downtown department store looking at rings, attended by a white-haired jeweler with a monocle and a bony thin nose.

"I'm looking for a ring that could look like an engagement ring to some people, but could also look like a regular ring that doesn't signify anything to someone else."

The jeweler raised an eyebrow. "Well, which finger will she wear it on?"

"Her ring finger. Is there such a ring you can wear on that finger that won't immediately look like an engagement ring to everyone, but will to some people."

"Hmmm," he said. He pulled out another tray from the glass case.

In a driven frame of mind, I pulled out my credit card and bought a ring with a fiery opal surrounded by little sparkling diamonds. Opal was her birth stone. When the jeweler ran my credit card—*please, please, please*—I crossed my fingers it would work.

That night, after she unwrapped the present, Eva chose her words carefully. "That's lovely." Without looking at me, she added, "I'll just get it re-sized for a different finger."

"You don't want an engagement ring?"

"I told you I didn't want one," she said, matter-of-factly, completely clear about who she was. "I'm not a piece of property that needs to be marked."

She bedeviled me. I didn't always grasp the flickering contradictions: she had one foot in our urban post-collegiate world, the potlucks with sassy friends who embraced feminism and questioned everything handed to them about being a woman, and one foot in the Methodist churches of Northern Illinois, attended her whole life with her mother and aunts. She wanted to live her life, on her own terms, but she also wanted to be a good daughter.

When we first met Gary, our florist, my bland world of primary colors was transformed into a graded rainbow of subtleties: "Summer Raspberry," "Evergreen Mint," and "Periwinkle" twinkled in his vocabulary. "Emerald Green" and "Precious Peach" fell like bejeweled syllables from his lips. He had expensive opinions about all aspects of wedding design—floral trellises, columns draped with creamy silk and filled with roses on the edge of blooming, elaborate lily centerpieces to mount on the wedding cake, and ivy garlands for doorways. Eva told him she was not going to carry a bouquet.

"The bride always clutches something in her hands," said Gary. "It signals appropriate feminine nervousness."

She whispered in my ear, "Do we have to work with him?"

"It's a beloved tradition," Gary coaxed. "Maybe just a few calla lilies?"

No flowers came the decision. They were "too feminine and frilly." When it came time to take Gary over to the chapel, I walked with him. Eva and the photographer trailed behind.

"This is turning out rather unconventional," he said, worried.

"Does the groom ever carry anything?"

"Never," Gary said. "His hands are just supposed to sweat."

Gary's fussy, strong-minded opinions reminded me of Father Sam. I wanted to tell him: *I am one of you. I get the thing about the flowers.* But that admission felt strange and it would make our ceremony look even weirder to him.

We arrived at the chapel that was part of the Chicago Theological Seminary, a multi-purpose building near the school, above the basement bookstore at 58th and University Avenue. The events scheduler had loud gospel music playing on the radio in her office and a broad smile that suggested that she herself was saved, but that she willing to talk to those who weren't. She took us to tour the chapel. The steel, gargoyle-covered gates creaked when she pulled them open. Inside, it was dark and gray. The maroon and purple stained-glass windows rationed any suggestion of daylight. The floor was cold, dusty stone.

"Wow," the photographer said, "wow." He squinted through his light measure.

"Cute little dungeon," Gary observed.

"It's affordable," the events scheduler said. "It seats up to one hundred."

It was the only chapel in Hyde Park that met the combined needs of seating capacity, budget, and location. Although the neighborhood teems with people pursuing spiritual discovery and inward searching, its chapel selection is not particularly suited to the agnostic lower middle class living off social worker incomes. Most chapels were either palatial and exorbitantly priced or uncomfortably cozy and cheap, like this one, tucked away in some forgotten corner of the Divinity School.

"We'll need it for Saturday, July 31st at two o'clock," Eva told the scheduler.

"No, eleven in the morning," I corrected her. "Before lunch, right?"

"Eleven or two?" the scheduler asked.

"Eleven," I said.

"Two," Eva insisted, with a touch of exasperation. "I thought we weren't doing lunch."

"We'll call you and confirm," I said. We were in a rush to meet a caterer. The list of details was exhausting.

As spring turned to summer we had several meetings with Father Sam; sometimes together and sometimes separately. His office on the second floor of Bent House felt comfortable and home-like. Lined with windows, the space felt like a spectacular tree house. A collage of green and yellow light refracted through the leafy trees outside covered the walls. On the bookshelf that reached to the ceiling, in a special place of honor, hung a photo of Quentin Crisp, still with wavy lavender hair in his eighties, from his visit to Hyde Park when I was a senior in college. I had helped Father Sam raise the money to bring him to campus. It was our father-son project. Naomi and I had taken Quentin Crisp and his purple hair to The Medici for brunch.

During one of my solo visits Sam looked me straight in the eyes. "So, what about fidelity?"

I hated this question. "Um." I fidgeted. My left hand, hidden in my pocket, clutched my thigh. I wanted a dream break. "I think there are ways to get my needs for male companionship met, without having sex with anyone else. I have a lot of warm friendships with guys. Well, gay guys." I hoped this was true. I wanted to please him. I didn't want to talk about it anymore.

He smiled and said, "OK, son."

"There is one other issue." I looked out the window, at the treetops and clouds that made the office seem so removed from Earth. "No one seems interested in getting together anymore. I'm starting to worry about losing my gay friends."

"With some gay people, you getting married will be upsetting, it's true," he said. "Some people won't understand. But I've been an openly gay man for thirty years, Wayne. It won't make any difference to me. The real friends stick. You're still you."

After we finished talking, he walked me to the door of Bent House. He had been in a relationship with Tim, a Presbyterian minister, for ten years. "You know, I didn't realize Tim had a sexual addiction when we met. I didn't know we'd have to grapple with that challenge," he said with a sigh. We walked down the stairs to the front door. "There are snipers in the bush, son, waiting to sabotage what brings you joy."

I looked at him, uncertain what to say next. I wasn't sentimental, not exactly, but I wanted to ask him not to mention snipers during the ceremony. Instead I moved to shake his hand. He pulled me into a warm hug. "You be careful," he said, patting my back.

The next time, just three weeks before the big day, Eva and I met with him together. We had written our vows and he asked to see them.

As Father Sam glanced over our notes, we looked at each other and we looked away. Eva still didn't have a dress yet and I had a shiny embroidered vest but no suit or dress shoes because I was waiting for her to get the damn dress. We told each other and all our friends we weren't panicking. That was for conventional couples. But we were panicking.

"Hmmm." Father Sam's eyebrows were raised as he turned over the pages. "Um, kids, there are two pieces missing here, and they're a pretty big deal."

"What?"

"God and fidelity."

"But we don't believe in God," I said. Eva nodded. "Not in any conventional sense." Neither of us said anything about fidelity. I knew it was important to religious people, but I didn't think it needed to be in *our* vows.

He pushed the folded draft over the desk to us. "I'm an Episcopalian Priest," he said. "I can't officiate a wedding unless the vows contain God and fidelity."

"Uh oh," I said. The breath left my body. Because his alcoholism was out-of-control and untreated, I hadn't invited Scotty. His mother was boycotting in solidarity. I needed Father Sam to be there. I was paralyzed about what to do.

Eva looked at Father Sam and said, "Then we'll re-do them." We took back the drafts and left his office. We walked down 57th Avenue to The Medici. It was bustling with Saturday morning brunch-goers. We sat in a wooden booth covered with drawings and messages, inked and carved over decades by students declaring devotions and curses, allegiances and rebellions. We ordered fresh squeezed orange juice and coffee. Eva had Eggs Florentine and I had Eggs Benedict.

"OK," she said. "So I've got 'To be faithful to you, to respect our differences, to accept and work through conflicts.' How's that?"

"Pretty standard." I took a bite of chocolate croissant. I was glad she was writing it down.

"We'll take each other 'to be my lifetime partner,'" she said. "No 'husband' or 'wife.' I doubt anyone will notice."

"Sounds right."

"And then we've got the social work-y 'peaceful world' stuff at the end," she continued, looking at her notebook. "To honor our covenant as a small piece interwoven in God's promise to all people."

"That's the God part?"

"Really I'm just working in the word for him," she said, taking a sip of peppermint tea. "More democratic and people-oriented than patriarch-in-the-sky focused."

"I can live with it," I said, sipping my coffee. "Your mom and aunts will be happy, right? The faithful part sounds so clichéd. What about 'To be faithful to you, and to receive your faith'? The second use of 'faith' as a noun opens up other meanings of the word faith. Belief in each other. Trust. Sincere intention. I'm tired of being sandwiched into other people's dogma."

Sexual fidelity was important to Eva. It meant safety, not getting a disease, devotion, being special to each other, and not worrying about being abandoned. For me, the scent of her sparked a kind of wild unconsciousness: I would do anything to be with her. I couldn't imagine a future where I would not desire her. I knew I would never leave her, but I also knew my desire was bigger than just her. Would it be difficult to be faithful? I wanted a definition of faithful that was more expansive, I thought to myself.

Eva was tired from writing and eating and too much tea and a long to-do list, including no dress yet. "Fine with me," she agreed, adding it in. "I don't think anyone but us will care. He'll have his God and fidelity."

"Thank goodness," I said. His presence at the ritual felt more essential than any of the other props or flowers or conventions that had been pushed on us.

The big day got closer. My family flew into town and stayed at a vintage downtown hotel called the Blackstone, host to mobsters and writers since the twenties. On our way to a restaurant the night before the ceremony, I walked through downtown Chicago, arm-in-arm with my mother. Eva was walking ahead with Bruce, who had flown in from San Francisco, and Dean and Bernadette Marie, just arrived from Baltimore. Watching Eva a few steps ahead of us, I felt strangely like I had to keep some distance. She and my mother were still figuring out their relationship.

Amazing Grace: therapist and confidante, protector from the brutish cruelties of other boys and men; shield against my father's more flawed humanity, his cruelties, his absence; a woman alone in a very big world. We had never talked about the role I played in her life: husband proxy, confidante, co-parent to my brothers. It was impossible to know how to mourn that unspoken, ever-present bond. She was happy for me, but she was guarded.

When I had finally told her, at nineteen years old, that I was having a relationship with Cass, she paused to reflect. "You know when I was your age, I had an experience like that with one of my girlfriends," she said. "We got anxious and stopped what we were doing, but I've always wondered what might have happened, if I had lived in a different time."

Throughout college, to test her professed acceptance, I brought home a succession of witty, amusing boyfriends. Sometimes I brought home boyfriends because none of them believed I had a parent so tolerant of my gay friends. Some of these young men Grace liked; some she wished I'd leave. When Stefan visited, he found it hilarious to teach my mother's two black cats to masturbate with their tails. His ribaldry was one of the few things that ever pushed her patience. "Why can't you go out with clean-cut guys like Roy?" she asked when Stefan was out of the room. "He dressed so neatly and he wore his hair short."

That night in Chicago, I asked her, "Would you do me a favor?"

"What's that?"

"At the reception after the ceremony, when you make the toast, would you mind outing me?"

"Outing you?"

I thought for a moment, tried to slow down and analyze this impulse. "Not really *out* out, just a little out," I said. "Make some funny, indirect allusion to my gay life. Some of Eva's older relatives wouldn't understand, but I don't want my close friends to think I'm going in the closet, or that I'm becoming someone different from whom they've known. Do you know what I mean?"

She thought for a moment.

"Maybe something campy about how I was growing up," I said. "But I don't want George to figure it out. He'll kill me. So kind of gay-ish, but not super obvious."

We were crossing the bridge over the Chicago River. Eva and my brothers had already reached the restaurant and were going inside, so our conversation would have to end. "I'll think of something," she said, squeezing my arm.

The night before our ceremony, on the twelfth floor of the Blackstone Hotel where our out-of-town family members were staying, Eva and I lay in bed under soft sheets, holding onto each other, unable to sleep. The sex we had had earlier drew on some boundless, nervous energy that seemed to come from the city itself, glittering and chaotic and bustling in the background. It was two in the morning. "We *really* need to get some sleep," I said.

"I'm going to have circles under my eyes," she said. "I can't settle."

Sometimes after we had sex, I would sit in a sense of rich irony, the same surprise I would feel on the most daring amusement park rides, jolting my body, suddenly, in directions it was never supposed to go. Even five years into our relationship, I often felt after sex as if I had somehow tricked my body, my most apparent desires, and the mythic, faraway Gods of social identity. "I am a *gay* man," the tribal mantra drummed inside me. But right alongside that declaration, my heart thumped; I was sweaty; my body swelled with yearning ("Honey, do you want to do it again?"); the scent of her dismantled any logic. Those thoughts—"I am a gay man" and "Honey, do you want to do it again?"—seemed to erase me, yet, uncannily, I emerged, fully myself, in that fleeting moment of contradiction.

I rolled over in bed to check on her and noticed that, yes, she was awake, anxious about tomorrow, which was now today. She kissed me. "Do you want to do it again?" she asked.

The next thing I knew we were driving to the big event on a hot, bright summer day. I was praying there weren't sweat stains on my new linen shirt. Eva wore a cream-colored lace sheath that exposed her strong collarbone. My linen suit matched. In all our finery we climbed into my soon-to-be mother-in-law's car for the drive to the Chicago Theological Seminary.

There had been so many hand-wringing arguments leading up to this moment.

What kind of dress could she tolerate, that would make her look like a bride but also not like a bride? If she stayed in a bridal shop for more than fifteen minutes, she became nauseous. Everything was a despicable, glittery, lace-exploding meringue. Naomi would scout out shops first, select the sleekest, least lacy concoctions for review, to maximize our narrow time window before Eva bolted.

"We can't push her too hard," Naomi said.

I liked shopping for wedding dresses. This irony helped no one.

Would we ruin the ceremony if she didn't carry a bouquet? You will, Gary continued to insist. With so many elaborately dressed women, and a spouse-to-be who eschews a traditional gown, the guests will be confused. *Fire the damn florist,* Eva kept whispering in my ear.

Would male relatives resent being without boutonnieres? Without a doubt, Gary insisted. I wouldn't do it, agreed the photographer. It is a beloved tradition, Father Sam said. Otherwise you will be encircled by resentful men who don't know who they are.

As we neared 57th Street, Eva asked, "Do you remember that argument that we had about what time to schedule the ceremony?"

Amidst the swirl of so many arguments, I did recall it. *Would our older relatives feel slighted by a midafternoon reception with light hors d'oeuvres, or did we need an earlier event with a full-blown lunch?*

"Why do you ask?"

Before she answered, I could see. On the lawn of the Chicago Theological Seminary one hundred guests, in their finest church attire, languished under the July sun. In the one sliver of shade, four musicians, brows glistening, rehearsed, like those musicians that played while the *Titanic* slipped under ocean waves. Sweating, red-faced, furious, Gary leaned against a van, monstrous wilting flower arrangements at his feet.

Immediately I dashed inside the Seminary followed by Bruce, Dean, and the photographer. The first-floor chapel was impenetrable, locked, secured behind iron bars. Inside I could see wooden chairs in rows; the stone walls; a bar of sunlight, coming through the stained glass, piercing the shadows, insisting on an antique stillness.

In my cream-colored linen suit, with the embroidered vest that I would never wear again but that conferred specialness if not ridiculousness on this day of days, I grabbed the bars. Much to the consternation of my brothers and the photographer, I rattled them and grunted like a mad prisoner on the opposite side of his confinement. It made a metal jangling sound.

Dean said, "I thought you didn't care about this stuff."

At that time, in the basement of the seminary, was an academic bookstore, much beloved on the South Side of Chicago. The labyrinthine passageways and narrow crannies were crammed with colorful titles and curious words like "grammatology" and "phallogocentrism" and "historicity." During my undergraduate days these rooms had been the places where I loved to linger, delightfully lost, thinking and exploring. That Saturday, students waited in line for the cashiers, books in arms.

I shouted. "Does anyone have keys to open the chapel?"

The two cashiers eyed me in my fancy garb. "Sorry."

"Do you know anyone who can find the people who can open it?!?"

Again, they were useless.

An impatient undergraduate whispered to the person beside him, "Heteronormative sheep."

Outside, guests melted like ice cream cones. I glimpsed Father Sam: black vestments freshly starched and ironed; a crisp gleaming white collar; Bible under his arm. He was talking to Eva's aunt who gazed at him with rapt attention.

I touched his shoulder, he leaned into me, and I whispered, "Do you know any place where we can get married?"

"*Fuck*," said the priest.

Along the tree-canopied, mansion-lined streets of Woodlawn Avenue a long line of guests and musicians and florists and amused brothers traipsed to the backyard of Bent House, four blocks away, for an impromptu service.

Everyone knows what a wedding is supposed to look like.

It was a mad, loud beehive of consternation: the panic of needing to look normal, puffy-white-cream-frosting-wedding-day beautiful was palpable on every face. It was a cultural emergency. With an authoritative sense of *feng shui* and an impeccable sense of last-minute design, Father Sam launched into high command mode. Chairs appeared in rows on the grass. A path was marked for the bride and groom. The photographer positioned himself behind an azalea. Musicians settled and played under an awning. George sat in the front row with other older relatives. I had never seen him smile before this. Younger guests stood behind them, sweating. Father Sam pursed his lips and wiped his brow with a handkerchief.

The service started only an hour later. In the center of the garden was a gold, sun-shaped mandala on a pedestal, a memorial to congregation members who had succumbed to AIDS. While Father Sam spoke, those languid looping sentences in that drawl of his, we stood in front of it, only half-hearing what he was saying, all the religious stuff. Finally relaxed after the frenzied, last-minute search to find a place for the ceremony, I glanced at Father Sam as he spoke, so grateful, at the mandala which absorbed the sunlight, at the ex-boyfriends and brothers and family surrounding us, at her dad looking satisfied and dignified, at my mother blotting her eyes, and at Eva in her dress. It was perfect. She wore a simple strand of pearls. Although Gary had insisted on providing a bouquet, even when we said we wouldn't pay for it, she had handed it to Naomi who chucked it behind a tree.

Dressed in a flowing gown, pastel flowers blossoming brightly on an indigo background, Naomi, victorious matchmaker, smiled and read one of the "Twenty-One Love Poems."

> ...*show me what I can do*
> *for you, who have often made the unnameable*
> *nameable for others, even for me.*

Then we said our vows under the hot sun on the bright green grass.

People took many lessons from the day we were locked out of the church. The photographer confessed that he thought the chapel was a dusty prison cell. For weeks he had had nightmares about terrible, shadowy photos. Aunt Shirley said, "It was so beautiful and perfect, like it was supposed to happen that way." My friend Scott mused about the Japanese aesthetic of *wabi-sabi* that values flaws as a part of the beautiful. Mary Jo consoled: "Sometimes it is a gift when beautiful things begin imperfectly."

Gary had dropped off the wilted flowers at the second destination, his invoice attached, determined never again to work with couples who wouldn't use the words "bride" and "groom."

Four years later, I was in a sterile white room in an assisted living facility holding my daughter, Rosie, just over a year old. Eva's and my mantra—*No marriage, no kids*—had withered beyond recognition.

Exhausted, tear-spent, Eva had left for the cafeteria. It was just me, my sleeping child, and my bedridden father-in-law. George was riddled with cancer. He couldn't talk. He could barely move. But his eyes were wide and he was alert. He had expected to have so many more years. In this stray, atypical moment, he was alone with his literary, do-gooder son-in-law who was still so different than who he imagined his beautiful daughter marrying. I struggled whenever I was alone with him.

In only a few hours I would be getting on a plane with my small family. Almost certainly, this was the last time I would see him alive. The gravity of the deathbed confounded me. For years we had struggled to communicate. Now I had to figure out the last thing I would ever say to him.

There was a long, strained silence. He stared at me, eyes moist, mouth open, with an expression that looked like pleading. He was in pain. I shifted Rosie in my arms. Perhaps it was the new, humble wisdom that accompanies having a first child, but I wondered: *What would I want someone to say to me, if I were on my deathbed?* And it came to me, miraculously, the promise I needed to make, an echo of those vows we made on that improbable lawn, when we were locked out of the chapel:

"You know, George, I am always going to take care of her."

It was no longer an act of translation, but the truth, stripped bare of any distracting decoration.

He couldn't respond with words. His eyes teared. He squeezed my hand.

Then we left.

PART TWO

—

AVALANCHE

There is a long time in me between knowing and telling.
Grace Paley, "Debts"

5
—

THE NIGHT GRACE PALEY DIED

Portland, 2007

The night she finds out, I am running in the dark.

Four or five times a week, after the dishes are cleared and washed and put away and Rosie, Louis, and Philip are tucked into bed, I run this same path. The centripetal routine of raising children and maintaining a home and working a job to pay for the home and the children and the two sickly cats from the rescue shelter who need constant medical attention pushes out this one precious hour to the end of the day when it is dark and I am tired, but it is, it seems, the only hour I get. It is nine o'clock.

The streetlights, few and far between, create dappled, orange flecks on the ground. This is a neighborhood of grand trees, gnarled bodies wrestling with tight sidewalks, their canopies obscuring the sky. Here and there a square of sidewalk buckles, broken by tree roots, hazards that could catch a runner's shoe unawares. But still I am running—heart thumping, running shoes pounding, autumn leaves crunching—picking a path out of the darkness.

This will be the joke about my midlife crisis in the emergency room. Running in the dark? Seriously? I could come crashing down on the cement, wrists splayed to break my fall, the thud of my body landing on the hard, rough ground, a "Fuck!" heard by dozing children in their bedrooms. Limping home, I might wonder: How will I explain to anyone that I was running at night, without even a head lamp?

Why do men do reckless things?

I arrive at the high school and hop down the cement stairs that lead to the oval-shaped track. Within this bowl surrounded by massive shadowy pines, it is even darker. The lights over the tennis courts, just north, extinguish at nine o'clock. There is only a hint of the lights that line the nearby street. No one can see me here.

After I circle the track several times, I head back through the leaves dappled with flecks of orange light. My pace is slower. My brick house comes into view. Though it is after ten now, there are lights on in every window except the children's bedrooms. This is the first sign.

Wiping my forehead, I stop running and walk up the sidewalk, panting, sweat catching up to me. I turn the key in the lock on the oak door, and I enter.

Eva is standing there, waiting, a look of fury on her face, holding a photograph she has printed out on a piece of paper. It is a picture of my face with a flirty message, one I emailed secretly to a man I found on a gay hookup site.

She says in an otherworldly voice: "GET. OUT. NOW."

The same night my marriage as I knew it ended Grace Paley died. She had breast cancer. She was eighty-four. Even though my life plunged into crisis, one that would last several unbearable years, I spent any extra time I could find re-reading her stories and essays and thinking about her: the spare, slightly fatigued language, awash with the plainspoken quirkiness of life, the antics of the neighbors, the spinning, up-and-down musical carousel of family bonds. In Grace Paley's world, they say, everyone is eloquent when telling their own story.

It is a common occurrence in her essays that people come up and tell her what and how to write. These conversations always give her pause, but she never actually writes what anyone suggests. Predictable parts of other stories you read—things like plot and character development and epiphany—hold no interest for her. She has a pure allegiance to the quirky, unexplained, unapologized-for ordinariness of life in which her characters are immersed. Her people are equal parts foolish and wise. What shines in her stories: the triumph of voice, characters whose sentences pulse with loss, Yiddishkeit. I read these stories in the aftermath of my own denouement. They act as a kind of spiritual salve, but I can't understand its chemistry or why.

In the sad, numb days that follow, living outside the house, I play a translation game. I take a passage from one of Paley's short stories and re-imagine it with my own falling-apart life. I try to sanitize the perverse details, re-see them through the kinder eyes of an old neighbor who is amused by the particularities of the human condition. If my story began like "Wants," for example, where the woman runs into her ex-husband at the library, it might sound like this:

In many ways, she said, as I look back, I attribute the dissolution of our marriage to the fact that we stopped having Scott and Ann to dinner.

That's possible, I said. But really, if you remember: first, we moved to Oregon, then the children were born, then the internet got big, then there was 9/11. Then they didn't seem to enjoy children so much. But you're right. We should have had them over more.

Maybe I knew this day would come, a far-flung, trampled moment at a dark end of the day's rhythms.

"I'm sorry," I stammer to Eva. I don't know who I am anymore, but I know that I am wrong. Wrongness is all of me. "Nothing happened."

"Get. Out. Now."

I do not question her authority, its intensity. I will not argue or deny. I need to leave, quickly. I walk upstairs to find a suitcase. Lights are on everywhere, except the children's rooms. I hope they are sleeping. In our shared office, the computer screen blazes hot colors, red and yellow. I see two words:

DIVORCE LAWYERS

I find a duffle bag in the closet, but I cannot think what to put in it. How long will I be gone? Where will I go? What do I need? Shaking, I toss my running clothes in a wicker hamper and pull on a gray sweatshirt and sweatpants. I grab a few shirts, underwear, some jeans, a toothbrush. I grab several books of poetry cracked on the nightstand. My heart is beating like a mad man banging the bars of a cell, fear welling up in my throat. I resist the temptation to look in the children's rooms: Philip and Louis on their bunk beds; Rosie with her head under the covers clutching a monkey called Mr. Milsen. At this burning moment I cannot bear to kiss them goodnight. I cannot slow down. Before the duffle bag is even half full, I head downstairs where she is sitting at the dining room table, posture alert, staring at the wall. I see her profile: the short tousled blond hair, the high cheekbones. I do not want to talk to her, do not want to hear the words again, their cruel inevitability.

Get.

Out.

Now.

But a decent man would say something before he leaves, even though I am not a decent man anymore. "Can't we at least talk?"

"No," she says, without looking at me. "It's over. I want you out."

She has her father's white-hot temper. I have always been afraid of it, just like I was afraid of him when he was alive. Once, while studying in Mexico City, a man put his hand on Eva's butt and, without thinking, she punched him in the face. Bam! She is no man's fool.

The moon is a silver thread. Walking to my dusty green car, I glance one more time at our house, windows blazing at this dark hour like it's burning down. My hand shakes uncontrollably when I try to put the key in the lock of the car door. I drop my bag to use my other hand to steady it. I lay my forehead on the cool side of the car. How did this happen? How did I get ripped out of my home? Why did I go so easily? Everything pivots on a contradiction: I knew it would happen, that I was on dangerous, desperate ground, but I wanted to stay, to hold onto the rhythms of child-rearing and doing the dishes and folding the laundry and feeding the hermit crabs who never seemed to die and taking the cats to the veterinary emergency room again and spinning on the mer-ry-go-round and noisy family dinners. Sometimes I suffocated in the routine: there was too much; it was unrelenting. But I loved everyone and I loved being in the sloshed-together comforts of family life.

I must leave.

In 1994, when I was a student in my MFA program, I met her. Grace Paley was diminutive, with a round face, wispy white fly-away hair, a fine nose, eyes that crinkled with kindness. A humble radiance shined in her. I had drafted a short story that left me feeling anxious and exposed. The protagonist was a teacher in an obstetrics and gynecology training pro-gram, a woman who uses her body to instruct medical students how to do a patient-centered pelvic exam. To research the story, I interviewed our friends who did this kind of medical school instruction, including the girlfriend who became my wife, to discover what it felt like to be a naked teacher, to have someone invade your body for a good cause. What did it feel like to have a woman's body and to allow it to be touched in this way, to be both subject and object, to be violated and empowered? For so long I was mystified by the uses of a speculum. I felt presumptuous, like I was on territory where a man shouldn't enter.

Grace Paley was a famous feminist and anti-war activist. I wanted to please her. I worried about offending her. The night before the workshop I barely slept. What would she say? Had I taken the wrong risk and ruined my one opportunity for her to want me to be her special male feminist protégée? And what do special male feminist protégées do anyway?

There were eight of us in the workshop, mostly women. Under my shirt I could feel beads of sweat dripping down my sides. I barely heard what anyone else said. I worried that everyone could see my wet panic. I read a page.

As is customary, students commented before the teacher. There was a mad volley of commentary, constant interrupting. I took notes furiously, tried to check my defensiveness. Some of the commenters objected for feminist reasons. It wasn't a man's story to tell. It had a certain arrogance. Could he really, authentically—within the limitations of a man's experience of the world—understand the woman's perspective, especially in this intensely vulnerable position?

Like a mother watching her children argue and pacing her energy, Grace Paley listened and nodded and smiled and nodded. Her unflinching gaze communicated steady compassion, like we were in her Upper West Side neighborhood watching the circus spectacle of the neighbors being their crazy selves. I was just one of the local curiosities. Finally, she spoke. "I like this, Wayne," she said quietly, the one exception in the room. "It's real." That was all she said. It was weirdly anti-climactic, like my story, so perverse for a man to want to tell, was just another interesting tale in the world, acceptably odd, from an unexpected but interesting angle. She didn't say anything more.

I search for my cell phone and punch in numbers. The phone picks up and I hear sleepy fumbling. "H-ullo?" My mother is on the East Coast where it's three hours later.

"It's me."

"Are you OK?"

"She threw me out of the house."

"What?" I can hear the rustling of sheets. *"What?"*

I don't know what else to do but blurt out the crude, jagged details which had been secret up until now. "Eva threw me out of the house," I repeat. "She was looking through my sent emails. She found an email to a man. I was looking for sex."

"Oh no." That's all she says. She divorced my father when I was fourteen. He is dead now. She lives alone. She never wanted to remarry.

"I don't know what to do."

"Where are you?"

"Driving." I start to cry. "I ruined everything."

"Should you pull over?" she asks, and I do. She listens. She has deep reserves of kindness. For two decades she loved a handsome, funny man who was an alcoholic, a womanizer, an out-of-control gambler. She tracked him down at night and drove him home from bars. She took him back after he had affairs. She patiently tried to make their marriage work—she tried to change herself, she tried to change him, she had another baby, she moved to another state with him to see if their luck would change—until he left without a word.

I wonder what she thinks of me as she sees my father's destructive DNA playing out in my own life. "I can't make myself fit into this mold," I say. "I tried it and it didn't work for me. I wish I could."

"Maybe you two need to find a different way of being together and parenting the kids. But not married."

"I still want to be married," I say, between rough sobs. "I don't know why."

My mother knows this isn't the first time that I have strayed. "Are you really sure?" she asks. "It doesn't seem to me that it works for you."

I am quiet, taking in this pronouncement. Usually, she is neither an advice-giver nor a judge. When she offers an opinion, it is hard not to listen. "I need to find a place to sleep tonight."

"Where can you go?"

"I guess a hotel. Somewhere."

"Do you have enough money?"

"I'm OK."

She reminds me she loves me. "Take care of yourself," she says. "And be careful. You need to stop driving and get to sleep."

I promise to call her in the morning.

I want to get as far away as possible.

It is after midnight and I am driving on deserted, treeless streets under yellow streetlights. I want my geography to match the fractured map of my mind, a map that can only lead to different versions of lost-ness. Driving up Sandy Boulevard through northeast Portland, farther and farther away, I pass small hotels—they get shabbier the farther I go from my home—but they are still too close. I want to be more lost. I want to be someplace unfamiliar, where no one knows me.

Suddenly I am aware of this sense of crumbling in my body. My skin burns as if the boundary that defines me is disintegrating. My stomach rolls in rebellion. My heart pounds louder than ever. Could I have a heart attack? I cannot calm myself down. I cannot breathe slowly or deeply. It doesn't work. The thought that my breath doesn't work—a sputtering engine on its last legs—intensifies the shock of the world breaking apart.

I drive up 82nd Avenue, a stretch famous for drug deals and larceny. Here and there I see a woman with a mask of hard routine waiting in a short skirt or cut-off shorts. Finally, I am driving through the desolation of Marine Boulevard, one of the industrial arteries on the edge of the city, far from any real neighborhood with people. I pass shut-down sawmills and refrigerator stores and industrial appliance supply shops. Then I see a barely lit white building, a boxy hotel with an office with a sleepy attendant behind bulletproof glass. I am so tired. I pull into the parking lot.

People asked Grace Paley to tell their family stories. They wanted to give her their projects: memorabilia, letters, family archives. Kind as she was, she always refused.

Immersing myself in Grace Paley's stories is like listening to a local elder recount the goings on of all the eccentric neighbors; parents arguing with children, husbands cruelly patronizing their wives, mothers in the kitchen exhausted by arguing children and panicking about missed periods or worrying about deadly cancers. There is never judgment or alarm at any cruel spectacle, just cool, sometimes weary observation, perhaps a hint of irony. Usually there's no plot, no reach for epiphany. "Everyone, real or invented, deserves the open destiny of life," she writes in "A Conversation with My Father." And maybe that's the pleasure and that's the relief.

There's a story called "Living" about two women, friends, mothers of young children, who both think that they're dying young. I am looking at the structure of their conversations, the catalogue of ordinariness. One character tells the other: "Life isn't all that great...We've had nothing but crummy days and crummy guys and broke all the time and cockroaches and nothing to do on Sunday but take the kids to Central Park and row on that lousy lake."

"I want to see it all," the friend answers. Of the two, only this friend will actually die.

I play with translation again, fit myself into this sad conversation about maybe-endings. *Marriage isn't all that great,* I think...*We've had nothing but working days and worrying nights and broke all the time and nobody remembers sex anymore and pushing baby carriages through numb exhaustion those ten blocks (and they walk so slowly!) to see a neighborhood pig named Mooshie who never came out of his distant pen to see us anyway.*

But I want to be married.

I try to match the weary, curious, near-defeated tone. I do want to be married, I think, but not in the narrow sense that I've been suffering with so far; more in the sense of those spilling-over watershed moments, the near-impossibility of loneliness, that these fellow-travelers, my family, bring to me.

Her stories are a kind of salve for a hard life. They hint at the possibility of breaking free from shame. When I translate myself into a Grace Paley story, I feel like an ordinary fool, not a cruel freak.

Does it matter that we exchange text messages into the night? Does it matter that they contain words like *narcissist, sociopath,* and *fucking bastard*? Or my apologies that make no difference? Does it matter that I take a shower, with the cold water on full-force, to purify, to obliterate? Does it matter that my skin burns like the boundary between myself and the world is disintegrating, that no amount of water makes the fire diminish? Does it matter that I don't sleep? The text messages stop at about three o'clock.

A few hours before dawn I get a text alert from *The New York Times* and read that yesterday, while my life was falling apart, Grace Paley died. There will be no new stories about those far-away neighborhoods with their world-weary inhabitants trying to figure out how to live. Outside the sun has not yet risen, but in the distance there is a glimmer of yellow.

I take another freezing shower.

6

SERAC

The glare of sun presses against my eyelids. The room grows warmer. I open my eyes, hoping I am not where I am, that I had a nightmare where my life fell apart, but I wake up in a tiny white room, barely separated from the rush of pick-up trucks. The ground rumbles with their early-morning industry, an earth tremor rumbling through my body.

I grab my cell phone, look for more texts. Nothing new. The words dwindled. *Narcissist. Liar. Sociopath.*

I miss my home in the morning: the stillness of the high-ceilinged rooms as I come downstairs before the children awaken. Outside the window: birds call to each other, a gentle flute-like competition of conversations; leafy tree branches sway; pink sunlight peeks over the roofs of neighbors' homes. Usually I wake up before anyone else, boil water, and turn on the radio. In the morning they often play Baroque music—harpsichord, lute, delicate wind melodies. I glance at the newspaper, then pour hot water into the French press, set the timer, and wait. I am a creature of rituals, a lover of habits. Ironically, I am also a follower of rules; someone who wants to do right and to be a good person.

Lying in bed, in this hotel cell, I am paralyzed by a list of tasks. Take stock of the damage. Try to see Eva and talk. Come up with something to say to the kids. Find a place to live. Reach out to a friend. And then, looming, the biggest task: How am I going to live my life now?

My skin burns. Is it the sunlight that pierces the curtains or the epithets heaped like wood on a fire? Language—harsh condemning words pile up in my mind—traps me like a wet, writhing bug on corkboard.

Cad

Philanderer

Adulterer

Rake

Alley cat

Faggot

There is no shortage of words for me.

Deadbeat dad

I am a terrible father who has left his children. I had not even said goodbye.

Earlier that week there was a newspaper story about a young man who had gone snowboarding with friends to the western edge of the White River Glacier on Mount Hood. The three had entered a snow tunnel bigger than a school bus: glowing walls, blue shadows, bright sky peeking through its door, the shattered glitter of sun on snow. They were looking for a place to snowboard, perhaps through the A-framed tunnel, and to take pictures.

They played. Then the roof of the glacier collapsed. The beautiful day ended. Two of them were injured. One man, just twenty-five, was crushed by a block of ice, a *serac* that fell from the ceiling. Seracs form when glaciers move over bulges in the ground, cracking the glacier ice into blocks.

In that slow, rumbling, split-second before the tragedy, was there some flicker of awareness? Did he suddenly realize the danger? The glacier's smooth glittering walls through which the bright sky shone might have fooled him into seeing an illusory permanence, reassuring him that he would be safe. He had seen the stunning enormity of the structure, but not the fissures in the ceiling, its vulnerability to collapse.

Was there another flash of awareness, when he lay crushed beneath the hard snow, when he realized the beautiful glacier's destructive power?

I can't stop thinking about the snowboarder. I think about the limits of human understanding. We do not see all of the beautiful structures that surround us, towering above us, enclosing us, burying us. We see aspects of them. We see more of ourselves and the ways we can or can't navigate these enormous structures. When tragedy happens, we blame ourselves and what we didn't see, even though the edifice is so seductively big, it's not seeable in its entirety and brokenness, the subtle fissures mapping eventual collapse.

I can't stop thinking about him, trapped, suffocating in those moments before the breath left his body.

Sometimes, in the most unlikely moments, we get a flash of insight, shining light on a piece of our lives that had bedeviled us. That morning in the hotel room, awash in searing light, I remember my own father, Scotty, that stubborn ghost. He died seven years ago. At his funeral all his friends told me how they loved him: his warmth, his laughter, his joke-cracking energy. I was not sure I loved him.

I remember the awful morning, when I was fourteen, when I asked my mother where he had gone, see her sitting at the dining room table, drinking coffee, eyes tired and gray, her mouth a grim line. In the kitchen Bruce and Dean were fixing their cereal and hot chocolate, pretending that this conversation about my father's whereabouts was as uninteresting as a conversation about chores. No one wanted to admit that we were becoming the kind of fatherless family we had become.

"I don't know where he is," she said. Each word had a lurching truth. "He hasn't called."

"Are you worried?"

"I'm worried," she said. "But there's nothing I can do."

He is gone, he is gone, he is gone.

I hugged her. I sensed that maybe she had started to cry. I held onto her tightly so that I wouldn't have to see if there were tears. In that moment I hated him for putting us through this ordeal of not knowing. I hated the depth of his secret-keeping, his arrogance to leave her to take care of us.

"I'm so sorry, Mom," I said. "We'll take care of you."

Thirteen-year-old Dean broke out of his complacent cereal-fixing, orange-juice-pouring routine and also put his arms around her, and Bruce, only ten, joined, and we were all holding onto each other in the terrible storm of his betrayal.

Now, forty-three years old, alone in a hotel room, I understand. I know why he didn't come home. Suddenly one of the defining stories of my life becomes a different narrative. A story that I had no other way to tell, other than to impute a cruel narcissism, becomes softer, more human. It wasn't villainy. It's this same crushing paralysis, this serac, that's keeping me in this room, under the covers, shielding my ears from the rush of traffic, hoping the day won't arrive, that time will stay as petrified as my mind and body feel.

Ignorant of how to reverse the damage.

And then, as that old story about father-absence and father-rage softens, the paralysis shifts. I see another truth, inarticulate in the tumult of past events, becoming clearer.

Even though I was angry at him for leaving, enraged about every way he'd broken my mother's heart, bereft at the casual way he left me to grow up mostly without a father, worried that he had left because parenting an effeminate son was disgusting, there was one truth from my fourteen-year-old life I could no longer ignore:

I wanted him to come back.

In spite of his glaring mistakes, I wanted him to try again.

In my hotel room I pull down the covers and open my eyes. The light from the sun, unforgiving, floods my body. But I know what I need to do. I need to find my way back home.

I know I am wrong. But I am also devoted. I am wrong and devoted. I pick up the cell phone and stare at it. I know I have to call her, that we have to negotiate the next steps, but I am terrified. There is a poverty of language. I remember a sign I saw once above a quarry. It showed a stick figure man tumbling into a chasm with exclamation marks flying from his head.

"Hello?"

"Hi."

"We have to talk sometime today."

"There's nothing to talk about anymore."

"We have to talk about what we tell the kids."

"I told them you went on a business trip. That something came up."

"We need to talk about what's going to happen."

"There's no talk. We're getting a divorce."

I wince at the word. I take in the dark flip side of moral certainty— that core piece of who she is, that once drew me to her—which is condemnation. I bristle. I have to remind myself—maybe I *am* narcissistic?—that today's judgment isn't about some petty domestic failure like neglecting to take out the trash or fill up the gas tank. I have betrayed her.

I don't want to divorce. I want to make amends.

My voice shakes. "I ruined everything. You're right to be furious. We still need to talk about how we do what we're going to do. I want to see the kids. I miss them."

"You should have thought about that when you couldn't keep your dick inside your pants."

Dick. Divorce. I don't know what to say. Contemptible sex. Contemptible men. I am nobody.

"Will you meet me at the track by the high school this afternoon? There's a bench under the big tree."

"My mind's made up."

"I know. Eva, I'm really sorry. I wish things were different."

"So do I."

"Will you meet me please?"

"I'll be there. Goodbye."

I shower and pack up the few possessions that are scattered in the room. I don't know where I'm going, but I'm not coming back here.

I call my friend Scott. I have known him since I was nineteen. He knew me from our college days, when the world thought I was gay. Like me, he is a writer who does many other things besides writing to make ends meet. We get together every two weeks for lunch; always about an hour; vegetarian fare to suit both our allergies; and talk about how we are writing or not writing. He reads and edits everything I write. He is steady Charlotte, writer-friend-spider with boundless compassion who never lets me down, to my worrying Wilbur, dusty pig racing around his pen.

"Can you meet today?"

"Hey, I'd love to, but I've got errands..."

"Eva threw me out."

"What?"

"She was searching in my sent emails for some correspondence related to a bill. She found an email where I was asking this guy about sex. She kicked me out last night."

"Jesus."

"I don't have any place to go."

"Shit," he says with a tone that means: I get it; the spinning world just stopped; this is not our usual conversation.

We meet at Costello's, the neighborhood café, four blocks from my house, where I sometimes come when I have breaks from parenting. The ambience is dark. The tables and café chairs are distressed antiques. Screens flash with filmed street scenes from cities around the world, souvenirs of the owner's travels: Paris, Buenos Aries, Athens.

Scott has a goatee with hints of gray and a blue tattoo of a vintage post mark with his birthdate on his forearm. He smiles uncomfortably and gives me a hug and we order coffee and sit down and I look at him from my stunned place. I wanted to get together to talk. Now I have nothing to say.

He is in problem-solving mode. "Fred thinks you can stay in his father-in-law's apartment," he says. Fred is a mutual friend, another writer who works most of the time at things that have nothing to do with writing. He does not have a tattoo. "His father-in-law is out of town for a month."

"Really?"

"Fred's mother-in-law has the key. They're not married anymore. It's odd. Anyway, she's watching the place. You can meet her this afternoon. If it feels OK to her, she'll let you stay."

"That would be a relief."

"How are you doing?"

"I don't know." I can't meet his gaze. "I really don't know." At first I think that I am too shocked and numb to talk, but then it hits me: this is not the first time Scott has been my confidante after an infidelity. He is a good husband to Ann. He is steady and loyal, though I am not. If I were him, I would judge me, but he never makes judgments.

"Did you actually meet with that guy?"

"He never responded."

"All this and you didn't even meet?"

I shake my head. Would it have been more awful if we had? "It's ironic."

I try to talk to him, to unburden, but the words are fitful, imprecise. Scott nods, searching my expressions, trying to understand what I don't understand. I'm still not feeling anything, or I'm feeling so much that I can't name it. Shame, shock, crumbling, burning; sadness, sadness, sadness, sadness; a dark grief at the core of all the tangled confusion; in the background, barely admittable, relief. It is the most awkward conversation we have ever had. Why does he continue to be my friend?

"Let me know what Fred's mother-in-law says."

"I will," I say as we rise. "I don't know what I'm going to say to Eva."

He gives me another hug. "Just keep showing up."

It is the kind of perfect summer day—warm sunshine, pure blue sky, a gentle breeze, everywhere flowers bursting rainbow colors—that should make it impossible to talk about anything as ugly as divorce. I arrive first in a park, at the bench beside the track—the same oval I run at nights—under the canopy of pine trees. In the distance, before I can even make out her face, I notice her body, the determined energy and fast step. I know she has already talked to her friends in the neighborhood and contacted Naomi to come for a visit. Her powers of creating community are formidable. Growing up, it was just her and her mother, her father visiting weekends. When we talked about having children, she insisted on three. One might die, she said. Yes, I said, but then there would be one left. But when we die, she would be all alone, she said.

To be alone, disconnected, unseen, was the greatest terror.

"Hi," she says. No hug. I knew there wouldn't be a hug, but still I wanted one.

On a weathered bench we sit distant from each other. There is a hardness to her expression, like she is steeling herself against anything good about the two of us. It has been cast out by her discovery. She has a small purple pamphlet in her hand. It is a copy of Adrienne Rich's essay "Women and Honor: Some Notes on Lying." Years ago she bought a handful of these pamphlets, thinking it would make a ready gift for friends. "Here," she says, bitterness in her voice, and hands it to me.

I take the pamphlet. This is the first time I have not loved Adrienne Rich. Maybe I won't be able to read her again.

A serac crushes my heart. I need to say something. I have nothing to say. I hear her efficient declarations:

"We'll need to sell the house."

"We'll need to tell the kids we're divorcing."

"I'd like us to split our assets evenly. I'd like half your retirement savings."

The sentences are racing away from me. I struggle to respond. "I don't think we should make any decisions yet," I venture. "It's still too raw."

"I'm not changing my mind."

"I'm not trying to get you to change your mind. These are big matters. We need to be thoughtful and not rush."

"I don't want to talk about this anymore."

She needs me out of the house for a while. Our friend Callie has come to stay with her for a few days. Then Naomi, now married to the good Jewish man, the same lawyer who once broke up with her but then changed his mind and proposed, has plans to come into town to support her. We agree that I can come to see the children in a few days, then she rises and walks away, back to our neighborhood, leaving me alone.

When Fred's mother-in-law opens the door to her small second-floor apartment, all I can think is: I need to make a good impression. I need to come across as a responsible man. I need to leave with a key. I am shaking inside, trying to look like nothing's wrong although it's safe to say *everything is wrong*. I need to come across as stable, maybe even likable. I want to tell her as little about myself as possible because I don't know who I am anymore.

She has gray hair with tight curls and a man's flannel shirt, worn pink slippers on her feet. She is about seventy years old. "Have a seat," she says, gesturing toward the couch. It's pink and cream, overstuffed, with a pattern of green ribbons and red roses. This is a woman's apartment. It's crammed with antiques and striped afghans and doilies and knickknacks, too much stuff, like she's trying to downsize but hasn't quite done it yet. She sits in a weathered armchair and looks at me, unimpressed.

I try to smile but it's the last thing I feel like doing. I have nowhere to stay tonight. Maybe I can stay at Scott's, if I'm desperate, but I sense that Ann doesn't want to appear to take sides. I am on my own. My stomach rumbles. I want this woman to like me, but I'm not sure she likes anyone.

"Fred told me about your situation," she says blandly. "Some trouble at home?"

"My wife and I are separated," I say, not because I want it to be true, but it sounds sanitized, close enough, and doesn't necessarily mean I am the fuck-up that I am. "We need some time apart to figure out what we're doing."

"Marriage is difficult," she says, still staring at me. There is a world-weary flatness to her.

"How long have you lived in Portland?" I ask.

"I moved here from New York less than a year ago," she says. "I'm retired. I wanted to be closer to Sarah, Fred, and the kids. My ex came about six months ago. He likes being close to the grandkids too. He's not fully retired yet. He's away on a work gig."

"It's nice that you can be close to your grandkids," I say.

"The apartment is his, but I'm keeping an eye on it while he's away."

"So Fred asked you about me staying there?"

"I think my ex would be OK with it," she says. "He knows how marriage is. We've been divorced since Sarah was a teenager. If you stay there for the month he's away, you can bring in the mail, water the plants. It'll save me a trip. Would you do that?"

"I'd be happy to do that."

"Do you think you'll use it the whole month?"

"I can commit to that if it helps you," I say, wetting my lips, wanting to be helpful, desperate. "I don't really know how long we'll be separated. I hope not too long. But I'll keep watering the plants, no matter what."

"I don't know what makes marriage work," she says. "You stay connected no matter what, even if you don't like them. Sometimes just in your head. I like having him around. He takes me to the doctor. We go to family gatherings with the grandkids together. But I'm glad we don't live together. He drinks. Everybody has to find their own way."

"You're friends."

She pauses, looks away. "No, not friends. We do take care of each other, in a way. He lives a couple miles from here." She takes the key out of her pocket and nudges it across the coffee table.

"I appreciate your generosity," I say. "We have little kids. There's not a lot of extra money."

"You're going to be OK," she says, the first cheerful statement she's made. "Eventually. You'll be surprised."

I do not know my father's story. He never gave me advice or guidance or wisdom. In Grace Paley's world, the father looms, a formidable opinion-maker.

In "My Father Addresses Me on the Facts of Old Age," the narrator, a middle-aged woman, tells her father that she and her husband are divorcing. He yells at her, "What? What? Are you crazy? I don't understand you people nowadays," then lectures, "My advice to you—stick it out. It's true your husband, he's a peculiar fellow, but think it over. Go home. Maybe you can manage at least till old age. Then, if you still don't get along, you can go to separate old-age homes."

In the midst of marital crumbling, we are in the last stages of building a beautiful garden. It started as a common project that gave us both delight.

Five years ago when we bought the house—a clinker brick structure, the smallest house, circa 1905, on an avenue of grander homes with taller ceilings, more generous porches, set back from the street by wider lawns—the backyard was uninhabitable, bringing down the cost of the property and enabling us to worm our way into a neighborhood we couldn't otherwise afford.

The backyard was shaped like a bowl, with old, crumbling concrete steps descending to the bottom. The sides of the bowl had eroded. Soil had bled onto a makeshift patio made of the same broken, clinker bricks as the house. The patio's edges were obscured by mud. Here and there on the periphery a straggly rose bush or a purple hydrangea, ill-matched to the soil and sun availability, had been allowed to grow wild. Framing the space was a hedge of laurels that sprawled out of control. They cast shadows on the yard. When he razed them, the arborist found rat carcasses and dusty, antique toys.

We had replaced the laurels with a cedar fence. Wide, heavy Prichard slabs—rust-red, bronze, and blue with gold veins running through them like threads in a tapestry—had been laid on top of each other to create regal-looking stairs. The stone mason cut flagstone into puzzle-pieces and laid two patios, one round and wide at the bottom, another smaller two steps above it like a stage. Basalt boulders had been arranged around the diameter, defining the edge and holding back the soil.

Now that the transformation of the garden is nearly complete, Eva decides our marriage is over.

A few days later, while the children are at school, we meet with our friend Ann, Scott's wife, who also happens to be the garden designer, for an update on the work. She had just planted a short Japanese maple, its burgundy branches an airy umbrella. Her overalls are covered with dirt and she wears yellow garden gloves with dirt between the fingers. As we examine the space, she says, "We should talk about installing a sprinkler system, before the rain starts."

"I don't want one," Eva says, her expression hard. "We need to finish. We're putting the house on the market when we divorce."

The word punches my stomach. Definitive and angry—and now public. I know better than to argue. The outcast husband, I creep on the side of their conversation, listening, not hazarding to participate. Ann looks away from us, the storm of who we are now, looks away from the word *divorce*. She surveys the garden, nearly complete, a work of art.

Noticing Ann's discomfort, Eva says, in a softer tone, "I don't want to do anything ambitious. We need to rein in expenses. What are the main things left to do?"

"The flagstone's laid and it looks beautiful," Ann says, smiling. "You still need some kind of path for people to walk on so they can get to it. Otherwise you've got bare soil and it'll be mud."

Eva sighs. Nothing is ever done. There are too many frayed edges in her life. "I don't want to spend any more money."

In the corner of the yard are remnants from the stonemason's work: stacks of weathered bricks from the old patio, piles of flagstone, leftover, pieces of every shape and size. "I talked to the stone mason," I offer. "He said those flagstone pieces are ours. He can teach me how to put in a stone path."

"You *never* work in the garden."

She's right. I never do home projects. Ever. Our realtor joked with us: There are two kinds of men. Those who are handsome and those who are handy. Never both. Every heterosexual woman must make the choice. You'll have to settle for handsome, I had chided Eva once, when we still made jokes. "I'll be the handy one," she had said.

Now, I say, "The stone path would start in the front of the house and circle around the periphery to the back patio. The stonemason said it's not difficult. He said I could learn."

"How long will that take?"

"I can work on the path after work. I can finish by end of summer." I am buying time, bargaining. I want to have a reason to be at the house. It is obvious that I am a failure at fidelity, at marriage, but I want to be relevant, even if it is attempting to do something I have never done before.

She knows what I am doing. "I don't know."

"We can ask the stonemason to bid the job," Ann offers. "It wouldn't take long. Maybe a couple thousand dollars."

Eva purses her lips. Having me lay a stone path delays a neat end to our crisis. "OK," she says weakly. After Ann leaves, she pauses by the gingko tree, fingers one of the leaves, and speaks in a softer tone. "I've been through a lot," she says looking away, "with you." Tears form in her eyes. She wipes them away and tells me, "I love you but I can't do this anymore," and she retreats to the house where I am not welcome.

7

SET ME FREE

Chicago, 1990

Early in the evening when it happened the first time, I was watching the local news. There was a story about a notorious exhibitionist who was finally caught in a suburban neighborhood, far from his home (where he had driven, I was sure, because the farther away you drive the more likely you are to go unrecognized). Exhibitionists are master escape artists.

I knew so much about exhibitionism.

My heart thumped: drums on a battlefield. My chest felt thin, like it might not contain the furious rhythm. He was my client Max.

I saw the back of his head as the officer guided his body into the police car. He wore handcuffs. His wealthy parents, who thought therapy was helping, who believed in him, would be mortified. This time they would hesitate about bail. His girlfriend, who had never grasped that this—this kind of shame-saturated crime scene—was what his offenses involved: pedestrian terrorism; soul-cleaving humiliation. She would think carefully about how to call off the engagement.

Max and I had talked about this issue once. The whole group of men who had committed sex offenses had done an exercise on accountability and consequences. Then it seemed so theoretical.

Just a few days ago I had written a letter to a judge saying Max had completed all assignments. He had grappled with his rationalizations and excuses. He was done with treatment, I asserted with a little pride. I wanted to have one client from my group be successful. It would give hope to everyone.

I wondered if I would still have a job on Monday.

Max was young, white, professional, soft-spoken, introspective, clean-cut, a boy who clearly all his life had played by the rules (except when he didn't or couldn't). He appeared and acted like me.

So it looked like I lied to the judge.

I was so tired of shackling my trust to someone who was fooling me. To be lied to in any relationship was crazy-making.

I turned off the television, tried to steady my breath, and sat down on the couch and picked up *Giovanni's Room*, which I was re-reading for the fourth time, and I wondered if I could lose myself in scenes of Parisian cafes and cruisy gay bars and the drama of cruel David who strikes up a romantic friendship with Giovanni while his fiancée Hella is vacationing. It was impossible to like David. He is cruel, egotistic, duplicitous, full of self-loathing.

> *That door is the gateway he has sought so long out of this dirty world, this dirty body.*

But I could not concentrate, and I could not get my mind off Max's betrayal—his hard pink penis peeking out of his jeans as he glared, eyes glittering with otherworldly arousal, at an onlooker who for a minute could not believe what she saw, until she did and screamed—and I threw the useless book on the floor.

On the windowsill our black rescue cat, Oscar, startled. Eva was not yet home from her internship at the shelter. Oscar preferred Eva.

I did not know what to do with the fury building in my body. I grabbed my red down coat and walked out the door of our apartment. I needed to go somewhere. The cat hissed. It was dark and bitter cold on the busy streets on the North Side of Chicago.

These were the ponytail years. The longer it grew, the more I hated it. I spent hours with my therapist Jack, obsessing about how feminine it made me look, threatening to have it cut off. But I knew that if I didn't have it, I would lose the sign that marked me—somehow—as different.

To my female coworkers in a non-profit agency that helped families hurt by interpersonal violence, I was the Sensitive Man, the Male Role Model, the Man Whose Behavior Would Pave the Way Toward Change. And although the counseling agency where I worked had placed a want ad in the newspaper, for so long I was the only man: The Only Man at Staff Meetings, the Only Man in a Roomful of Angry Women, the Expert on Why Men Were the Way They Were. And I knew it was dangerous to speak for men, no one voted me their ambassador, but it was seductive to feel knowledgeable, and focusing on my specialness helped me forget one fact: to be the only one was lonely.

Two years into our relationship, Eva and I were well-matched in our exhaustion. She was in her first year of social work school, the same program I had just completed. She was interning at a domestic violence program, advocating for women survivors. The counseling agency where I worked referred most of the mandated clients to me. I was surrounded by sex offenders.

We were both disgusted by men.

Not queer men as much as straight men. Most of the domestic violence abusers and the sex offenders we met said that they were heterosexual. To mention my disgust with men, my disgust with myself, was to give it time and power and language it did not deserve. The silence that contained our unspoken disgust about men was a weird kind of annihilation. The sex we had was dwindling. I was trying not to take it personally.

The way straight men had sex was furtive, predatory, violent.

Each evening I arrived home late from work looking white-faced, tie loose around my neck, collar stained from perspiration. Out of habit I picked up a water gun from the basket by the door, in case Oscar jumped me. In the kitchen making dinner, always experimenting with a new seasonal vegetable, Eva asked, "How was your day?" as if there was an interesting story on the other side of the question.

I looked back at her, as if from some parallel world, and, searching my mind, answered, "I don't remember." Even the facts of the previous hour eluded me: how I tidied up the office after the last therapy group, how I climbed into a cab (too exhausted to consider the subway), how I asked the driver not to talk to me.

"I'm talking to you!" Eva shouted angrily, interrupting the stunned blankness of this other world I inhabited.

Late into the night, I buried my attention in the television—I watched reruns of *The Mary Tyler Moore Show* that my mother taped for me—sheltering myself in flash and noise and laugh tracks. Later, long after Eva retreated to bed, I marveled at the simplicity of talk-show conversations, the straightforward way participants threaded together their stories: question, answer, question, answer. I stayed awake until, exhausted, I was certain I could sleep without having a dream I would remember.

When I stood to go to the bedroom, the cat's eyes narrowed and he hissed. Whenever he suspected one of us was leaving, Oscar clawed at us. Eva and I argued. I wanted to get rid of the cat. She insisted that he was scared and traumatized and needed consistency and love and then he would heal. She was the moral center of this one-room apartment where we were trying to become the people we wanted to be. She did not give up on anyone. Her kindness almost always brought me back to my better self.

I walked down Broadway, the street on which we lived, to Unabridged Bookstore. Once a week I visited to pick up *The Windy City Times* to see if my review got a good placement. The bright, colorful, book-filled windows were like a literary hearth on the cold, bustling city streets. A bell jingled when I entered the store. Two skinny men with buzzed hair and tight pastel t-shirts, gay twins, looked up but didn't say hello. A kind of anti-customer service that lent a chilly ambience: a fertile site for longing. In the background the Communards were singing "Don't Leave Me This Way" as if it was a gay bar. The two men danced behind the cash register. I thought this must be a fun place to be employed. *Set me free, set me free, set me free, set me free, set me free.*

Tonight I wanted to console myself with James Baldwin. I had read so many of the famous essays and *Giovanni's Room*, but there were other novels I hadn't read. A copy of *Giovanni's Room* was shelved on the "Gay Men" bookshelf—everything was so neatly labeled—but the book cover said that it is a "bisexual novel." I had not decided if it was a real bisexual novel or a story where "bisexual" was a suspect transitional identity, a cover, a passing, cloaked in self-loathing and guilt and indecision. There was so much shame in this distant world in Paris. It started and ended with the narrator regarding a prison. Why were there always prisons in gay men's writing?

I wanted there to be a real bisexual novel.

My friend Al, from my college days, had told me a story that I could not get out of my head. As a student, he worked with the Organization of Black Students to bring James Baldwin to campus for Black History

Month. At the apex of his career, Baldwin's speaking fees, which included traveling with two assistants in first class accommodations, were exorbitant. Al and other students lobbied the university to pony up the money (just like Father Sam and I had done a few years before to bring Quentin Crisp to campus to speak).

The famous author came to Hyde Park the year after I moved to the North Side. I was so out of touch with the gay community there, living on the North Side with my girlfriend, I didn't even notice he had come to town. I missed the speech. When I found out it happened and I hadn't known, I was distraught. Why didn't anyone tell me?

After Baldwin delivered a fiery speech to a packed auditorium, Al brought him back to the Organization of Black Students office to collect his coat. Baldwin told Al that he was handsome—Al has a smile like summer sunshine—and stole a kiss.

"James Baldwin kissed you?" I asked.

"I didn't wash my face for weeks," Al said sheepishly.

Baldwin died less than a year later.

On the shelves of Unabridged, there were so many titles by James Baldwin. Each had a picture of him with his wide, all-knowing eyes. Always, he had a cigarette clasped between his fingers.

I tried to imagine that kiss. The full soft lips. The faint smell of cigarette smoke. The sweaty musk of his body, adrenalized after speaking to a house of adoring fans. The eyes that saw more than the average human. I imagined he kissed with his eyes open, staring straight into your soul. I kept replaying the story of James Baldwin in the office with Al. It was hard to recall without a bitter selfishness. I should have been the one James Baldwin kissed.

I took *The Fire Next Time* and sat on one of the couches. I wanted to stay here, reading Baldwin and listening to The Communards and stealing glances at the two dancing cashiers and forgetting Max and handcuffs and the worry about getting in trouble at work and feeling left out and longing for missed kisses.

Every day while Eva was still asleep I woke up and beat off in a fever in the bathroom, like I wanted to get rid of sex. By midday the feeling built up again, it magnified and consumed and blocked my vision of anything else, especially if the day was bad, if there was a surround of sadness and suffering, and I escaped to the men's room on the floor of my office building, and I beat off again. My dick was becoming chafed and red and it hurt to the touch. It started to hurt when I sat down and got up, and you might have thought that that would make the fever diminish. I didn't know what to do with myself except tuck in my fitted shirt, tighten my ponytail, straighten by shiny tie, and emerge a respectable professional.

From my clients I heard stories about older men, men in their forties and fifties, about how the sex drive would slow down and disappoint. When my own dick was chafed and red, I consoled myself that someday this irresistible fever would dissipate and I would have a life of productivity and purpose, not the fury of this endless beating off.

After I watched the film "Prick Up Your Ears" about British playwright Joe Orton, I resolved to stop beating off. "Have a wank," he suggested to his sometimes lover Kenneth Halliwell. It sounded like something that would occur at teatime over scones. So I started wanking instead—one, two, sometimes three times a day—thinking that this, *wanking*, was what gentlemen in business dress do.

At twenty-seven years old, you never knew that lying could be so casually regarded, part of your professional routine, your boring everyday, nothing to take personally, just the stuff of work. Your job was to "invite responsibility": to create room for self-reflection about how denial and rationalization and all the fictions we spun about our darkness served us in some way but also was the stuff of ruin.

The way you worked with sex offenders focused on their stories, moving from fiction to memoir. Through a combination of trust and pressure to tell his story—the story of how he had hurt someone—you prompted and cajoled and invited a sex offender to tell truths. ("Clear, specific, detailed," you used to say. "Show don't tell.") That would light the path toward healing and responsibility. You stopped taking their lying to you as an affront. (Well, that was the lofty goal.) Never short of a quick opinion, Mary Jo advised, "Lying is what they do. Your job is to figure out how to invite them to a more responsible version of themselves."

Lying was what they did.

You studied the categories by which to sort and arrange and control the lies they told you: Denial of facts, denial of impact, denial of awareness, denial of arousal, denial of responsibility. Session by session you sorted all the sentences of their stories into these tidy categories, and each category cued your next strategic response. Each conversation was a slow, belabored, painstaking journey through shame and obfuscation. But you were never sure if you would actually arrive anywhere.

The truth was: I missed Eva. She worked, she interned, she studied, she hopped on the bus to help her eighty-year-old grandmother with groceries, she grabbed the train to help her mother move to an assisted care facility, she boarded a different bus to go have dinner with her father who was lonely and demanding, she wrote another paper in graduate school that got an A (I got Bs), she talked on the phone to Naomi about moving on from her breakup from another perfect Jewish man (a lawyer!), she read *Street Level Bureaucracy*, she returned to the shelter with the secret address and when she came home she fell into bed by nine o'clock with Oscar cuddled by her side.

In the sliver of time we had together she apologized endlessly. She was still The Woman Who Blames Herself for Everything

"No, it's fine," I told her, feeling like I didn't want to be another demanding man, when we drank coffee in the morning, before she caught the bus and then the El, and then the other bus that took her to the South Side for a class on social policy.

In her whole dutiful life, I was the only one who knew her truth: the energetic warmth that radiated from her core was not in fact endless. My understanding of this truth gave us an ironic intimacy. In our rare moments together, I was the one who understood and forgave.

"I don't know what else to do," she said, and I believed her. "I don't know how to stop." Who would she say no to? Neither of us could imagine. Oscar meandered into the dining room, glanced suspiciously at me (he hates men too), and sat on her lap like it was his throne.

Unabridged was notoriously cruisy, even during the week. It was Communards night. Jimmy Somerville's falsetto filled every book-lined aisle with sadness and longing. Behind the counter the gay twins were lip-synching and dancing, as if ignoring customers was part of the job. *There's a very strange vibration/Piercing me right through the core.*

There was a lean man with curly brown hair in a London Fog raincoat looking at a book by the shelf labeled "Art History—Modern." Reading his book, he turned in profile. At first, I didn't recognize him because of a soft sadness in his features, a handsome melancholy.

I stared unabashedly. It was a mark of the strange times—every night was littered with more nightmares about clients than sleep—that a few minutes after I noted the chiseled jaw, the dark stubble, the sparkle in his alert eyes as he fingered one of those coffee-table-sized books on Kandinsky, that I realized: *Oh, it's Ivan.*

I had never—even when we were waiting together, in the clutch of such doom, for our HIV test results—seen him sad. Almost as if he had the ability to refuse sadness.

"Ivan?" I asked, but I knew it was him. I had not seen him—except once in passing on campus—since I dropped off my copy of Madonna's *Sex*.

He smiled when I said his name. "I heard you live on the North Side now?" His voice was not effusive, as I remembered it, but he still looked perfectly coiffed, in the elegant coat, his black shoes shined, the professor-in-training.

"Yes," I said, "just a few blocks north of here. Are you and Drew still in Hyde Park?" Since I moved in with Eva, I had let my appearance go, by gay standards. I was not as fussy as I used to be about my rumpled ponytail. My clothes were more unkempt. I hadn't gained weight, but I was not a gym rat in the same way.

His eyes softened when I said Drew's name. "We're not together anymore," he told me.

"I'm sorry."

"I'm living up here too now. I'm working on my dissertation, so I don't need to be full-time on the South Side."

He smiled and looked away awkwardly. I was unsure what to say: He was my ex who had just broken up with the boyfriend who came after me. I couldn't really ask what happened, even though I was curious. Did Drew also think he was remote about his feelings? Ivan and I were not close anymore, but it felt like we should be. Our bodies had been so close once.

He exchanged the Kandinsky book for another oversized volume on Matisse. I didn't know why he was looking at Modernists; his period was the Renaissance. I looked down at my Baldwin, unsure if we were going to say anything more to each other. I stole another glance at him. Was it still cruising if it was an ex? Ivan walked to the cashier with two books and one of the gay twins smiled and winked. They never looked at me that way. Sitting on the couch, I pretended I was immersed in Baldwin.

Before he left, Ivan walked over to me. "I saw him when he was on campus," he said. "He's fucking brilliant. Al introduced us. I shook his hand."

"I'm envious."

Then, out of nowhere—

"I could tell you more about it," he said casually. "Do you want to hang out? I have a bottle of wine back at my place."

At the end of *Giovanni's Room*, Giovanni, in his despair at losing David, has committed a murder. He has killed Guillaume, an older gay man, his employer who had harassed and exploited him. After his fiancée returned to Paris, David wanted to forget about their affair, and he was waiting anxiously for Giovanni's execution in the same room he had once shared with him. In that anguished moment it was as if they were the same body, because they were the same body.

> *The body in the mirror forces me to turn and face it. And I look at my body, which is under sentence of death. It is lean, hard, and cold, the incarnation of mystery. And I do not know what moves in this body, what this body is searching. It is trapped in my mirror as it is trapped in time and it hurries toward revelation.*

I disliked David, it was true, but I resembled him: a body trapped in history. I was searching for a revelation that would make it easier to live with this swirl of contradictions: to be in love with Eva; to feel this other furious desire, for so many things, in so many directions; to feel criminal and ashamed, as if it was my inheritance, even though all I had done was to be born in a restless body.

In that last Thursday night group therapy session that I had with Max before his arrest, I could tell my irritation was cresting, but I was trying not to let it show. Before group, I thought if I wanked—*twice*—that I'd be able to manage my ill-temperedness. It wasn't working.

My clients joked that whomever I focused on was on the "hot seat." I pressed one man to clarify his recollections about a nighttime incident with his stepdaughter. "But do you remember being sexually aroused?" I asked. "Did you have an erection?"

A rustle in the room as men shifted in their chairs. Each man liked to think that he had been caught for a one-time, impulsive act, an experiment, inconsistent with his "true" sexuality. Admitting to arousal by his child victims was the most difficult hurdle. Max looked at me with those moist dark eyes, a vulnerable expression. The lone exhibitionist, he often got a pass in these conversations because he had not known any of his victims.

"No," the man insisted. "I didn't have an erection."

"But you ejaculated," I said. "The police report says there was semen in her underwear."

"I did molest her, but I didn't have an erection."

"How could you not have an erection?" I asked, thinking I was hiding my irritation but probably I wasn't. "That's why they call it *sexual* abuse."

"Oh, you *can* ejaculate without having an erection," another man piped in. Several men, all of whom were arguably in denial of arousal, nodded and traded stories.

I was lost. I was twenty-seven years old, in a roomful of men, most of whom were the same age as my father. When more than two of them insisted that a man could ejaculate without an erection, I began to question my own experience. Had I been doing it wrong all these years? How had I come to assume that my own experience was "right"? I felt exposed, immature. As if they could see into the bedroom where Eva and I were supposed to be alone, where we cuddled, my dick pressed against her back, so hard.

Their rationalizations about "half" and "partial" erections clouded my mind. I didn't know what to say. Max, who was my age, looked at me sympathetically. *What a bunch of buffoons*, his expression seemed to say. We were in this together, my star pupil and I, although he did not say anything to the other clients, nothing to challenge their absurd rationalizations. I dropped the subject, like the bad, irresponsible, tired therapist that I was.

Because I was a good boy, because I was a rule-follower who was about to break the rules, and I wanted to straddle these two impossible worlds, I called home, talked to Eva.

"I ran into Ivan at the bookstore," I told her. "We're going to hang out for a bit."

"What?" she asked confused. "You have work tomorrow. It's already nine o'clock."

"It's fine," I said, as if this were a casual transaction. "It's nice to see him, to catch up. Don't wait up for me. I'll be late."

"This doesn't make sense," she said. I could hear the mounting distress in her voice and I didn't care, I wanted to block it out and do something different than us. "What are you doing, Wayne?"

"It's fine. I'm just needing some space. I'm hanging up now."

"Wait!"

I put down the phone, the good boy deciding with one swift move to be a reckless asshole.

In the bitter cold Ivan and I were walking close to each other on West Roscoe toward his apartment. He lived so close to Eva and me, and I hadn't even known. Of course, we were not holding hands, but our shoulders bumped frequently. His James Baldwin story was briefer than I thought it would be. We settled into a yearning kind of silence.

"You're sure you're OK with this?" he asked, putting the key in the lock, and I nodded, not OK, but also not turning away.

In the living room of his third-floor apartment, we took off our coats. Ivan switched on only one glowing lamp. I sat on his couch and waited while he put a Roberta Flack tape in the recorder and she sang "The First Time Ever I Saw Your Face," which recalled the time, three years ago, when we were boyfriends.

I did not know the etiquette of exes.

The loaded silence annoyed me. I wanted to talk about what was in my mind. "When we were together, I was always a top," I said. "I had been the top for years in all my relationships. With a girlfriend I feel like I am always the top."

Ivan smiled. "Well, hetero sex, right?" He sat beside me and said, teasingly, "You had a reputation. You were the one who was good with first timers, right? Even guys who never thought they'd bottom would try it with you." He laughed with genuine warmth. He did not seem sad now. "My god, we were a gossipy bunch!"

"That's true," I said, smiling. "But now I'm tired of being a top."

"Ha," he said, putting an arm around my shoulders, squeezing my neck gently. "That's a coincidence, Wayne. I haven't bottomed since we broke up," and he leaned in for the first kiss. The scratchy roughness of his face surprised me.

One evening, during another group therapy, I explained "transitional objects," cuddly belongings that give children and adults a sense of security. For a ritual to explore trust, I told the men, each should bring one of his own transitional objects to group next week. He would tell a story about its meaning to him, then explore how it would feel to allow someone else to hold it for a week between sessions. We were building trust so that we could eventually hear each other's honest stories.

"Do you want to see my transitional object?" one man asked. He was new to the group, referred by his probation officer. His eyes glittered with a criminal intensity. "I brought it tonight."

Before I answered, he showed me, but I didn't see the object itself, only the flash of light on the blade.

"Please put that away," I told him, trying to steady the trembling in my voice. I hated this job. The consummate professional, I continued my explanation about teddy bears, heart thumping fearfully, ignored again. This moment epitomized the psychological trap of working with sex offenders: feeling frightened and vulnerable and yet obeying a mandate—from a supervisor? from some unwritten code of masculine conduct? from some God? or from myself?—to appear cool, unaffected.

The white-faced expressions of the other men compelled me to be more honest. I was supposed to be different, after all. The Special Man. "That scared me when you pulled out the knife," I stammered, a show of vulnerability that was both performative and true.

"Were you scared?" he asked, smiling. Now he had power over me.

"What did the rest of you feel about the knife?" I asked other group members.

No one said a word.

On his bed it was a weird reunion, between two bodies that were different, shaped by time, but also familiar. It had been seven years since I tried to do this—bottom—and I couldn't remember what I was supposed to do, except kind of surrender and let go and trust—and I still couldn't believe this was Ivan. Ivan, the fussy, well-mannered art historian, liked to top now, and he knew what he wanted to do with me. So I gave up. I did remember: there was a part of bottoming that was about losing control. You were the object. That was just so strange. To not be on top, taking the lead, setting the rhythm. I didn't even need to have an opinion. I had no idea how to position my ass at the angle he needed. I couldn't see what was going on back there.

I was a different animal. I was a shape shifter. I was mutable.

Just relax, he said. *Breathe.*

I think I'm really tight, I said, and my breath was somewhere between excitement and panic, but closer to panic.

You just have to ease into it, he said, putting on more lube, *just relax,* and I felt this pressure, like a mine wanting to explode, it grew stronger more insistent, then I felt the tip of his cock inside me. I gasped, and that was just the tip.

Take a deep breath. It'll be ok. I'm not going to hurt you.

It felt like I was cracking open. I winced. Was I bleeding? Did it used to hurt like this? Ever? Why was I doing this? He wrapped his arms across my chest, buried his mouth in the back of my neck, and I could feel my body relax and the relaxed feeling spread down my torso, loosened my sphincter. *I can make you like this,* he said into my ear, both reassuring and forceful, and I was trying not to panic, telling myself I might like this in a minute, that sometimes there was pleasure just over torture's horizon. The last time he and I were together, I fucked him, our usual routine.

"You have a condom on?"

"It's on, Wayne."

He pushed again and what felt like another inch slipped in. I used to like this. I used to ...

> *...and trembling, and tenderness so painful I thought my heart would burst.*

Oh god.

Somehow, I was hard now. I had no idea how that could happen while my asshole was being destroyed. Ivan pushed another half inch in—was he always this big?—and suddenly, I could deal with it. The pain relaxed, shifted, became something else, something that made me hard against my will.

(Cass, always the top, ever the professor, had tried to explain it to me once, when I was nineteen, days after losing my virginity. We were lying naked in bed. "Do you feel that?" he asked, the prostate docent, inserting his middle finger knuckle deep into my asshole, pressing in a way that hurt and aroused. "That's it: the prostate. That's why you love it. Feel it?")

Now I was more relaxed. Ivan and I switched positions, facing each other. Our eyes were fearlessly locked, wide-open stares; my legs encircled his hips; our arms were around each other; tighter, tighter; his hard dick slipped in and out of me; we were one and then separate, one and then separate; pulsing like a single organ; this rare moment when desire, intangible and fluid and hard to ascertain, left no question. It plunged. Insistently, truthfully. And I could will my body to open; to submit; to be entered.

But out of this astounding, intolerable pain came joy...

To be close, this close, to another man, still felt so forbidden. The male body as a warm shelter—for once—not a force to be fought and resisted.

I would never understand my dick.

I could never explain this to anyone.

There was a way that men touched sometimes: rougher. The way he kissed me scratched my face, left red marks, so that afterwards I thought everyone would know that I had been kissing a man. The strength in the arms as they wrapped around you. The way desire emerged, an urgency, not able to be ignored.

When Ivan touched me, it was the way my brothers and I wrestled as boys, every single day, with such ferocity—love and rivalry and anger all intermixed. It was the way our father wrestled with us, pinned us down, always reminding us that he was bigger, superior. It was the way he arm-wrestled us, week after week, a game but not a game, us boys hooting and cheering with the hope that maybe one of us might finally win—but we never won—until the day when Dean, at sixteen, did win and my father, so broken, an alcoholic, at forty-five, said nothing. On that day the game of rivalry that he always won, that kept us close, ended. We never played the game again. I never touched his hand again.

Ashamed, walking north on Broadway, I wondered if maybe I would get a pass, that maybe she would be asleep and forget the cruel clipped interaction on the telephone. I worried that, even though I had tried to wash up, I smelled like Ivan's cologne. I worried there were scratches on my face. Maybe she would be asleep and I would crawl into bed and we would agree, in that implicit way that couples sometimes have about painful realities, to pretend it didn't happen, that they didn't notice. After all it was two in the morning and tomorrow was a workday. She would go to the domestic violence shelter for her internship. I would go to the fancy building with the marble lobby and see a succession of men and we would tussle over stories of secrecy, rationalization, and denial.

When I entered the courtyard, it looked like a dim light was on in the living room of our one-bedroom apartment, but that didn't mean anyone was awake. We both were afraid about break-ins and always kept a light on somewhere. When I inserted the key in the lock, I tried to turn softly, the tumblers clicked too loudly and I winced, still hoping she was asleep. I wanted to get undressed and crawl in bed next to her and forget who I was, the confused mess. But the first thing I noticed when I got inside: Eva at the dining room table, eyes red, still wet; Oscar in her lap with no interest in me.

"What did you do?" she asked, eyes glimmering. Her face was pink with the crazy temple-pounding fever of someone who was betrayed by the person she loved.

I was twenty-seven years old. I did not yet know that this was the beginning of a pattern of confusion and wild impulse and cruelty. This was not the last fever. I did not know what to say. I was more like Baldwin's David than I wanted to admit.

"Why did you do that?"

That night she did not ask me to leave. That night it was an angry cruel story at the knot of who we were and we wanted to figure it out, to spread it out in front of us, to find some expensive, golden epiphany in a wise therapist's office that would ensure it never happened again because in the middle of the confused storm we still clung to a feeling of love.

That night she did not ask me to leave. And I started to cry.

I would not see Max again. I heard that he was sentenced to a short jail sentence and I knew it would ruin his life anyway. No one mentioned that reassuring false letter to the judge. Lying was what they did.

Two years later, the week before Eva and I moved to Washington, DC, I would take Oscar Wilde back to the Humane Society where we got him.

The woman behind the counter looked at me with judgment. I was a failed cat owner. In his purple carrying case, Oscar rustled, making a guttural sound. *Where the fuck was Eva?* "Does Oscar Wilde have any behavioral issues?" the woman asked. I knew what the answer to this question portended.

I would, heavy-heartedly, begin to lie. "No," I said. "He is a good cat. He is very attached to my girlfriend. We are moving to an apartment in another city that doesn't allow pets."

8

—

IN THE GARDEN

What word of grace in such a place
Could help a brother's soul?

Oscar Wilde, "Ballad of Reading Gaol"

That year, before I was thrown out of the house, I developed a terrible skin condition. My face flushed red perpetually; forehead and cheeks burned; bumpy rashes erupted all over my body. The itchiness worsened when the sun was bright, or when I was stressed, like at the end of a long day seeing psychotherapy clients. When I went on car trips, I stocked a cooler with bags of frozen vegetables. I would press them to my forehead and cheek, trying to soothe the burning.

No one knew what it was. No doctor—after seeing five dermatologists in white lab coats who barely looked up from their note taking—had made a difference. Except Marcie.

I got Marcie's name from a friend. Kate swore she was a miracle worker. Even when I wasn't desperate, I was susceptible to promises of miracles. There is a delicate line between the conjuring of a writer's imagination and a belief that magic happens. Kate had been infertile for years, but Marcie's intuitive mix of herbalism and acupuncture and optimistic determination had worked. "She was the first person I called when I found out I was pregnant," Kate confided. "Even before I told my husband. It was *our* victory."

On the front porch of Marcie's home a rainbow flag fluttered. The first floor was a waiting room and office. Her wife ran the business. Marcie's glasses were wide and round and they reflected the yellow light from the ceiling. Her brown hair was plain and short. She began appointments by holding my hands, thumbs on my wrists, and feeling my pulses. She listened with her fingers.

She paid attention. "You have a lot of heat," she said in the first appointment. "We have to fight the heat."

Over the course of half a year she would have me lie down in a darkened room and place fine needles beneath the surface of the skin: in my ears, in the fleshy pads under my thumb, on the tops of my feet, on my chest. Even though she explained why she was doing what she was doing, I never understood a word. The opaqueness of her descriptions heightened the sense of magic. Sometimes I felt nothing and sometimes there was a jolt, like a tiny, emotional bomb exploding, and I might wince or shout "Ow!" I loved the sweet subtle punishment.

"Now you rest," she would say, patting my shoulder, and I would remain still, afraid to jostle the needles sticking out at all angles.

She left me alone in the dark room with faint guitar music playing, and I had this sensation of my mind, its radar usually focused on the burning of my skin, opening up to the vastness of the world—the ceiling above my head, the roof over the ceiling, the shadowy canopy of the elms, sky filled with rain clouds, the dome of the earth—at the same time terrifying and yet tolerable. When the lights were back on and I dressed, Marcie assembled brown paper packets of bitter-smelling herbs with instructions to boil them and drink down the muddy-brown liquid. "This will cool the heat," she would say.

Later, drinking them, I gagged, hoping the awfulness was proportionate to their healing power. I trusted Marcie, her quiet conviction. I wanted her to be a miracle worker. Miracles shouldn't be delicious or easy to take.

A few days after my marital crisis, I show up for my appointment, pale and shaking. My skin—everywhere—is on fire. I want to cry.

I want to tell Marcie, but I don't know the words to say it. I don't know how to tell the story of who we are, because I don't know how to tell the story of who I am. The compartments by which I sort the incompatible parts of my life break down. I wonder if she will judge me.

I am gay-in-college-but-quietly-interested-in-women-especially-particular-acts-that-nobody-can-talk-about-politely-and-all-those-ugly-father-conflicts-keep-rearing-their-jagged-monster-beaks-whenever-I-get-close-to-a-nice-man-and-why-am-I-attracted-to-men-who-struggle-to-be-truthful-while-AIDS-is-wiping-us-out?-and-then-I-met-her-and-the-puzzle-pieces-of-who-we-were-fit-into-each-other-like-humans-spooning-which-we-also-like-to-do-so-she's-the-one-but-where-do-I-put-the-rest-of-me?-and-some-labels-are-so-unwieldy-that-you-just-can't-say-them-and-who-knows-when-people-will-judge?

All I know how to do during the crisis is blurt perverse details.

"Eva threw me out of the house," I tell her. "She found out that I was reaching out to men on the internet, looking for sex. I've had other hook-ups in the past. She was clear she'd never tolerate it again." It is the first time I tell Marcie about my struggles in my marriage, about the desire for men that I cannot ignore, even while I love Eva.

In college, my gay male friends were awkward around me and Eva when we started dating, as if I were being unfaithful to them. Our campus group, the Gay and Lesbian Alliance (the euphonious GALA), did not contain the word bisexual. Maybe this knot of contradictions is part of my sickness, the fiery breakdown of my skin, and it is OK to tell her, my healer.

I talk about how devastated I am. Marcie grows quiet. Perhaps it is just in deference to my pain? She listens to my pulses: that exquisite quality of attention that feels like the beginning of some subtle witch-craft. I must look very different from who she assumed I was.

"Your heart's not broken," she states with authority, looking away from me. This is the first moment that it occurs to me, at odds with her diagnosis, that in fact this is what a broken heart might feel like; this shattering inside; this ragged incoherence that makes me struggle for breath. But maybe you're not allowed to have a broken heart if you betrayed someone. Maybe it's selfish to think the brokenness happened to you.

She has me lie down and applies needles above my eyebrows, on my hands, on my stomach. Alone in the dark, a lute playing distantly, I wait, skin burning, tears pushing against the back of my eyes. For a moment some glimmering of the old peace eventually returns.

Twenty minutes later the lights switch on and Marcie quietly removes the needles and puts them in a plastic container. I stretch and sit up on the table.

"I checked your insurance," she says, her mouth a grim line, "and this will have to be your last session. The benefit is exhausted, so our work is done."

"Really?" I don't know what else to say. I long for her determination to heal me. I still want her to be a miracle worker.

She doesn't make eye contact or say anything more but exits the exam room and I can't muster the strength to question her. I know this interaction, our final one, has nothing to do with insurance benefits.

By this time I have moved again. I am living in a small, unfurnished studio in an anonymous brick building five city blocks from the family house. I sleep on an air mattress that deflates by the time I wake up every morning. Piles of clothes sit in stacks—rumpled shirts, dirty pants, wadded underwear—alongside the suitcase I used to transport them here. I don't know where the laundry room is and I don't care.

"Why is it, do you think, that you don't want to get a bed?" is one of the questions Michael, my therapist with the thick square glasses and the white goatee, poses, when I complain of soreness in my back.

Another: "What are you trying to prove by not having any furniture?"

And then: "What harm would it be to have a bureau for your clothes?"

I am the father in exile. The apartment is convenient, an easy walk home. It is a placeholder for some kind of marital separation, maybe even divorce. The meaning shifts daily.

Every morning, just after dawn, I walk through the neighborhood streets. The sun peeks over the horizon and Mount Hood, far away, glows ghostly and pink. At the family home I make breakfast and get three kids dressed and ready for camp. I move from bedroom to bedroom and kiss each of them, tussle their unruly bed heads, rouse them with goofy dad enthusiasm. "Time to rise and shine, mop-heads!" I create this illusion that I am still their in-home dad, ever attentive. Maybe they don't even think about the fact that I spent the night in a room down the street. I make oatmeal. I stir cocoa on the stove and pour it into sippy cups left over from their baby days. They come downstairs and Louis and Rosie drape themselves over couches and chairs, sipping cocoa. Louis gazes into space in a half-dream, Rosie reads *Cat Warriors*. Philip makes a tent with his baby blanket on top of the heat vent in the living room floor.

Nothing is more consoling than these chores.

When Eva comes downstairs in her bathrobe, she smiles and says "Good morning" in a neutral tone that is almost kind—it has no rancor or overt unpleasantness—but it also lacks any enthusiastic love as if she must titrate any affection, meter it out according to the day's particular memory of the crime. It is my new hobby: spending endless amounts of time parsing the tone of the words she offers me. Occasionally she kisses my cheek—an innocuous kiss that a friend might offer. That thrills me. Mostly she refrains from any physical contact.

"Don't forget their permission slips," she says, pouring coffee. "They're going to play in the Jamison Fountain."

After a noisy transition to the minivan, I drive the kids to camp and wish them happy days before going to my office.

Later in the afternoon, I am back in the family home. I help make dinner and set the table and hear stories about camp: the teenage counselors they adore and the buckets of water balloons they stashed on the school bus and how everyone got soaked in a surprise water battle at the fountain.

Together we shepherd the three of them through their getting-ready-for-bed rituals: putting away clothes, donning pajamas, brushing teeth, fielding complaints and refereeing arguments, reading stories, tucking in. They outnumber us. What would happen to us at this shaky point in our marriage, Eva and me, if there weren't three of them? What would it be like for only one of us to manage this beautiful, overwhelming tedium?

At the door, as I get ready to leave, Eva looks at me and sighs. No kiss tonight. Gratitude makes her angry again. She is no man's victim.

Later, back at the father-in-exile apartment, unable to sleep, I worry. Without any father-chores or children to check on or wife to cuddle in bed, I get up and wander the streets of Irvington, the neighborhood of turn-of-the-century bungalows and wide, canopied streets. I glimpse into some living rooms, where the lights are left on, jewel-colored tiffany lamps glowing in the windows, the comfortable hearths, bright art on dark red walls: evidence of a vibrant family life.

Late one night at the tail-end of summer, I near another man on the sidewalk, handsome, younger than me, another insomniac. We make a flash of eye contact, then turn away. We pass each other. Heart thumping, I pause beside a parked car and notice that he has turned around too, loitering by someone's poetry post. It's always Mary Oliver or Rumi or Rilke on this block. We steal another glance at each other. We lock eyes. It sends a bolt through my body. Is it a shudder of thrill or danger? At two o'clock in the morning, with no one else on the street, the possibilities are narrow.

It is a kind of sexual longing that cuts to the center of who I am: this desire to be close to another warm body. This stranger knows me, my primitive stirrings, the pitch of my loneliness. He walks toward me.

But it is too embarrassing to be seen, my hungers undisguised on the street. I turn away and quickly leave the scene. I am afraid of how much I want this stranger at this unconscious hour and that he saw that I want him, and that maybe he wants me too, and we don't even know each other's names, but we recognize that kindred despair.

I fumble to unlock the door of my studio, enter the room with the naked ceiling lightbulb, undress and get under the covers on the air mattress, body trembling. I try to fall asleep, imagining solitary men wandering the streets, so many ghosts moving over the planet, locking eyes, searching. The thin walls of the building where I huddle on the floor give the barest illusion of separateness.

Will, the stonemason, is a jovial soul with tree-trunk biceps. He is used to leading crews of young collegiate jocks who work on his team installing flagstone and boulder gardens. That Saturday, when I arrive in our backyard for my lesson, he might have been skeptical. I have the kind of body that looks like the life I've led, a bookish writer, a sedentary psychotherapist, a runner who hates fixing things around the house or working on cars: thin without much upper-body muscle.

There is a long, uneven stretch of grass from the patio, so new and perfectly laid, to the front porch of the house where the stone path must go. "Is it realistic I can do this?" I ask, not wanting Eva to hear.

"Anybody can make a path," he answers. "It takes time and perseverance. And muscle. Oh, and sweat."

It is a dry stack path, no cement. I create it one foot or two at a time. First, I dig out grass and soil, then layer a few shovelfuls of blue gravel. The tamper is a thick wooden stick that comes up to my chest, its base a flat, heavy, hammer-like surface. I use it to pound the gravel. Then I sprinkle a shovelful of sand and spread it around and use the hose to spray water on the gravel and sand so that the sand settles between the gaps in the gravel. The foundation must be packed tightly, Will tells me.

I pound and pound and pound.

I search among a stack of flagstone for pieces that will fit together. I can lay only one slab at a time. Then I continue the repetition of tasks: put down gravel, tamp with all my strength, add sand and water, tamp more; watch the sweat flying from my face; pound and pound and pound; stop caring about the neighbors and their need for quiet and peace; fix the next jagged stone in place. I like the way the broken edges of the slabs scratch my arms and hands. Blood runs up and down my dirty forearms.

I use the full weight of my body to jerk the tamper up and slam it down on the rock. Any other time it would have been exhausting, but I have reserves of fury. The sound of rocks being pummeled—metal hitting stone—fits me. Over and over and over I propel my body into this inarticulate crushing gesture.

As if to seal her resolve, Eva tells the neighbors about her gay husband and the coming divorce.

I do not feel gay, not exactly, but I don't feel like I can say anything.

The sound of pounding on stone connects me to *fin de siècle* convicts, sentenced to hard labor, and I imagine that Oscar Wilde, beloved author, queer martyr, after his trial, had spent similar time among rocks and gravel, pounding and hammering. Punishment and deprivation feel right. Suffering agrees with me. As long as I am pounding and lifting puzzle pieces of flagstone and jamming them into place, I don't have to think about anything too abstract, like the state of my marriage, or whether I am a good man, which I am pretty sure I am not. There is just the pure, gray, rough-hewn suffering of pounding rock—a resounding assault of thwacks, smashing wet sand and gravel into a flat surface— that echoes like an inmate's inarticulate rage throughout the whole neighborhood that might otherwise have expelled me.

Every day that fall, I finish work and return to the house where I no longer live to create the path until the sun sets and it is dark. Neighbors don't know what to do with me. The sound of crushing rock is incessant. The fury behind the sound coming from our garden poisons any peace and quiet they might want. Friendly pedestrians stop by to marvel at my dirty appearance, my scraped hands and legs, the blood and grime of who I am. I refuse to wear garden gloves.

"My goodness, look at you!"

"Shouldn't you wear gloves to protect your hands?"

"How much longer will this take?"

It is slow, painstaking work, like putting together a puzzle without a box cover that shows what it should resemble. The stone shapes are remnants left by the real stonemasons who put in the patio earlier that summer. I carry and sort pieces and arrange them, a few at a time; consider the fit and look; rearrange again; scrape my fingers; think about angles and curves and alignment. More than one neighbor, women who know the story, say things like, "You're creating your own path," with a wise nod. I cringe at the cliché, but I don't say anything. It's part of the punishment.

One day I come inside the house, where I no longer feel easily welcome, to get some water. No one else is home. The doorbell rings. It is Amalia, our next-door neighbor, who is also a psychotherapist, needing to see Eva. She wears lavender garden clogs and clutches a brown shawl around her thin shoulders because she is always cold. Usually we share cordial banter. Today she stares at me, the soon-to-be-ex-husband, at my dirty, scratched-up arms, my face dripping sweat. "Why are you here?" she stammers, as if I had broken in.

There is a long pause. "I'm finishing the garden path," I say.

The next weekend, as I pound rock on a path that is slowly finding its shape, rounding the turret on the east side of the clinker brick house, Eva putters in another part of the garden. We are not working together. She wears gloves and a broad-brimmed hat that shields her face.

The sunshine is bright and oblivious. A few late roses bloom pink on tops of long stems, bobbing in the breeze. The world goes on.

When I pause in my work, I steal glances at her. Sometimes her expression looks strained, but occasionally she looks serene, lost in the business of planting. Through the umbrella of the maple tree that Ann planted, I spy her, kneeling in the soil. We are not supposed to be looking at each other. We are stuck in it: her resolve to be divorced.

It is hard to break the habit of paying attention.

The black cat watches the garden from the kitchen window. Gray squirrels creep along the top of the new fence. The cat startles, eyes narrowing.

Stretches of soil lie blank like a canvas, waiting to be filled. Eva takes purple salvias, still in their containers, and arranges them in the dirt, considers the relationships, then rearranges, like art.

Bees and hummingbirds spiral around white stars of jasmine that climb the weathered bricks.

I pretend I am not looking at her, but I keep glancing over whenever I imagine she won't notice. She does not look back at me. I hope that she is stealing glances, too. I am wishing that she cares, but I suspect she does not.

On the other side of the new fence: the sound of neighbors talking while they mow lawns or prune hedges or rake brown leaves that have just started to cover the grass; snippets of friendly conversation that connect but will be soon forgotten; the simple, uninterrupted ordinariness of life. The world is moving and we are stuck.

It is hard to break the habit of paying attention.

As I pound rock, different images come to me, sustaining me: I am a superhero like Batman in a fight against evil, captions popping over my head (BASH! BAM! SMACK!); I am Vulcan at his fire, hammering with Olympic strength; I am an anonymous prisoner in a Victorian jail, doing hard labor; I am Oscar Wilde, outcast, in Reading Gaol, the "madman on a drum."

In the evenings in the bare-cave-like studio I read Richard Ellmann's thick biography, *Oscar Wilde,* and imagine the Victorian author in his prime: arrogant and aristocratic; bold and provocative and above the common hypocrisy of social mores; brilliant mind meting out witty epigrams; dashing in his floor-length black velvet cape. His comedies were the talk of London.

Then he was exposed and betrayed. The forces of social derision, incomprehensible in their power, rained down. No longer the writer who articulated a multi-layered reality though plays teeming with irony, suddenly he was labeled.

Bugger.

Pederast.

Sodomite.

People forgot that he was a father to two sons.

The jury trial humiliated him. People stopped flocking to his plays. All but two friends turned against him. Imprisonment, hard labor, and decrepitude followed.

He missed his sons when he was in prison.

I pick up "The Ballad of Reading Gaol," his poem about prison, which he named "the cave of black despair." He recalls how he and the other inmates wait on the execution of another prisoner who murdered his wife. "What word of grace in such a place/Could help a brother's soul?" He walks the prison yard with other convicts in gray uniforms. Just like David in *Giovanni's Room*, he feels for the man awaiting execution. "Alas! it is a fearful thing/To feel another's guilt!"

> *And I and all the souls in pain,*
> *Who tramped the other ring,*
> *Forgot if we ourselves had done*
> *A great or little thing...*

The dead man's fate is their own, because shame obliterates equally.

"The Ballad of Reading Gaol" is unremitting in its steely-gray castigation; not bed-time reading for the faint-of-heart, but perfect for me. The hopeless scene Wilde describes—the prison yard, the scaffold, the gray cell—is belied by a bouncy rhyme. The singsong no doubt enabled him to hold the poem in his head when he was forbidden to have paper and pen to write.

I am the man who murdered the thing he loved. I am the soul in pain.

Beyond the shame that nearly suffocates me with its wordlessness, there is a curious glimmer that I cannot deny. While I may have entered a no-man's land, robbed of any sense of belonging anywhere, the pressure of other people's expectations—the badgering notions of "What is a good man?" and "What is a good husband?" which once I could answer, but only with a dash of illusion and conjuring—lifts. The expectations no longer apply because I have failed, utterly, and failure allows me, mercifully, to give up.

And that is a relief.

I want to document a strange state of marital decomposition which, for lack of a better word, I'll call *liminality*, a confusing in-between-ness in which all contradictions are true, no matter who says them:

We are working on our marriage.

We are divorcing.

We are separated but working on reconciling.

Even though I am living in the studio a few blocks away, after working on the path, I feel entitled to shower here, in the house. When I emerge from the backyard, I am exhausted, dirty, and covered with scrapes. Afterwards, I change in a guest room where I am allowed to keep some clothes and apply antibiotic lotion to my arms. One evening, as I am changing, Eva opens the door and enters, looking wistful.

It feels wrong to be shirtless in front of her. "What?" I ask, then remind myself I don't need to start off defensively.

She rushes toward me and embraces me. We begin kissing, the movement emerging from some deep involuntary force within us. She pushes me onto the bed. We kiss as if we are touching some forgotten and displaced reality of who we are that we long to resurrect. She takes off her shirt. I wrap my arms around her and we are in the full ravenous cleaving of sex. The scent of her transports me: a place of blissful forgetting, outside history, outside time, outside wrongdoing and rightdoing.

As we roll around the bed, limbs entwined, hands roving, kissing as if we want to disappear into each other, I don't recognize the passion of our lovemaking. It is different from before. It is outside the usual habits and rhythms of how we held onto each other. There is a lawlessness and abandon about it, as if we are breaking rules. My head moves along the inside of her thigh, I am waiting for a "no," getting closer, closer, the scent so near that I want to cry for longing, and she doesn't pull away, and my tongue touches her in that pearl-center of her body and any sense of time, the before and after of who we are now, it melts, and there is no wrongdoing and rightdoing, only us.

These outbursts of sex go on, inexplicably, throughout the path-building season. We are creating something out of the damaged remains, illicit and wrong and wholly our own.

"This is confusing," I say one night, as I get dressed afterwards. The three children are in the living room, rapt, their one hour of television dedicated to *Avatar: The Last Airbender*. "What's going on?"

"I don't know," she says, pulling on her pants, then putting on her shirt.

"Are we getting back together?"

"No," she says. "We're not getting back together. It's goodbye sex."

"We're saying goodbye a lot," I say. I am also dressing. The show is over. I can hear the children playing in the living room now, building houses out of Legos.

"It *is* goodbye sex," she responds without looking at me, and the hardness returns.

I don't know how many instances of goodbye sex there will be. When she shows up at the door to the guest room, always a surprise, usually when I am dressing, I never know if she will be angry or arguing or talking about custody arrangements or if it will truly be the last time. I imagine that there is some number of times we will make love before

we reach goodbye.
    I don't know the number.
    I don't know if she knows the number.
    But there is a countdown.

9
—

ONCE MORE TO BREITENBUSH

*It is strange how much you can remember about places like
that once you allow your mind to return into the grooves
that lead back.*

E.B. White, "Once More to the Lake"

One evening, after dinner, while I am washing dishes under warm water
and looking out the window at the garden, covered in wet leaves, Eva
pauses as she wipes the counter. There is a gray flatness in her eyes. She is
wearied by us, the mysterious collision of tensions keeping us together.
"I'd like to go to Breitenbush," she announces.

"By yourself?" In the past we have gone as a family as well as solo
retreats to recharge and take a break from family noise.

She is not looking at me. "We could go together," she offers. "It's
pretty in winter. It might snow. The kids would enjoy it."

"I'll take care of it," I say, trying not to seem excited.

That winter we rent a cabin at Breitenbush, near Mount Jefferson in the Oregon Cascades range, for a week. Season after season we travel to Breitenbush, our family retreat, familiar to many in the Pacific Northwest, if not much beyond it. Years ago, on our first visit with just one baby, we met other families for whom Breitenbush was a touchstone. Their children were so wholesome and open-hearted, we chose to make it our touchstone as well, the place where we always return.

On the two-hour ride from our home, each mile taking us farther away from the city's clutter and noise, the three children argue, poke, throw wrappers from fruit roll-ups at each other, and wonder when we will arrive. Through the rearview mirror I can see their tow heads: Rosie's fine hair cut into a perfect bob, the two boys with rumpled bed heads. Philip has a splotch of grape jelly on the side of his mouth. We are trying to listen to a CD of *Harry Potter and the Prisoner of Azkaban*. This trek could be any journey to Breitenbush, even though the time is particular and a difficult one for our family. Just east of Salem, we pass the Correctional Institute that sits back from the road, behind high fences, surrounded by brown fields.

My head aches. I am desperate for them to stop whining. "Look, kids, a prison!" I call.

There is a pause in the bickering as everyone wonders about angry, tattooed men in orange jumpsuits behind bars.

"Just like Azkaban," says Rosie.

"Where are the dementors?" asks Philip sleepily.

"There are no dementors in the real world," Louis, the expert, corrects. "Can prisoners ever escape, Dad?"

"Almost never," I say.

Beyond the flash distraction of the Correctional Institute we drive through towns with small population numbers, on roads with ever-changing speed limit signs (40 to 30 to 20, then jumping back up to 40) watched vigilantly by the local sheriffs.

"Dad, slow down!" Louis, the sign-watcher, warns. "Dad, speed up! No, slow down again!"

"Can we listen to the *Cats* CD instead?" Rosie wonders. "When are we there?"

Philip's curly head droops on the side of the car seat.

The transition into the primeval forest is part of the experience. As our blue minivan snakes along the road that borders Detroit Lake, the children's noise quiets a second time, their gazes fasten outside. I can feel the nearness to the forest. Maybe, when we return, everything will be just like before? The city is far behind us. I wonder if the crisis poisoning our marriage will mar this holy spot in our family's memory.

As we ascend the gravel road pocked with potholes that jostle us, the van's progress is staggered at less than five miles an hour, and this slowing down, even slower than slow, is part of the ritual. We arrive. Eva is quiet—I can see the strain in her expression, her pale diminishment, and I can imagine her wondering, "Is this a mistake?"—except for reminders to the children about buttoning their coats. It is cold. Patches of old snow cover the ground. I park the van in the lot.

We deboard. Each child has a backpack that is supposed to be filled only with books and Legos and dolls and other non-electronic games. Philip glances at his brother with a breathless worried look, as if to say, "Are we really this bad?" Louis looks back at him remorselessly having decided stupid rules are for ordinary boys. They do not know that I know they have stashed game boys in the "secret compartments" of their backpacks.

The maple-red sign at the entrance reminds guests: "Please respect and enjoy this sacred land." We traipse down a long footpath, a carpet of decaying brown needles bordered by pine steeples, to the store. "Just listen," I say, like so many times before. The family pauses to take in the old-growth forest, the strength of centuries-old trees, standing trees, fallen trees, layers upon layers of shadows of trees; the intermingling of the living and the dead. For a moment, we are outside ourselves, eyes and ears opening to the chilly, dark depths of this forest.

On that path, that first walk whenever we arrive, what never fails to come over our noisy, complaining family is a serenity, as if the surrounding wilderness, with its green and blue and gray depths, overpowers all our clamoring. The three children, who rarely heed my coaxing to be quiet, sense it and comply. Our movement down the path is the barest scratch on the vast earth.

On our left, we pass the trailhead called "The Inner Path," a memorial to a long-time Breitenbush resident, Thor, whom we met once before he died. One winter he warned us that there had been terrible storms and that the Gorge Trail, which we love, was blocked with fallen trees and we wouldn't be able to hike it. We ventured out to explore anyway. I had never seen such destruction. I tried to imagine the sound when those mammoth trees collapsed onto the forest floor or the way the earth must have shuddered with the terrifying weight. I couldn't imagine the human task of clearing out the damage. Animal footprints circled around the fallen trees, the barest beginnings of new paths.

As we continue to the store where guests check in, I have that cozy feeling that we are doing something intimate and familiar. But I know something will be different. The grand lodge where residents and workers congregate and eat meals sounds the same: a guest picking out a tune on the old upright; workers bustling to clean the dining room for the next meal; reggae emanating from the kitchen where the cooks are busy. The children run to the steaming hot spring in the center of the commons, fenced in, with a sign: "Danger! Scalding. 180 degrees." They marvel, as always, at this exhalation of the earth's dark breath. It will always be new and amazing. Away from them, the conversation between

Eva and me is strained, limited to child-focused concerns: What will we feed Philip, the picky eater, tonight? Which hot spring will we visit first? Is there a dance this weekend? Don't forget to remind workers to bring the extra mattress to the cabin. Do we let them know we know about the game boys?

Inside my head, I am wondering, as I suspect she is: Should we be making this visit at all?

I did not want to tell the children.

Eva did not want to tell the children either. But she was more reluctant to delay the end of the painful disappointment which was our marriage. Telling the children was part of the ending, confirmation of the new reality.

Just a few weeks after The Night Grace Paley Died, we had our loudest argument in the garden. Brown and orange leaves were just beginning to waft downwards, covering the purple-red maple and catching in the rose bushes which were done with their blooms. "It's too soon," I said, thinking about goodbye sex. "We aren't even sure what we're doing yet."

"But I am sure," she said. "I want this to be over."

"Please can we wait?" I asked. "I'm not ready."

"There's no reason," she said, her expression hard, resolved.

We decided to tell the children in two rounds: first the older two, ten and eight, who would need more information, then Philip, five, who would need a simpler version and more patience. We called Rosie and Louis into the living room. They sat on the couch, legs dangling. Because I was overwhelmed and uncertain and angry, I deferred to Eva to do the telling. The five simple clipped sentences were anything but simple, but they followed a timeworn formula, as if we had gotten it out of a how-to-divorce manual.

We have some difficult news.

We have decided to get a divorce and live in separate places.

We still love all of you very much, but we do not love each other the same way anymore.

It has nothing to do with you.

You will live with mom and have time with dad throughout the week.

There was a shattering, inconsolable wail. Rosie and Louis both cried.

"What?"

"Why?"

"But this doesn't make any sense!"

"We don't want Daddy to leave."

"Can't you work it out?"

Then I cried and Eva cried. She hugged Rosie. I held Louis. Then we switched. No repetition of the five sentences that defined this new reality, so simple and clipped and clear, provided any reassurance or quelled the anguish.

Nothing made any sense to anyone anymore.

In the span of their short lives, they had never even seen us argue.

They say our brains are networks of grooves, like well-trodden paths: our thoughts and ideas flow in an endless circle, old yearnings emerge, habits and expectations comfort and assuage. Once you allow your mind to fall back into those grooves, memories return unbidden. You long for one thing. It reminds you of another. For example, at Breitenbush, in the morning before anyone is awake, I often rise and wander to the silent pool, the hottest, farthest away haven in the meadow, and find it empty and am the first to touch my toe to its smooth surface. I am careful never to enter it too quickly. A splash seems sacrilegious. Or that moment later in the day, at dusk, when a doe and her spotted fawns, sometimes two or three, venture onto the field, pausing to glance at the river, aware of the soakers in the pool and unafraid.

Amidst the din and confusion of that difficult winter, some instinct leads Eva and me back to Breitenbush, to the forest with its insistence on peace and goodwill and abundance, even though we cannot find the words to connect to each other without a fitful awkwardness. It is an age-old, ragged drama: the straying husband; the wounded, chagrined wife. The cliché makes it no less searing or exhausting. It is the fifth month of our separation. Our marriage is collapsing, but we have an almost somnolent attachment to familiar rituals. Although I still sleep in the studio, I am at the house every day before the children wake and after work I stay until they are in bed, helping with homework and chores and meals. What are we going to do with ourselves? How will we parent when we divorce? Will this be the last trip we do together? The questions hang in the background of everything, even while we doggedly do some things, like Breitenbush, that remind us of *before*.

We finish checking in and make our way to the cabin. Breitenbush is rustic, only a step above camping, off the grid, with no internet connection, no screens anywhere, except the boys' stashed contraband. Water from the same hot springs in which visitors soak is routed through the network of guest cabins, warming them in the chill mountain air. Daily the cooks prepare three vegetarian meals, using whatever fruits and vegetables are in season, brought up from two organic farms in Corvallis. Always, on the whiteboard that serves as each meal's menu, there will be a handwritten note from the cooks reminding guests that they prepared the food with love.

All the staff—cooks, yoga teachers, healing arts workers, administrators, water engineers—live in an intentional community reached by a footbridge across the river. Signs remind us to honor the quiet of their community if we are walking through it to the trailhead on the other side of the village. Just like the guests on the other side of the river, the workers, too, have limited access to phones or internet and live intimately in small side-by-side wood structures.

At Breitenbush, even the tense of one's sentences shift casually, seamlessly between the particular now of present-moment details, to the more declarative always, *this is how it always is*, an insistence on the durability of certain sights and sounds and habits and ways of being, irresistible to the agitated brain: the white rush of the river, always in the background, day and night; the falsetto call and response of the squirrels; the sight of men and women in their contemplative poses at a yoga class in the forest sanctuary; the certainty that it is rude to ask the soakers in the Silent Pool if we can talk just this once. Whether rain is falling or snow is pelting down or the sky is full of dark clouds or sunshine, strangers waiting for the dining room to open greet each other with smiles. "Another perfect day at Breitenbush," their expressions seem to say. In the dining hall, everyone sits at common tables. Newcomers quickly embrace the new rules of association. "May I join your table? How are you finding your time here?"

Mostly that winter escape we have a beautiful week in the forest. To our delight it snows and the children and I build snow people and igloos and bring snow balls into the hot springs to lick like shaved ice. We spend long blocks of time at the Medicine Wheel with the four tiled tubs filled with water from the hot springs (warm, hot, hotter, hottest) and Philip and Louis experiment with running back and forth, warming themselves in one of the tubs then running to a human-sized barrel filled with frigid water and dunking themselves and screaming hysterically, then running back to the hot tubs, back and forth, in endless hilarity. As usual, back in the city, the children insisted on packing bathing suits. "I don't want to be naked, Dad," Louis instructed. "And you and Mom have to wear suits too." But once at Breitenbush no child can resist the fun of having no clothes on in the tubs like everyone else.

That is another extraordinary thing about the place. Even though we are generally a modest family, being naked feels right in the tubs and springs and saunas at Breitenbush. It is what everyone does, no matter what age or body shape. There may be no place in this human world without shame, but here the spirit of the place declares a whole-hearted acceptance: the disabled woman whose friends lower her, naked, into a hot spring in the meadow and the smile that warms her face as she sinks into a throne shaped by rocks softened by the ages; or the stooped over man—is he in his eighties?—so unconcerned, strid-ing unclothed between the beaten-down, steam-blasting sauna closet and one of the pools, his skin loose on his frame, his white whiskers bristled and wiry.

Eva watches the two boys and laughs at their skinny bodies, bounc-ing between the hot and cold tubs, and I watch her, wondering if we will ever make love again. I am missing goodbye sex, which has dwin-dled. But I suspect it really is over. I wonder if we are just biding time, procrastinating, a marital pathology. We have played out the drama of marriage-and-its-broken-promises too many times. It feels as though, on some level, our marriage really is done, and I grieve.

The grooves, the grooves, the grooves: they surround us and pre-dict us and tell us when we succeed and when we fail. They reach back to one's own ancient time, the stories of one's tribe, one's own personal stories. Stories I read in obituaries praising marriages that ran fifty, sixty, seventy years; always the focus on duration, constancy. Then, my moth-er's sad marriage; Eva's mother's short marriage; men who left without warning; husbands who yelled and hit and drank. Even failed marriages create in the mind a groove of judgment, suffocating expectation, wells so deep with shame, they are immersive. We don't know anything differ-ent. Beyond that shame, there isn't anything except a punishing sense of failure: absence of words, collapse of meaning.

Everywhere we wander I have trouble figuring out what kind of family we are and will be. We appear and walk and eat our meals together the same as always. At night we sleep in the same configuration in the cabin: the oldest two children on the bunk beds; Philip sprawled on a mattress on the floor; mom and dad in the big bed as usual. The bunk beds have no guard rails. We borrow tall books from the library in the lodge and wedge them between the top mattress and its frame, creating a protective gate to keep Louis from falling on his brother on the floor. After everyone is settled and quiet, I reach out my hand to Eva in the darkness—a familiar gesture, but will it be OK anymore?—and she turns her back to me, reminding me that we are estranged, even though we are in the same bed. But then, maybe a half hour later, she moves closer, until her back presses against the front of me, and we are spooning like the old days.

A fragile clarity, like the wispy light of dawn, presses on my awareness—it will come and go over the next year of sorting out and re-becoming—that I am in love with someone to whom I cannot possibly be married. I am grieving something, but I am not sure what it is.

My right arm drapes around her side, pulls her toward me, and I press my cheek to the back of her head, inhaling deeply. She snuggles closer, so the curve of her body matches the curve of mine, and together we grow warm in the chilly dark night. I don't want to think anymore. Our breath synchronizes as we fall asleep.

The last night before we leave Breitenbush, they announce there will be a dance in the North Lounge. The children are ecstatic at the thought of rollicking to music through the huge open room with the slippery floor, and we decide to go. The music is rock and roll and reggae and Motown. Throughout the lounge residents and guests dance and dance, a kind of exploding and never-ending movement, with no sense of any division between them. Dancers may take a break, or pull back to sip water in the corner, but the music blasts, the dance continues, a pulsing energy like the heart beating, the five senses taking in everything about the world, the flow of warm blood transporting love to all parts of the body.

During the early days of our relationship Eva and I danced all the time in the Chicago clubs—Paradise, Berlin, Medusa's—until heading home just before dawn. We love to dance. After hours of dancing in groups bursting with energy—ecstatic marathons—I forget who I am. The boundaries between people dissolve. I expand into this drunken illusion of being larger than myself.

Wild with excitement, Philip, face flushed pink, who has never grasped the idea "marital separation" or "divorce," in spite of several patient explanations, is running around the lounge, darting through the crowd, and jumping on couches and yoga cushions. He is naked from the waist down, wearing only a tie-died T-shirt, in a moment of delirious joy. No one remembers the game boys, their secret sin.

Relieved at that moment of any conscious thought, I dance separately, then I dance with Rosie and Louis and Philip. Our wild adorable children. Our Miracles. Earth, Wind and Fire is singing "Got to Get You Into My Life." I hold hands with them like Ring Around a Rosy and we spin and laugh and spin and laugh.

Moving around the spacious lounge Eva and I keep circling back to each other. The movement enlivens her, and she loses that quality of strain and diminishment. We enjoy a fleeting physical connection through the music and the rhythm and a shared participation in the ritual. She smiles at me as we dance by each other, hands brushing. Her face is flushed, pink with joy. An unfinished meaning is forming between us, propelling us forward. The three children pull us into a circle and we spin like dancers in a Matisse painting. Consoled for a moment, I imagine the whole party's frenetic dancing as the heart of some massive body, pumping its warmth into the cold forest, to the trees waiting, wise beyond knowing.

10
—

GHOST TRIANGLE

*The whole past theory of your life and all conformity to the
lives around you would have to be abandon'd.*

Walt Whitman, "Whoever You Are Holding Me Now in Hand"

Washington, DC, 1996

No one was supposed to know why I was there. They had, it seemed
purposefully, tucked the lab away in a gray building where there was little
traffic. Too little traffic, really. When I walked up to the attendant's desk
to sign in, she eyed me knowingly. "You're here for the seventh floor?"

"Yes." I considered adding a lie. *I'm here for a job interview. I'm
meeting someone for lunch.* But she looked so matter-of-course, I gave
up. All day long she watches a stream of well-dressed, middle-class men
in their mid-thirties and forties—each no doubt more paranoid than
the last—traipse through this lobby and skulk to a destination that, like
an illicit sexual act, everyone describes with a vague label.

The seventh floor.

As I walked down the hallway, everyone who saw me appeared to know something. I was second-guessing their thoughts, their voyeuristic curiosity, their pity. What was so odd for me was not that others might guess my secret, but that, most irritating of all, they were guessing the *wrong* secret.

When I arrived at the door, labeled only 714, I tried to knock with confidence, hiding my embarrassment, but the knock came out too loud, entitled, and insistent.

There was no way I could be myself.

A woman opened the door. She smiled with friendly warmth that was clearly intended to put uncomfortable men at ease and so it didn't. I noted that she was attractive, then remembered that this fact had nothing to do with my purpose.

"You're here to produce a specimen...?" she told me, almost a question, but why bother. "Just a minute," she said, returning to the lab. Behind her I glimpsed hundreds of glass vials, microscopes, pipettes, and other dripping contraptions. I wondered about all the anonymous men before me. Were their random specimens cluttering her desk? Or did sperm need to be refrigerated? She handed me a plastic container and a brown paper bag. "After you produce the specimen, you seal it in the container labeled with your name and place it in this bag."

I nodded. I took them. I have evolved from beating off to wanking to producing a specimen.

"How many days has it been since your last ejaculation?"

No one had ever asked me such a question and she did it so casually, I cringed. On this day of so many pretenses, another lie seemed negligible. "Um, three," I answered. The right answer.

"Perfect," she said and handed me a key. "The room is at the end of the hallway. Room 745."

Room 745 looked like a storage closet that someone had redecorated to appear romantic in a hard-edged, Spartan kind of way. The walls were concrete block, painted a soft eggshell. A print of Georgia O'Keefe's *Music—Pink and Blue, 1919* hung on the wall, from an exhibition at the Art Institute of Chicago: a mystical, pastel breast; a vaginal cave. The furnishings consisted of a battered couch, a coffee table, and a bureau with labeled drawers:

LINEN TOWELS
KLEENEX
PLASTIC GLOVES
MAGAZINES

I opened the drawer labeled MAGAZINES. With O'Keefe's pastel daydream blossoming over my head, I flipped through a copy of *Penthouse*: air-brushed women's bodies; bodies flattened on glossy pages; objects for men's study and arousal. Their stares seemed to guarantee, almost reassure, they had no personality to consider or neglect or shock or hurt. Searching the dog-eared pile for something different—*I should probably be wearing those plastic gloves*, I thought—I couldn't find any pornography that I liked. After a while, the silence and isolation and anonymity of the chamber sunk in. The emptiness of the women's expressions settled in my gut.

We lived on NW Connecticut Avenue, on the outskirts of Washington, DC. I was studying for my MFA and working part-time as a family therapist at a psychiatric hospital. Eva was working with an advocacy group. The good daughter, she frequently traveled back to see her mother and father, both of whom were in uncertain health. She worried about getting pregnant soon enough so they could know a grandchild before they died.

Our apartment was a mile from Rock Creek Park, where on

evenings and weekends I went running. That spring in my T-shirt and running shorts I ran long distances to forget my patients at the hospital, the basement-level apartment that seemed suddenly empty, and Eva worrying about her eggs. On the paved paths and stone footbridges, I ran past sumacs and ancient oaks reaching for the sky, azaleas exploding in burgundy and lavender, and alders and birches and holly. The crisp, cool air filled my lungs. My heart pounded and I couldn't worry anymore, not here.

That spring I was reading Walt Whitman, part of a graduate seminar. I thought often of his time in the nation's capital, where he migrated during the Civil War in search of his brother, a soldier. I imagined him wandering in the same wilderness trek, a wilder one, by the same quiet creek. It would have been so different from these manicured paths, maintained by the park service, that I ran. By the time he arrived in the city, he had already written his Calamus poems, named for the cattails that bobbed in the water, which celebrated, at the same time they obscured, his "need for comrades." I read and re-read the poems, pored over their hidden meanings: the codes he used to describe his intimacies with men, occasionally interrupted by a phrase so bold, there could be no doubt.

> In paths untrodden,
> In the growth by margins of pond-waters,
> Escaped from the life that exhibits itself,
> From all the standards hitherto publish'd, from the
>   pleasures, profits, conformities,
> Which too long I was offering to feed my soul,
> Clear to me now standards not yet publish'd, clear to me
>   that my soul,
> That the soul of the man I speak for rejoices in comrades,
> Here by myself away from the clank of the world

His poems were a consolation and an opening, his celebration of an unmapped wilderness. With every poem he broke free from heavy-handed European conventions of meter and line breaks and rhymes. The lines were endless, overflowing, a bright effusion of consciousness, of fierce body-love for, well, everyone. In this imaginary realm, unlike in life, Whitman will not be contained.

Eight years into our relationship, I was struggling with my own desires for comrades, the ways they burned in my body, struggling for expression. I remembered my conversation with Father Sam, about the solace of male friendships. Why wasn't it enough to know the desires were there, to acknowledge them without acting? Why was the pull to touch another male body so powerful? I didn't know how to explain myself to Eva or to say what I wanted. Were these the same limitations— the "standards not yet publish'd," the constraint of words, hidden excesses of shame—that prevented Whitman from more direct expression of his desires?

Somewhere on the northern end of the park there was a windowless restroom with gray concrete walls which was often left open for hikers and runners to use. It was a place where men loitered, sometimes men like me, running or walking the paths, who stopped to pause in a quiet place, with barely disguised yearning. Late one afternoon, near dusk, when the paths were more deserted, I noticed a man near my age, with a runner's compact build. His dark eyes had a serious glint. He was alone. He lingered outside the rest room, shifting from leg to leg, pulling his hamstrings.

I perceive one picking me out by secret and divine signs...

He looked at me and I looked at him. I slowed my pace and entered the rest room. My heart thumped in my chest: some combination of adrenaline, fear, and loneliness; insistent desire. While I stood at the urinal and peed, I heard the creek of the door, my muscles tensed, and someone walked to one of the stalls. I did not glance in his direction.

Little you know the subtle electric fire that for your sake
is playing within me.

While I stood at the sink washing my hands, the same runner emerged and stood beside me, washing his hands. He stole a frank glance at me, and I looked back and I felt a jolt. I bolted from the restroom, but slowed down again, couldn't run away, my curiosity piqued, heart both open and afraid.

When he came out of the rest room, he walked over to me. "Having a good run?"

"It's perfect weather," I said, my voice shaking. "Not many people. I like it this way."

He stared at me, leaned closer. "Do you want to go back to my apartment?" he said in a low voice. It was almost kind. "It's not far."

All the breath left my body. Even though I thought he might say something like that, I couldn't speak. I shook my head and backed away and took off running again. This time I didn't look back, but I wondered. I did not tell Eva.

That year I spent hours shopping for pearls. I was shopping for a gift to console Eva; I was also going for myself. My passion resembled an addiction. There was a secret ritual attached to it, a heady anticipation, an urgency I didn't understand. Once, when we were driving in another city, I shouted to Eva to stop the car. I hopped out and told her I would rejoin her in an hour. Like a junkie on his way to meet his connection, I didn't tell her I was going to a jewelry store I'd just spotted.

No visit to a city was complete without a survey of the jewelry stores. I took copious notes, comparing prices, strand lengths, pearl sizes, luminescence, nacre quality, and hues like "creamy pink" and "antique white." When I walked into a shop, a newly married man in his thirties, the jeweler assumed I had romantic intentions. "Do you know how a pearl is cultured?" they would inevitably ask. And I would listen, as if to a grandparent's story, aged perfectly from re-telling: Under exact climatic conditions, a grain of sand, called a "nucleus," is introduced into an oyster, irritating it, causing it to coat the object with nacre. Most pearls result misshapen or "baroque." Even the most desired pearl, a nearly perfect sphere with a smooth, uninterrupted sheen, has dents or tracks of roughness that hint at the natural process behind its origin. A cultured pearl is a carefully orchestrated accident, a product of both nature and human artistry.

As I became more and more obsessed, my visits to jewelry stores, these furtive conversations with jewelers, resembled an affair. Pearls became an escape, a distraction, a dazzling hobby that transported me from a home that seemed suddenly, inexplicably empty. We both worked long hours. We didn't have any children. We worried day and night. Shopping for pearls, I became, momentarily, a different and more interesting person: the dashing, romantic, pearl-buying lover that the jewelers assumed me to be.

Few processes in life are as vulnerable to superstition as the effort to conceive a baby. Notwithstanding the best explanations of doctors, fertility specialists, nurses, support group members, lay experts, people who'd conquered it, and even old wives' tales, Eva and I entertained all the stock superstitions:

As busy professionals, we were "unable to relax."

As perfectionist worriers, we found it impossible to "forget that we were trying."

Although anathema to the young, professional couple, the element of spontaneity, everyone agreed, appeared to be a vital ingredient.

My head spun with the catalogue of my inadequacies as an American male: At thirty-three, I had only recently learned to drive a car. Being a sensitive man in an atypical profession—family therapy—I did not fit a traditional mold. I was disappointed with my dwindling number of gay male friends, the frustrations of bonding with straight men, my burgeoning loneliness. I didn't own a house. I was struggling to maintain a savings account. My biceps were too small. My chest was too narrow. Only when I had corrected these defects, I believed, might we conceive.

The most powerful superstition was that we were infertile because having children had never been the story I told myself about who I would be. Though right now I wanted a child, because Eva wanted a child so badly, for most of my life the thought of having one never occurred to me. While the doctor insisted on some biological cause, in my mind I wondered whether our infertility was about a failure of wanting.

And then there was the fact, growing fainter with each year of marriage to Eva: I used to be gay. Sometimes I told myself I was still gay. (The bigger more encompassing word *queer* hadn't yet been embraced so I still toggled back and forth between more polarized words.) Like a Jewish man who marries outside his faith, I told myself, I'm gay in a cultural sense. But there were no winter holidays for me, no rituals or special food dishes to moor me to my origins. Except those friends, my literary ancestors, like Whitman. I was drifting.

Before I'd met Eva, I'd expected to enjoy a certain kind of lifestyle: expensive urban condos, antique shopping, nights at the theater, gourmet cooking, vacations in lesser-known niches of Europe, inspired dinner parties with over-educated guests and witty repartee. I wanted to question the status quo, the supplied ideas of who I should become, where I should belong. None of the typical bourgeois worries.

No marriage, no kids.

As she and I rode that monthly carnival ride of accelerating hope and crashing disappointment, I wondered, in the primitive, self-blaming way of infertile folks, whether our problem was rooted in my gay identity. Gay men can't have children, I told myself. We can't become fathers because we are radicals, queers, outsiders who don't belong in these places, with these experiences. It's not part of the script.

Chambers and Sons was a venerable Washington, D.C. jewelry store that catered to congressmen, professional athletes, and other elite gentlemen of the capital. Leticia was their most successful seller. A petite woman with sculpted hair dyed a bright, unnatural gold, who could have retired years ago, she had once owned a jewelry store, but it had fallen on hard times. She wore half-moon eyeglasses encrusted with tiny diamonds that slid down the tip of her narrow nose, rings set with precious gems (opals, rubies, sapphires) on every finger, and delicate gold chains that gleamed around her neck. As she pulled out strands of pearls to show me, her bracelets jangled so many charms. "Of course, I'm not beautiful like a young woman anymore," she told me, displaying them against her neck, "but you get the idea."

I made so many visits to Chambers and Sons. Like most retail people and other strangers I encountered, Leticia liked to unburden her soul with me. No matter how hard I tried to hide it, people always intuited I was a psychotherapist. One day, she confided, "You know, you remind me of my son."

"Do I?"

"You're just the age he was when he died."

At first, I didn't comment, afraid of what other intimacies this relative stranger, dear as my own mother, might disclose.

"He was an artist," she continued, spreading out two eighteen-inch strands against a black velvet cushion. "A wonderfully gifted painter.

He had a beautiful wife and, just like you, he bought her pearls—a gorgeous twenty-four-inch creamy pink strand. I helped him pick them out myself." She shook her head. "He was my only child. But he didn't value his own precious life. He took it himself one evening. No reason. No note. He just did it."

"I'm sorry," I said, focusing on the glimmering pearls in my hand and trying to imagine them against Eva's neck. Secretly, I rehearsed all the prejudices I found impossible to resist: What had this lovely woman done wrong? What had it been like for her artist son to have a mother so invested in beauty?

"They say mothers never recover from the loss of a child," she added, her eyes watering. "My husband had a nervous breakdown. He stays at home all day, doesn't know what to do with himself. But I work here all the time...and it helps."

She was putting away the pearls. "You think about what you want," she said. "Take your time. Your wife will have them for the rest of her life."

For days afterward, I found myself imagining Leticia and her husband, stranded in their separate orbits. I wondered about her husband, shifting around an empty house, unable to face what was left of his life. I thought of Leticia, putting in long hours at the jewelry counter, holding pearls to her neck and reminding gentlemen buyers, "Of course, I'm not young anymore..." as if apologizing for time's passing.

Robert Woodruff Anderson, the American playwright, once wrote, "Death ends a life, but it does not end a relationship, which struggles on in the survivor's mind toward some final resolution, some clear meaning, which it perhaps never finds." There was a phrase that family therapists who worked with me used—*ghost triangle*—that described Leticia and her husband. Their son, the third point of the triangle, was a ghost, an invisible but real presence that absorbed their attention. Although no one could see or talk to him, he hovered in the background, haunting even the simplest interactions, stranding them. Triangles evolve, they said, at times of heightened grief and anxiety; beautiful distractions that keep people from talking honestly to each other.

Together for eight years, Eva and I had been waiting for something to come along long before that something became a baby. For two years Eva had been looking for a new job, but with no luck. Her parents had had a series of life-threatening illnesses. At work I had mastered my responsibilities, but the next step, moving into a higher clinical position, was proving difficult. Near the end of my MFA program, I was struggling to finish a novel. I was lonely. The stranger in the park spurred a realization: I didn't know what to do with my longing for comrades. I wasn't sure how to speak about it, without seeming to break a rule. It hovered, trembling, unfixed, without any place to land.

Against this backdrop of uncertainty, getting pregnant gave us a fresh focus, distracting us from the passing of time, signs of our own age.

Like Leticia and her husband, Eva and I were stranded in our own ghost triangle, one certainly less tragic, but still painful. The drama of infertility was an endless series of ghost triangles, except the triangulated spirit wasn't dead. It was unborn. From the moment we tried to get pregnant, this unborn being we were grasping for became the third point of our triangle. Lovely fantasies developed about it, like the luminescent nacre that coats the grain of sand. As our peers conceived, gave birth, and raised healthy children, we waited, hoped, took pregnancy tests, catalogued our shortcomings, collected myths, old wives' tales, and superstitions, visited our doctor—and tried and tried again.

At the doctor's instructions, Eva, the A student, transformed her desire for a baby into methodical, daily rituals: She studied the process of conception in books, bought ovulation kits, took prenatal vitamins, visited an acupuncturist, and visualized herself pregnant. She counted and subtracted days, monitored the consistency of her vaginal mucus, waited for the tenderness in her breasts to signify the descent of a microscopic egg. In the back of her calendar, she kept a labyrinthine monthly chart on which she labeled the days of her cycles. Hollow dots represented pre-menstrual symptoms. Solid dots represented menstruation. Asterisks meant intercourse. Crosses meant waiting.

Our lives became tethered to these routines. The quality of her attention to them was exquisite. Even in her sadness, which was dark and unrelenting, she seemed beautiful to me.

She resented not being able to share any of her worries with me. She couldn't even talk about the struggle to pinpoint ovulation, because too much scientific talk interfered with my job, which was to have sex on schedule. If I knew that she was ovulating, I felt pressured and couldn't perform. Sexual desire was becoming tenuous.

To treat a luteal-phase defect—an obstacle to pregnancy, but not necessarily the sole cause of our infertility—we embarked on a series of injections, which lengthened her menstrual cycle from twenty-three days to twenty-eight days, allowing the lining of the uterus to build up to support a fertilized egg. The day of an injection, we would buy a bottle of Zinfandel. Because she needed the anesthetic effect, Eva had two glasses, while I, needing to stay sharp, had one. She held an ice pack to her left or right buttock while I mixed the powder with sterilized water and drew it into a syringe. I tapped the needle until a bubble rose to the top. Then I expelled the air, along with a single tear.

"Are you ready?" I asked.

"I told you not to ask," she said, looking away. "Just do it."

I looked away, hurt.

"I'm sorry," she said, "I'm sorry for all of this."

"It's not your fault," I said, which is what I always said when she apologized. "A little pinch now." I jabbed the inch-long needle into her upper hip.

Over the six months of injections, we never got used to it. We were embarrassed by the extreme efforts we were taking to conceive, ashamed that we could not simply "get over" our inability to have children. Weren't there other ways to have a fulfilling life? Were we so dull and uncreative? Somehow, these injections made the depth of our narcissism too transparent. There was an absence of grace.

To my amazement, we became a cliché infertile couple. We obsessed about our infertility the way other couples talk about their children's potty-training practices or taking their dogs to obedience school. Except for occasional mood flares, I was emotionless. Because of prescribed hormones, Eva was volatile, sometimes inconsolable. Neither of us could believe the people we were becoming. Infertility was now part of our identities. It defined my sense of self in the same way that "sensitive male" and "gay" and "writer" and "psychotherapist" did. Ironically, sometimes paradoxically, identities accrued, like strata of rock, each documenting the unique interaction of soil, weather, and time. Of self and circumstance.

To pass time, I made lists of baby names: Adrian, Sebastian, Gideon, Rupert—names that were British-sounding, perhaps somewhat effete and artsy; Wilde, Whitman, Lawrence—the favorite authors of my young adulthood, all either gay men or men who questioned conventional heterosexuality. Listing baby names—all boys—became another type of spree. I wasn't simply choosing names. I was designing an identity. And it was becoming plain: Not only did I want a child who would be creative and artistic; secretly, I wanted a child who would be gay.

Baby names provided a road-map through my own inarticulate, thwarted desires. Confounded by multiple, contradictory identities, I was pulled in too many incompatible directions at once: Gay and heterosexually married; radical and conventional; writer and therapist.

I was haunted by the past selves I had compromised, neglected, or abandoned.

There is a story that, shortly after Whitman's first meeting with Oscar Wilde, who emulated him, the poet and essayist John Addington Symonds, also gay in a Victorian kind of way, pressed Whitman to acknowledge that the Calamus poems described a homosexual affair. Afterwards Symonds also cattily claimed to have gotten a kiss.

Taken aback, the poet, so bold and exuberant in his poems, bristled "No, no, no," and called them "morbid inferences;" even "damnable" and "disavowed." The paradox of Whitman: he wanted to risk talking about something without talking about it, to speak through his poetry without analysis or direct language. How did those pieces of who he was—that exuberant desire that bounded through long lines of poetry; the coded words for his desires; and the angry public denials; the silences—commingle in his being? There was safety in poetry. That was the only place where love of comrades could be openly celebrated.

What poetry was to Whitman: what pearls were to me. The Magical Realm.

My semen, tests indicated, was normal. Much to my surprise, gay semen can make a baby. The situation was becoming desperate. The doctor recommended Eva undergo surgery: a laparoscopy, hysteroscopy, and pelviscopy. A camera would be inserted through her navel and directed down her fallopian tubes. He would run a blue dye through the tubes to check for blockages and examine for any signs of endometriosis.

Eva wanted the surgery. Even with the prospect of anesthesia, incisions, recovery, and stitches, she considered the surgery option less painful than the ambiguity of not knowing why we couldn't conceive. She hated not having a reason. While I felt the same way, I didn't want someone cutting into her body. What had begun as a simple desire to have a child had become a surgical assault, desire gone awry.

The night before her surgery, I broke down in tears. I hated my desire for a child, hated the narcissism behind it, hated the urgency to understand what wasn't working, hated the family and peer pressure rushing us along this path. Most of all, I hated that time was passing. We had no control over it. I was frightened by the prospect of growing old with only my partner's company. Would we ever stop worrying?

My obsessions with expensive jewelry bordered on campy. Once, beholding a beautiful strand—way outside my price range—I squealed. I loved the splendor of jewelry, the vicarious pleasure of wearing things that glittered. Acting this way helped me transcend that narrow person I had become, a man focused on a desire to have a baby. I thought it was obvious I was gay. But in spite of these pretensions, my fussiness, I wore a plain gold wedding ring. "What type of lifestyle does your wife have?" a jeweler in Manhattan asked, reminding me that I looked like an urban husband, not a drag queen. "Does she dress professionally for work?"

When I opened my notebook to take down prices, business cards from jewelry stores in Washington, D.C., Chicago, San Francisco, and New York City spilled on the counter. Inside the notebook were pages and pages of notes, illustrated with drawings of matching earrings and fancy gold clasps. For the two years we struggled with infertility, I had been searching for, admiring, and rejecting pearls.

That fall, on a trip to Jewelers' Row in Chicago, I encountered a shop owner who forced the issue. I had been in his store twice that week-end to look at two strands. He took me aside and said, "Mr. Scott, what do we have to do to get your business?"

"What do you mean?"

"You obviously like these pearls," he said, "and have been shopping for a long time. Tell us what you want to pay, and we'll work with you."

He was inviting me to bargain, giving me what he thought I wanted. "This is the price they gave me in Washington, D.C. for an eighteen-inch strand," I said, pointing to the back of a business card. "I want these two eighteen-inch strands strung together for the same price." I knew I was being preposterous.

The jeweler thought for a moment. "We can do that," he said.

"Oh."

"We can have them strung and sent to you in D.C. within the week."

I fumbled with my notebook.

"Mr. Scott?"

"Could I just take one more glance at the shop down the street. I saw something there—"

"It's a one-time deal, Mr. Scott," he said. "You need to decide now."

Up to that point, I had imagined that the purpose of looking at pearls was to buy them for Eva. Now, with this offer before me, I was hesitant. If I made a purchase, I would no longer be searching, examining, questioning. The hunt would be over. But my urge to go to jewelry stores—sparkling realms of taste and beauty that summoned my gay identity—would remain.

"It's a deal," I said.

"Congratulations, Mr. Scott," the jeweler said, beaming. "You got yourself a gorgeous strand of pearls." He and another salesman shook my hand. "Congratulations," they said, as if I had announced my engagement, or that my wife and I were pregnant.

After Eva's surgery, the fertility specialist, wearing green surgical garb, invited me into a consultation room. She pulled down her mask to talk. The operation, she said, was a success. The examination had uncovered no functional abnormalities. She had detected a trace of endometriosis on Eva's left ovary, but nothing that would explain our difficulty conceiving. She showed me color photographs of Eva's insides. Her ovary was a pale gray bulb hanging against pink tissue. Its smooth surface glowed white in the light from the camera. The doctor took a pen and pointed to some vague marks on the ovary's side. "This is the endometriosis," she noted. "An extremely mild case."

Eva's ovaries were beautiful, I thought, like pearls with their opalescent glow, the rough tracks, necessary flaws interrupting otherwise-perfect globes. What were we doing? How had we been fooled into thinking there was something *wrong*, just because we couldn't get pregnant quick enough to suit the urgency of our wants? As the doctor talked and Eva lay asleep in the recovery room, I thought, *We're done. I can't do this anymore. No more tests. No more injections.*

That Christmas, when she opened the box and saw her pearls, Eva cried. "Oh my god," she said softly. Under the twinkling lights of the pine tree, I was finally able to share about my ardent, secret search, the shopping excursions that, like a love affair, had taken me away from her and into places where I'd become a fussy gay consumer and a married man in love. Both identities were true. In this stray moment I was grateful for my many-layered sense of self, it felt true and deep and complicated, for it allowed me so many ways to express my wanting, which was never so simple as having a child, or having sex with a man, or purchasing pearls for the woman I adored.

For I am the new husband and I am the comrade...

As I shared about my journey, Eva experimented with the long, glimmering strand of pearls: wearing it loose, knotting it, twisting it, and doubling it. Through the story of the pearls, we were discussing all it had meant to search and to want. As we talked about what it meant to

be infertile and how we would move beyond it, the ghost of our uncon-
ceived child wavered in the background. Then we drew closer, and for
a moment there were just the two of us, alone together, under the tree.

PART THREE

—

MOUNTAIN, UP CLOSE

I want to travel with you to every sacred mountain
ADRIENNE RICH, "Twenty-one Love Poems"

11

—

THE COMMON STORY

Greetings and Happy Holidays! In keeping with tradition, we will try to summarize an adventure-filled year in one page...

In spite of everything that happened we decide to send a holiday card.

It is the same ritual of composing every year; one and then the other of us sitting in front of a laptop, expanding or contracting details from the past year; the pleasure of reminiscence, of editing and distilling; the imperative to contain everything to a page so as not to strain the reader's patience; the debates about what's important; playing with em dashes and semi-colons and just the right sprinkling of exclamation points, which suit Eva but not me. (The age-old argument: are exclamation points effeminate?) Always striving to write a letter that sounded not like me, not like her; like both of us.

We finally took the plunge and redesigned an uninhabitable jungle, otherwise known as The Backyard. An arborist took out an ill-placed oak tree and a long stretch of monstrous laurels.

Both of us enjoy words and stories and finding humor in the

everyday. We did in the past, before we had children; in spite of our present-day dilemma, we do now.

Not long after viewing the documentary "March of the Penguins," we suffered our own arctic hardships. Without really thinking through the logistics, we booked a cabin on Mount Hood—a habitation that requires its occupants to park their van and then ski in with all food, supplies, and children. It was only a mile and a half up and down snowy hills through a somewhat well-marked forest trail.

Mostly the letter writes itself—the word *we* occurs eighteen times—until Eva and I grapple with how to describe anything after The Night Grace Paley Died. The argument starts. How do she and I depict the strange state of our relationship? Will we say anything about divorcing? Does this news fit in this kitschy genre? She drafts three sentences about what happened, my betrayal.

I stare at the sentences, their cold sting. *Wayne had an affair. We've decided to divorce. I'm doing OK.*

I look like a perverted monster. Merry fucking Christmas.

"No," I say. "People will take sides if you blame me. Someday the kids will read this letter. This is private." I go to the laptop while she goes to the kitchen and grates cheddar cheese for quesadillas. I change the three sentences to one, a more cautious statement about separation. There is the word *amicable.*

We exchange places at the laptop. "I'm sorry, buddy," she says, "That's not honest." Our lives these days teeter between routines that circle around chores and children, punctuated by rage. "You're sugar-coating it. We're divorcing." She counters that over the years I have written many essays that grappled with messy personal dilemmas. Why not be honest now? Isn't this another form of authenticity?

We should have gotten the clue when the two younger boys—then aged 4 and 7—showed no interest in cross country skiing on earlier test runs. We made it OK—Wayne dragging the two boys in a sled—but the trek back to the van at the end, during an ice storm, was brutal and unforgiving, with the two boys crying hysterically, "My butt is frozen!"

Up until now I have been quiet about my hesitation to get divorced. It doesn't feel right. It doesn't feel like us. But I can't imagine what us, our present moment mess, is. I don't want to leave. She wants me out, but she likes that I stay. The patterns of our lives, already in motion before the betrayal, still in motion now, keep pulling us back.

We argue. On some days we abandon the prospect of a holiday letter, not speaking.

It seems to me we don't know what we're doing, but in her mind public statements must be emphatic, clear.

Somehow bound up in the dissembling edifice of our marriage there is an embattled pride. An ancient word, dating back to the year 1000. *Prüde.* Derived from the Old English, the word *pride* falls on a continuum, denoting either a positive regard for one's accomplishments or an inflated vanity, the outward expression of ego. One's pride, a flourishing state, the expansion of the blue and yellow tail of a peacock. For both of us, pride lurks in the deeper, unconscious strata of our damaged marriage, beyond words. It is the story of our marriage's public value; the ideal marriage as a kind of gold standard; the public perception of it in a world of narrow options for looking upright; and by proxy our individual stock.

Pride cannot survive, it seems, unless the terms of her liberation from me—*liar, cheater, narcissist*—are clarified.

In addition (and possibly not entirely appropriate for a holiday missive), we grown-ups have decided to amicably split. And so we enter this new year with the intent of continuing our friendship and our well-honed co-parenting of 3 energetic, funny, kind, intelligent, and wonderful children.

It may read smoothly to someone outside our marriage, but to me the two sentences pulse with all the haggling and punching and taunting of a boxing match. In the end, it is just a blip of a passage that could even almost be missed if the letter were read quickly.

But it isn't.

The flood of emails and calls starts.

That winter, I am reading E.M. Forster's *Aspects of the Novel* for the fourth time. Truth be told—I don't like to admit this nerdy fact to anyone—the book is a kind of comfort food for the mind, like *The Great Gatsby*, which I also re-read every few years. Again and again I read *Aspects of the Novel* because somehow, in breaking down the behemoth of The Novel into its parts—people, story, plot, pattern, and rhythm—he makes novel-writing seem simpler. Whenever I stop writing my own novel, I read Forster and am able to start the story again.

One afternoon I am sitting in my favorite back table in Costello's, surrounded by books, notepads, and pens. I can see the whole cafe, patrons talking and gesturing and drinking and eating. I am sipping my coffee and reading *Aspects of the Novel* and thinking about Linné's challenge from our first session: The Common Story.

I am musing on whether what Eva and I have together—what any married couple has—is a story or a plot. Forster has a famous formula to describe the difference. "'The king died and then the queen died' is story," he tells us. "'The king died and then the queen died of grief' is a plot." If I follow his formula, I can reduce our dilemma to two possible sentences:

STORY: The king cheated and the queen divorced him.

BOOM.

PLOT: The king cheated and the queen divorced him, because they had forgotten who they were.

Forster elaborates:

> *The time sequence is preserved, but the sense of causality overshadows it. Or again: 'The queen died, no one knew why, until it was discovered that it was through grief at the death of the king.' This is a plot with a mystery in it, a form capable of high development.*

I want to be in a form capable of high development.

In Forster's formula, human beings have stories, a sequence of facts (*And then...and then...?*), but characters in a novel have plots (*Why?*). The sequence of facts is colored by the mystery of who they are, undiscovered parts of themselves, inner worlds and secret lives, the meaning-making wheels that turn in their minds, the winding ways of what he calls their "self-communings." This depth of character, Forster tells us, makes the people we encounter in a novel rounded, not flat; more compelling folks whom we might befriend. "The test of a round character is whether it is capable of surprising in a convincing way," Forster tells me. Flat characters are literary shortcuts; quick sketches that draw on the reader's grasp of common stereotypes and caricatures. Rounded characters have depth, oddness, and idiosyncrasy.

Humanness.

Marriage, that word that floats between two people and defines who they are to the world and themselves, in fact, is a story. It sits in photo albums or framed on the walls of their living room. It is marriage certificates and mortgage deeds and birth announcements and holiday letters. Plot emerges in memories that couples share at dinner with new friends, in which they become characters to each other. They tell it jointly and often interrupt. They correct and argue about what really happened, and why, and how did you know? What did you do on that first date? Did you both even like musicals? Did she plan to stay the night? Are you saying the course of your lives was determined by the sorry state of public transportation in Chicago? Mostly there is a harmony of narrative: maybe different sounds, bass and soprano, but altogether a lyrical chord.

Maybe instead we are searching for a common plot.

Every day it rains. The gray surrounds us. I forget what the sun looks like.

Linné is quirky and mysterious. She does not schedule her sessions. It is an online scheduling tool which offers few openings every week. Like tickets for an exclusive rock concert, each week I jockey to find a time for us. Eva and I rearrange our lives to see her this morning or that afternoon or that late evening. It's never the same.

Tonight the appointment begins at nine o'clock, which I didn't even know was possible for counseling. Sitting on the blue ball between us, she leans in so close, it feels like we are in bed together. Her expression is soft, her gaze intense, unfaltering. Does she ever blink? She often seems inexplicably sad, almost teary; maybe this is the look of compassion, which makes all real conversation possible. It's as if she's telling us she's not afraid of any of this, this dark territory of transgression and anguish. Maybe she is a witch? Each meeting she starts by asking us to form an intention for the session's dialogue. No matter how upset Eva or I or both of us become, Linné brings calm.

Outside, raindrops run in crooked lines down the windowpane: a melting, liquid geometry.

We are not talking about custody arrangements or divided property. This does not feel like mediation yet.

We are trying to listen to each other. We share shards of our individual stories of what happened, fitfully building something common. Every few sentences Linné pauses Eva and asks me to say back what I heard without interpretations, judgments, or any reaction.

The thing is: I cannot hear her. Eva's words begin, my concentration perks up, I know what is expected—*This is your job,* I tell myself, *you need to listen*—then some feeling spikes in me, words scatter like alphabet soup, my mind drifts. Shouldn't I, as a psychotherapist, be better at this? I start thinking about my story, which is so different. Her story is about betrayal, abandonment. Mine is about loneliness, adriftness, the intermingling of love and disappointment.

"What did you hear Eva say?"

Shit, I lost track. Again. I shake my head, mention that I heard words like shock and anger. *I am in fact a terrible husband, just like the story goes.* "I'm sorry."

"It's OK, it takes time, practice."

"Damn it."

"It's really OK."

Eva is crying. I need to up my game. For her. I am determined to pay attention, to get outside my head. Her story of betrayal, of my badness, of her disappointment in me, in the marriage, is awful. I hear pieces, repeat them back. I am getting better at this. "Did I get that right? Is there more?"

She continues. I throw myself into forgetting the crazy, fretting sentences spinning in my head; into listening with my whole body.

"Before we end, I want each of you to share something about the other person for which you're grateful," Linné announces. It doesn't make sense. Damn it, we are breaking up! There is no gratitude in that. But Linné waits, unflappable. Like a magician casting a spell, she is powerful in the force of her conviction that, in this dark place, there is gratitude.

"You work hard for me and the kids," Eva says. She starts crying. "You really do take care of us."

"You do listen to me," I say, wiping a tear, "even though I know it's hard to hear."

Linné smiles. Another session ends. We walk onto Southeast Division Street. Cars whiz by, a few pedestrians saunter at this late hour, and we stumble, shell-shocked, which is what we usually are afterwards, like we don't know who we are anymore.

"We've never even paid her," Eva says out of nowhere. Her eyes are puffy and pink.

"She never says anything about it."

"Should we bring it up?"

"Yes, I suppose..."

Here is one truth of our common story: Neither of us wants to talk about the fee. Eva wants mediation to divorce, she says, but mediation is more expensive, and she is frugal. If we raise the question of the fee which we never pay, we will be forced to decide. Maybe, in spite of her pronouncements, Eva doesn't want to decide. Or maybe she really is that frugal. We do not know what we are doing—what the label is, therapy or mediation, healing or ending our relationship. We are just three humans sitting together in a room, outside any known economy. Every week we return to Linné, diving into the ambiguity of ourselves, our story, without mentioning the fee.

What is also clear: We are trying to listen to each other.

The rain is splashing down, sheets of water, without any sign of stopping, and I am so tired of the city and the season and my sad, confusing life. The gutters of the house overflow, spilling at the corners like waterfalls. The drains in the street, still clogged with autumn leaves, form small ponds that vibrate like timpani as drops pound their surface. Every morning there are low puddles in the basement to be vacuumed.

Eva takes the bus to work. Then it is morning drop-off time.

"Kids, we need to go!"

I help button raincoats and fasten book bags and try not to yell when everyone moves so slowly and the hands of the clock move so quickly. "Kids, NOW!"

For a father of three children, with a job, a falling-apart house, two sick cats, and a wife who wants a divorce, I have little time to untie this knot of confusion that's making my skull swell. I rush Rosie and Louis, complaining, out the door, load their squirmy bodies into the blue minivan, strap Philip, the tiny kindergartner, blond hair flying in so many directions we don't even bother to comb it, into his car seat. When finally I face the windshield, it is, in flashes that will be interrupted, as if I am alone.

My pre-divorce morning ritual, I put in a CD of Sarah Brightman and Andrea Bocelli. The violins swell with a pitch of nearly unbearable mourning. The drum beats like endurance, the battle lost, the warrior returning home. And then her voice, otherworldly perfect, breathlessly rushed, in Italian and one phrase in English: "Time to Say Goodbye." His tenor joins, triumphant and strong, like he is catching up before she leaves him.

I sniffle and wipe my nose. We are driving through a waterfall. It is one mile to the kindergarten: drop-off one. Six miles to the magnet elementary school, so far from our neighborhood: drop off two. Then three more miles to work. My vision is obscure. The wipers cannot sweep across the windshield fast enough. In the background, there is an argument brewing; something about a cheese stick.

> *Quando sono solo*
> *sogno all'orizzonte*
> *E mancan le parole*
> (When I am alone I sit and dream
> And when I dream the words are missing)

"WHY is that lady screaming?" Rosie asks. "Can we listen to James Taylor instead?"

I wipe my eyes, flip the turn signal, ignore them for as long as they will let me. I lead Philip to his smiling teacher. Nothing happens fast with him. The rain pounds our heads. I dash back to the car. I play the song again.

> *Sì, lo so che non c'è luce*
> *In una stanza quando manca il sole*
> *Se non ci sei tu con me, con me*
> (Yes I know that in a room so full of light
> That all the light is missing)

This is so operatic and gay, I think. *Is my misery really this campy?*

I don't care. It is. I am, I am, I am. I hide my face, wipe a tear, play the song again. I convince myself that Rosie and Louis are oblivious to the drama in the driver's seat.

"Can you play the *Cats* CD, dad?" comes the request.

"Yeah!" Louis chimes in. His voice is high-pitched, insistent.

The more I listen, the less I understand the lyrics of "Time to Say Goodbye." Later that night, by myself at the laptop, I will research the English translation, to see if I can decipher the song's mysterious hold. Even in English translation I don't get their story. Are they breaking up but still singing, in such harmony, together? Are they leaving a homeland together? Or going to another country as exiles? To whom is this goodbye directed?

> *Se non ci sei tu con me, con me*
> (But I don't see you with me, with me)

I pull the minivan beside the school and Rosie and Louis unbuckle themselves. Maybe it is the song beneath the incoherence of the words

that speaks to me; harmony pulsing in confusion; the notion that goodbye will bring clarity; a disjointed farewell, *to something*, between a
couple who is neither together nor apart.

Con te partirò
(It's time to say goodbye)

On the seven-minute walk to the bus stop; in the garden on weekend
afternoons behind the Japanese maple, where no child can see; on her
bed in the attic, under the heavy orange and brown afghan her grandmother crocheted; after the children are in bed, with an adoring cat
kneading her chest; in the locker room before a workout, when no one
else is looking; with her gynecologist during a routine pap smear, when
she is caught off-guard, supine, by sneaker waves of grief; over the stove
making dinner, when the children are watching *Bear in the Big Blue
House*...

...These, I imagine, are the places where Eva cries.

"We cannot understand each other," Forster tells his students in *Aspects
of the Novel*. "Except in a rough and ready way; we cannot reveal ourselves, even when we want to; what we call intimacy is only a makeshift;
perfect knowledge is an illusion."

I am back in the café, a half-drunk mug of coffee by my side, my
favorite table against the wall. Re-reading *Aspects of the Novel* is like
following a map inside the head of a man who longed for human fellow-
ship; a man who kept his homosexuality largely a secret, who did not
have sex until he was thirty-seven and struggled, during a morally constrained era, with intimacy. Forster was sixteen when Oscar Wilde was
imprisoned. He died two years after the Stonewall riots. It is hard to read
Aspects of the Novel and not sense the pitch of his loneliness, the brutal
absence of enduring love in his life, and to realize that the rounded

characters in his novels were a consolation. Novels were a refuge where he assuaged an unbearable loneliness.

To be a sensitive soul, full of compassion and love, alert to feelings in others, and to be denied deep connection, is a tragedy.

I do not want to be a lonely man.

Maybe I am falling in love with Forster, I wonder, in a literary kind of way. I hear a kind of sweetness in his lectures, a gentle humor, a mix of timidity and courage that seems similar to me, a depth of wisdom. I wish he and I could be sitting in Costello's, drinking coffee, talking about Eliot and Dostoyevsky. I think he would like this place. He would make passing comments about the televised scenes of Brussels and Istanbul. I want to ask him about the distinction between life—which in his mind is confounded by secrets and illusions, which feels like my life too—and novels, where there is a more perfect truth and intimacy. I want that intimacy, however imperfect and searching, in life. I want to be a rounded character to Eva, just as I want her to be a rounded character to me. I know omniscience isn't possible in life as it is, they say, in fiction, but maybe a deeper fellow-feeling.

Flatness is the enemy. Flatness is the story of divorce.

Suddenly I understand why it is hard to listen when we see Linné. I have writer's block in my marriage.

At this moment we are flat characters caught in a story, but I want us to be round characters unfolding in a plot. Maybe a marriage in crisis does not need a therapist to excavate the collective unconscious of two people, but a novelist who can reimagine their story.

Maybe marriage, like a novel, should be an act of imagination.

Week after week we keep coming back. Linné the Magician, our Cheerful Witch, seems to say: *Nothing is impossible.*

This Saturday afternoon session we are sitting in our arrangement, the three-legged stool, heads circling the invisible problem. Outside the rain has stopped and the sky is overcast white like a canvas. I am leaning in towards Eva. I find it helps me remind myself that my focus is her. When Linné cues Eva to share her story, I know my job is to track what she says, to ignore any rebuttals that circle in my mind, to listen intently. She tells a story from her childhood. It is a familiar family secret, but it means something different when she tells it here, with Linné nodding, with the stakes so high.

"There was a minister of our church named Baron," Eva begins her memory. She needs for Linné to understand for the first time and for me to hear it differently. "He was the minister for most of my childhood. He was married but he told my mother that his wife had lost any interest in sex. At night he would come to our apartment and my mother would ask me to go to bed early so that they could have time alone. I didn't like going to church on Sunday and hearing him preach and I did not like seeing his wife gaze at him with this admiring look. I would look at my mother and she would be gazing at him too, with the same look of admiration. It felt like I was drawn into their hypocrisy and lies. I was nine."

My chest swells with a heaviness. I remind myself to breathe. It's her story. I say it back to her. "Did I get that right? Is there more?"

"Baron was handsome, and my mother was lonely, and there weren't many options for a divorced woman in our town in that time," Eva continues. "He said that his visits were part of his minister's duties. At one point he had another affair, with another woman in the congregation. She was my mother's friend. I complained to mom that I didn't like Baron. I did not like being sent to bed early. I did not like his betrayals, of his own wife, of my mother, of all the women in that congregation. He lied."

I know this story. But this is the first time I am hearing it after our crisis. She reminds me that she was nine years old when Baron's attentions trained on her mother, and everything—the humiliation and anger—makes sense in a different way. We have a nine-year-old daughter, so principled and clear like her mother. I cannot help but re-imagine the story through Rosie's eyes: my daughter feeling trapped in an immoral situation, the concoction of these lonely adults, the forced duplicity, and resenting it. She would hate being sent to bed early; the humiliation of being treated like a younger child.

And then the truest sentence:

"I can't be weak like those women. I don't want to feel trapped like that ever again."

Subtle as the wave of a wand, Linné nods at me. I could flinch—I don't like the picture of Baron, I don't like the comparison to me I am making in my head, I don't like the conclusion the story implies—but I don't flinch. I listen. I say back the exact words. It is her story. It does make sense. It runs alongside my story, which is also true. "You want to be strong," I say. "You don't want to be trapped."

"Yes."

I know why she wants me to leave.

I know why divorce makes sense.

I lied to her. I humiliated her.

In my heart there is a grim glimmering of acceptance that this, Divorce, the inevitable end of the path, is part of the Common Story.

> *To discover that one has been lied to in a personal relationship, however, leads one to feel a little crazy.*
> Adrienne Rich, "Women and Honor: Some Notes on Lying"

The four bedrooms in this house contain secrets.

At first, when I was working on the garden path, I convinced Eva to allow me to stay the night on occasion. No one knew. It would be more practical, I told her. I could be home earlier in the morning to help with rise-and-shine. I will not come near your bedroom, I promised. At first, I slept in the extra top bunk bed in Louis' room. Eva slept in the attic bedroom that had been our room, which she was redecorating to be a room for a woman alone. She bought a batik poster showing a woman leaning against an open window frame. The woman's room is dark. Outside the day is happy yellow. The woman's expression is pained but she is looking to something outside the window. Another framed postcard is a collage of a woman's face emerging from darkness with the words: *I'd like to find the way back to myself. I'm listening.*

As a kind of placeholder, I keep the studio apartment seven blocks away, but I spend nights there less and less.

Eventually, I persuade Eva to let me convert the room we use as an office into a guest bedroom that for all purposes becomes my room, even though I am paying rent on the studio. I buy a queen-sized bed.

She worries about the cost. Do you need such a big bed? Big enough for me and all three children, I rationalize, for times they want to cuddle with their father.

She shifts uncomfortably but doesn't say anything.

And then...

Sometimes, at night, after the children are asleep, she comes to my room. This is one of those stray moments in our lives, beyond notions of wrongdoing and rightdoing, when we are ourselves. "Can I sleep here?" she asks. There is no pride. There does not need to be. She climbs into bed. Our bodies mold together, me outside, she inside. We are one body. It feels precious and true. No one can see that we are together, holding onto each other in an uncertain, incoherent world.

Sometimes the truest things, the body truths, have nothing to do with language.

She relaxes into my body like we belong together. Eventually, the front of my body presses against her back. I grow hard, that familiar persistence, another body truth. I know she can feel my desire. She does not turn around. She does not move away. These are the two realities streaming into the new truth: hers and mine, side by side, not always the same.

She does not turn around and we are together.

She is liberated, and we are together.

A sadness arises in me and mixes with the desire. In these stray moments I want more, like the old days. I want the rest of her. I want the past. But the days of goodbye sex have ended. I hold onto my desire.

Even though I have read the chapter many times, I struggle to understand the one titled "Prophecy." Forster calls this lecture "so strange and grandiose." Prophecy is another piece of the novel, the most difficult to define. "Prophecy—in our sense—is a tone of voice," he explains. "It may imply any of the faiths that have haunted humanity...or the mere raising of human love and hatred to such a power that their normal receptacles no longer contain them."

Here's what I think: Prophecy is a kind of intelligence, glowing between the writer's words, that pushes human understanding beyond its limits, that sees something new. It's a gift to the reader and not always obvious.

There was, I discover, a special relationship Forster had, beautiful and doomed. They met in 1916 on the tram in Egypt. Mohammed el Adl, a young, handsome Egyptian conductor, a Christian in a Muslim world, acutely aware of how the British colonized and oppressed him and his people, recognized a fellow traveler in Morgan, who routinely rode his car, sometimes just to watch him. Throughout their "forever friendship," the two men moved closer to each other, then became sexual, though at first Mohammed called it "foolish." Their courtship was happy and fitful, separated by so many layers of difference: language, world views, prejudices, privilege. Mohammed had no frame of reference for being gay or for homosexual romance. Morgan was beginning to see these things as central but secret parts of his identity. Theirs was a love no "normal receptacle" could contain.

In spite of these differences, Mohammed awakened hope in Morgan in the possibility of enduring romantic love between men. It inspired his gay romance *Maurice*, although he kept the manuscript hidden during his life. ("I was determined that in fiction anyway two men should fall in love and remain in it for the ever and ever that fiction allows," he noted in the hidden pages. He dedicated it "To a Happier Year.") Over a span of five years, the men arranged numerous rendezvous, Morgan often traveling across continents to see his beloved. Eventually Mohammed married a woman, Gamila, and they had a baby which they named Morgan. It isn't clear what Gamila knew of the men's relationship, but she accepted her husband's friend's visits to their home.

A few years before Morgan delivered the lectures in *Aspects of the Novel*, Mohammed contracted a lethal form of tuberculosis. Morgan visited frequently, brought comforts and gifts, even nursed him in the presence of his wife. Morgan was out of the country when Mohammed died. Before his death, he sent Morgan a note which ended:

> *My love to you*
> *My love to you*
> *My love to you*
> *Do not forget your ever friend*

There were no periods.

Several months pass and we are seeing Linné again. It is her earliest appointment and it starts at eight o'clock. We are still not paying her. She is not asking us for payment. It is the great unspoken issue. We don't use either word: mediation or couple's counseling. It is magic. We are still working on listening. We are getting better at it.

"I feel inadequate," Eva says, "like I'm not enough for you."

"There's nothing wrong with you," I say. Sometimes Linné lets us talk back and forth, without listening and summarizing. We have graduated to conversation. "It's about me not fitting in a heterosexual marriage."

In a rare moment of diagnosis, Linné says, "It seems to me that the two of you *are* together. You're just struggling to make sense of it on the terms that have been supplied to you."

"What are we supposed to do then?" Eva asks and only I can hear the tone of contempt. "Have an *open* marriage?" Other couples' therapists we had seen over the years had talked with disdain, even disgust, about open marriages, as a kind of cultural pathology. They never work, our last couples' therapist John pointed out. They are delusional. The jealousy and insecurity are unbearable. All the books I had ever read about marital counseling in graduate school focused on couples needing to make monogamy work.

"Oh sure, many couples have open marriages," Linné says.

Eva grows quiet. I am confused. Linné does not see our souls rattling in the wake of this comment. Sometimes naming a word as something true is the magic.

"They're more complex," she continues. "There's not the same support from friends and family. They take self-awareness and communication, but regular marriage does too." Her tone is cheerful and upbeat, as if mentioning a new ice cream flavor. "I've worked with people who make them work."

This pronouncement, simple and matter-of-fact, has the weight of a spell. It slipped so cavalierly into the river of the conversation, just another string of words really; but there were deep ripples through our bodies.

The session ends. As usual, like dumbfounded zombies, we walk onto Southeast Division Street, in that wordless, shell-shocked state. The street is quiet. The sun is in the east. We can see the ghost of Mount Hood against the pink sky. Eva's mouth is still open, though she doesn't realize it. I am afraid to say anything. Could Linné be a quack? Where did she get her degree again? Is she licensed? But she has helped us so much.

"Did you hear what she said about open marriage?"

I am hesitant to answer. This may be a trap.

"I did," I admit. Truthful, neutral, non-committal.

"No one's ever said that before," she says, and I sense confusion in her voice.

"No," I agree.

We walk to the blue van which will hold only the two of us. We board and fasten our seat belts and lock the doors without even glancing at the empty snack boxes and tattered books and toys on the seats behind us. We drive and do not say another word.

That spring evening we are sitting on the porch swing under the yellow shine of the porch light. The glow from the streetlamp turns the street blue and silver. The house is three blocks from a street lined with bars and restaurants, and we are close to the hour when people stagger back to their cars, inebriated. The swing creaks like a loud cricket in the night, steady, insistent. I know it is time to talk, to push the issue, but I am afraid of the conversation. But we are in a window—that mix of relief and triumph after we have gotten children into bed.

"I'm wondering," I say, taking a sip of *Grüner Veltliner*, a crisp white, the new favorite. "I'm wondering if we could try what Linné suggested. Maybe she could help us figure our way."

Eva gazes at the street. The streetlamp gleams on her goblet. "Open marriage?"

"Just try it, to see if we could make it work."

She shakes her head vigorously, pauses. Her eyes soften, then she looks away. "I guess...I don't know, Wayne."

"It could be an experiment," I offer. I am not sure what we are getting into, but we have to try something. This limbo feels unbearable. "We can always decide it's not for us, and I'll give you the friendliest divorce there ever was."

"Maybe," she says.

I have to be careful about pushing. "There's nothing that you've discovered about me that you didn't know when we first started dating. I'm the same person."

"I'll think about it."

My breath quickens. I wonder if this is her first or second glass of wine. Since I've already ventured this far, I decide to say everything on my mind. "The thing is," I add, "if we were going to try a nonmonogamous marriage, to date other people, even as an experiment, you would have to be the one to go first."

"I know," she says.

We sit and sip and stare. A racoon creeps along the fence, heading for the neighbor's compost bin. The porch swing creaks like the pendulum of a clock.

On Saturday the neighbor's daughter, Sylvie, nine, is visiting. At the dining room table, she and Rosie are making art. Overhearing their conversation, I am in the living room reading the newspaper. Outside my view Eva is in the kitchen chopping vegetables for chicken soup, her Sunday winter ritual. There is a muffled thumping on the old cutting board her father made.

The wind is roaring. On this stormy winter day the girls are working on watercolors at a low table. Sylvie is mixing pink and blue above the horizon of a perfect black line. "What do you think your wedding dress will be like?" she asks Rosie in a kind of pastel dream. She loves nothing better than to engage in rapturous imaginings about bridesmaid's gowns and floral arrangements and towering cakes with cascades of flowery buttercream icing. In a few years she will dive into Jane Austen's novels and not emerge for the remainder of her adolescence.

Rosie, the same age but her mother's offspring and skeptical about anything typically feminine, murmurs "I'm not sure" with barely masked frustration. With precise strokes, she is painting a striped tiger on a plain.

Sylvie cleans her brush, dips the bristle into the orange, stirs up the fiery color. She is creating a sun. "I'm going to wear a white dress with old-fashioned hoops and a pearl necklace that my father buys me for my special day." Sylvie likes to note discrepancies. Nothing that is curious and out of order with the way things are supposed to be escapes her attention. "Why do your parents sleep in separate rooms?"

There is a pause. Rosie, I am guessing, has not taken time in other family's homes to observe their sleeping arrangements. "I don't know."

"My parents sleep in the same room," Sylvie pronounces with authority, "because they love each other very much."

From my peripheral view I see the pink rise in my daughter's cheeks. Maybe she remembers that horrible conversation about divorce; such a confusing memory now.

Before I can decide if I need to say anything, I hear Eva. "You know, Sylvie, it's true Rosie's dad and I sleep in different bedrooms," she tells her gently. "But that doesn't have anything to do with how we feel about each other. We love each other too, just like your parents. We just have a bedroom arrangement that's different, that suits us. But there's nothing wrong about it."

Sylvie, the neighborhood know-it-all, does not know that I can hear their conversation. "I thought you were mad at each other," she says.

I cannot see Eva. I do not know if she remembers I am nearby. "No, we're not mad at each other," she answers. "Not now. All mothers and fathers get angry with each other sometimes. It doesn't mean anything is wrong. There are lots of different ways to be married."

Rosie looks back at her tiger, calmly painting an alert black eye, satisfied with this response. I raise up my newspaper again and try to read, as if this were any other innocuous conversation on a weekend afternoon, as if the world had not shifted in its complacent, uninteresting orbit.

And she becomes round to me...

And I become round to her.

And then...

12
—

BLUTSBRÜDERSCHAFT

"You know how the old German knights used to swear a
Blutsbrüderschaft," *he said to Gerald,*
with quite a new happy activity in his eyes.
"Make a little wound in their arms,
and rub each other's blood into the cut?" said Gerald.
"Yes—and swear to be true to each other, of one blood, all
their lives. That is what we ought to do. No wounds, that
is obsolete. But we ought to swear to love each other, you
and I, implicitly, and perfectly, finally,
without any possibility of going back on it."

D.H. Lawrence, *Women in Love*

We are running in the forest.

We meet on the Wildwood, the trailhead on NW 53rd Drive, early
Sunday morning. Blades of sunlight cut through the steeple-like firs.

Fog hangs in the air, touching the green moss in the branches. To either side of the trailhead the fern-lined path meanders along a precipice. It is summer. The trillium, peeking out between the ferns and dark ivy, have turned dusty pink.

Colin wears black running shorts and a sleeveless shirt that exposes round biceps. He is doing a gentle backward lunge. It is hard to look at him and not to feel inadequate: his compact, athletic body, the flinty eyes, the buoyant energy.

I do some squats to get ready, then stretch my hamstrings.

"We'll start at Wildwood and head west until we get to Fire Lane 1," he tells me. "Then we go down Nature Trail and run along the creek which'll take us to Leif Erickson—that's a flat gravel road that goes on FOREVER" (he yells the important words) "and you think it's NEVER going to end. But then, just when you feel the MOST hopeless, Alder Trail appears. Here is where your calves are going to hate you, because that hill is so STEEP even when your mind thinks you're running as fast as you can your legs are going as slow as walking. How does that sound?"

All I can think, secretly, is: *NO. FUCKING. WAY.* Then: *How long?* And: *I don't think I can't do this.* "Let's go," I say. We take off, at a brisk pace, into the forest.

Rocks and exposed tree roots make the going uneven, almost dangerous. Dappled shadows—morning sun peeking through the firs—camouflage these trip hazards, make the path tricky to read. Run, but run carefully. Keep up on this tandem journey, but don't trip. Look down to avoid the roots, yes, but don't look to the right if you can resist—that drop is two feet away—and don't forget to catch a glimpse of sky through the trees. Ignore the queasiness boiling in your gut.

As we run, uphill or down, Colin talks, observing everything, without breathing hard. He leans close. "Did you see that guy? His chest? Those thighs?"

I glance at the runner zipping past us. "Wow," I whisper.

"Holy," he mumbles.

We keep running and talking, two dads in their mid-forties on their Sunday morning jaunt in the woods.

In the northern part of the forest, near Fire Lane 1, the Wildwood Trail pauses in a meadow with two forgotten picnic tables, damp and decaying, and a dead tree, humbled by age and an attack of fungus, upended long ago by a storm. The enormous trunk lies on its side and the vast ball of roots, cut off from the ground, creates a partition that hides a shadow space from the rest of the meadow: perfect for a mid-run pee.

Like gentlemen, we take turns.

I walk between the ferns, avoiding the brambles, and I slip my penis out of my running shorts to pee out the two and a half cups of coffee I drank earlier. Steam rises from the grass.

"How are you doing?" Colin asks when I return, stretching his hamstrings.

I hate these hills. I don't want to admit it. I mimic his movement and feel my own tight hamstring. "I'm OK," I say.

"You keep a good pace," he says. "We're well-matched."

I want to keep listening to him.

We descend a muddy slope, ripped apart by trailbikes, slipping and stabilizing ourselves, to another round meadow by Fire Lane 1 and find the trailhead for the Nature Trail which zig zags, hill after winding hill, a descent of stone- and root-encrusted paths to the creek. Sun sparkles on water dribbling over the rocks. My running shoes are splattered with mud.

Leaning into me Colin whispers, "What about THAT guy?"

"Is this some kind of model runway for REI?"

"OH. MY. GOD."

"Keep your voice down!"

Running downhill exhilarates me. My limbs stream with pure joy. It's the conversation with Colin, this beautiful new friend who talks, effortlessly, whether we are going up or down. I luxuriate in this illusion: I am athletic and fast, like him, my almost-doppelganger, even though the ease of descent is more about the slope, the pull of gravity, a warm unadmitted love.

We met in the dark forest of the internet, on one of those sites where men seek each other for sex and mindless hook-ups and sometimes dating. Most messages cited height, weight, hair and eye color, some favorite sex acts. Everyone included dick size.

Eva had begun to see a man, Henry, whom she met online. I was trying to be my best self. The loneliness was becoming unbearable.

I titled my message "Looking for a Fellow Traveler."

There were only a few people interested in me. Some were other bi married men. Some were gay men who regarded closeted married men as an exotic fetish. Mostly the messages were crude. One writer had an odd screen name: *Ignotus Peverell.* Where have I heard that name before? I do a search. Of course, he was the wizard from the *Harry Potter* books, this year's favorite bedtime story. The Cloak of Invisibility enabled Peverell, its original owner, to escape death. The Cloak was passed onto Harry who used it to penetrate places where he was not allowed, without being seen.

A Harry Potter reference in a gay hook-up site?

I contacted Ignotus Peverell, whose real name was Colin. He has two children at home, around the same ages as my two oldest. They have just finished *Harry Potter and The Goblet of Fire.*

"Well, you sound like someone that I would like to get to know," he wrote. "We are similar age, height, and weight. I too am married to a woman and we are just starting to open up our relationship. I'm looking to get to know someone before my pants are coming off."

They were discussing the rules for an open marriage. They were bogged down in a quandary about whether kissing would be allowed. "I came out to my wife about three years ago," he wrote. "A few years prior I realized that I was bi/gay and that I had to do something about it. I finally had to tell her as I was getting close to breaking my vows. That seems like a long time ago and we are still together and in better shape than we were. We still have sex and sleep in the same bed."

The flurry of email exchanges continued, sometimes several in a day. Every hour I checked my phone or computer, to see if he had written.

"My partner and I have been married 15 years and together 20," I wrote back. "We 'separated' a year ago when she discovered some of my activities on the internet. We are very close and love raising our kids together. I am home so much, helping with the kids, that sometimes she lets me sleep on the extra bunk bed in my sons' room. (We even still share the same bed occasionally, though we won't admit it to anyone.) She has a relationship with another guy, Henry. It's hard on me, but I have held back so far from other relationships out of shyness and fear. In the last few months we've come to realize that we might develop an open marriage of sorts—an economic, parenting partnership—with romance pursued with other people."

After a series of exchanges, we finally met at a coffee shop on the East Bank Esplanade, by the Willamette River. Colin arrived on his bicycle, dismounting in one gallant swoosh. He looked like me: sandy blond hair (thinning on the top); blue eyes; freckles; angular chin; runner's build (strong legs, thin chest). We were both wearing khakis and button-down oxford shirts (his white with black stripes; mine solid blue); standard, no-nonsense, working-dad uniforms.

"Good to meet you," he said extending his hand.

"Yeah, finally," I answered, fumbling to shake his hand, trying to contain my excitement.

We ordered coffee and settled into the first, long conversation. The similarities seemed endless. We were both runners. We both experienced weekends hijacked by the demands of parenting, suffocating swaths of time consumed by kid-focused activities. We both had wives at different stages of disappointment, who struggled with loving us. Like me, he was a queer man and a dad. He was a queer man. He was a dad. Queer dad. *What? How do those things go together?* His heart had expanded once, twice, the way it did for men when their children are born, so he had a different, safer kind of heart, a heart like mine. In those days I had a fantasy that the personalities of men who were fathers were different than childfree men. A switch had turned on in them, that released a kind of warmth and caring and safety. He did the things dads do: endless chauffeuring to soccer matches and chess camp and the climbing gym; the sacredness of midweek family dinners; the night-wakings that test the last thread of patience.

We discovered that both families attended the downtown Unitarian Church, sitting in the same section in the balcony, designated for parents in case the Sunday School teachers needed them for a crying child. "Let's just tell anyone who asks that we met in church," I suggested. It sounded pious and above-board, the kind of thing two middle-aged dads would do.

"We met in church," Colin agreed.

Going for long forest runs becomes our weekly ritual. The next Saturday we meet in the gravel parking lot at the Lower MacLeay Trail Loop, above one of the rockiest and slipperiest descents. The plan is to run to the Birch Trailhead, at the end of a four-mile climb up an almost never-ending hill.

There are dozens of running paths that intersect in this part of the forest, and Colin knows these paths intimately, never even consults a map.

He once bragged that the trail maintainers, who work for the City of Portland, check with him on the trail conditions, asking about landslides and downed trees and eroded banks that might need bolstering.

He is the old man of the forest, I tease him.

Colin loves running uphill. He never shows weakness or suffering. He plods with steady determination—the defiance of gravity seems to inspire him—while I imagine the whole listening forest—every squirrel, every deer, every coyote—can hear my gasping, my struggle to keep plodding forward, in spite of my body's resistance and the badgering in my mind: *Is this who you* really *are?*

Amidst a chorus of sounds there is a high-pitched fool's laughter. "What's that?"

"Pileated woodpecker," he answers, the assured birder. "They're huge, like crows, with red heads."

With each run on a different trail, I grow to love the forest more: the stillness far removed from city noise; a place where somehow we are just ourselves, unmoored from any duties; a sweet momentary forgetting of who I am supposed to be; the witness of ancient trees, standing and fallen and about-to-fall; and the shrieking squirrels and the occasional deer and the rippling creek that leads to the path ahead. It reminds me of the forest in Shakespeare's plays: that magical otherworldly place where misfits dance and play and fools tell jokes and sing with abandon and everyone forgets the unforgiving rules of urban life. In high school we had to memorize passages from *As You Like It*. I still remember that serene speech that Duke Senior, banished to the Forest of Arden, delivers to his fellow exiles:

> *And this our life exempt from public haunt,*
> *Finds tongues in trees, books in running brooks,*
> *Sermons in stones, and good in everything.*
> *I would not change it.*

But I am lagging on this stretch of the Wildwood, which seems endlessly uphill. He is a few feet ahead of me. I decide not to mention the words from Shakespeare.

We confide about our marriages in ways we would never want our wives to overhear. "Elise has some seriously wenchy days," Colin confides, loud enough for me to hear, "but overall she is pretty even-tempered. I think the big thing women want is to know that you love them and that you won't leave them."

From behind I can watch his tight runner's butt and it takes my mind off the agony. We hit an even stretch and I catch up to him and my breath grows more regular. We are side by side again. An army of firs surrounds us, sentinels, listening without judgment.

"I believe in the primary-secondary model," Colin says. "I don't see it working any other way for Elise and me. The biggest issue for you is whether you really want her to be your primary. Do you love her? Do you want to stay married? Is this only for the kids? These are core questions that until they are answered it is difficult to move forward." He coins the word *man-ogamy*, where a heterosexually married man has one outside relationship, exclusive with another guy.

"Yes, I'm crazy about Eva," I tell him. To save money, I have just given up the studio and am now sleeping in the guest room at the family house. More of the warm loving feeling between us has returned. "Can't explain it and it doesn't always make sense, so it must be love. We've been through too much. It's not just for the kids. But she can be frustrating and uncompromising at times. So I struggle and she struggles. We are seeing an amazing counselor. I have to admit, Eva has really been pushing her limits, so there's hope. But we're not out of the woods yet. I don't know for sure it will work."

We pause at the halfway point and decide to walk for a stretch. There is quiet between us, although I know we haven't run out of things to say.

I take his hand.

"Oh," he says. It is the first time he seems daunted. Suddenly the roles shift and I am the leader, taking him to an unfamiliar place. "I'm not sure what I think about this," he confesses. "I've never held hands with a guy."

"It's just being friends," I offer. He has a firm grip.

There is another silence.

"Have you read D. H. Lawrence?" I ask. He is my literary soul companion, the one who opened my eyes to a world that was more expansive than "gay" and "straight." I read him in my graduate seminar on British Modernist Fiction. "*Women in Love*?"

"Never heard of him," he admits. "What does he write about?"

I tell him about Lawrence's attractions to men and women and his struggles to fit himself into a conventional marriage and the friendship in *Women in Love* between Birkin (who is really Lawrence) and Gerald (his real-life friend John Middleton Murry, to whom he was attracted). Birkin longs for an intense physical friendship with none of the barriers built into conventional male upbringing.

"Interesting," says Colin. I cannot tell if he thinks it is actually interesting.

No one is nearby. The trees are filled with bird chattering.

"Gerald and Birkin are in love, but it's not like gay romantic love."

"I don't understand," he says.

"They talk about a *Blutsbrüderschaft*, German word, a kind of brother-bond-vow they make to each other, to be loyal and true."

"Well," he says. "I do like that."

The bold experiment continues: we are still holding hands.

He is confident, athletic Gerald and I am sensitive, uncertain Birkin. He is my Gatsby. He is my Phineas. He is not my perfect doppelganger because he does not read the kind of books I read, but he is my fellow traveler.

There is really no place to go.

We are talking about how to get more physically intimate outside of bumbling late nights in the front seat of the car. It is frustrating that two men with a four-bedroom home apiece have no place to go to have sex with their boyfriends-on-the-side. We can't go to my house because it violates the terms of Eva's and my agreement about not bringing "special friends" to the family home. Colin has told Elise about me, but she says she is not quite ready to meet. He keeps our friendship separate from his home life. The idea of hotels embarrasses both of us.

The parking lot is high above the hill that descends to Oaks Bottom Loop. Today we are hiking the long path along the edge of the Willamette River. It is Friday afternoon. It is almost autumn now but it is bright outside and the rains have not started yet. Colin carries a backpack.

He has just returned from a weeklong hike by Anthony Lake in Eastern Oregon. Every summer he does one solitary backpacking excursion. I cannot imagine leaving Eva with the children, on her own, for so long. "You don't know how many times I thought about how great it would be to have a Brokeback buddy along with me," he says.

The literary reference sends a thrill through my body. He has only ever talked about books on gardening or birding or hiking.

"Did you read *Brokeback Mountain*?"

"I can't read it," he confesses. "I've read about it. I saw the trailer for the film. I know it's about guys like us and it ends tragically. I didn't think I could handle it."

We descend the hill. An older man with binoculars is paused on the trail. Immediately I think he must be gay—he has a flower print shirt and artsy glasses with a dark purple stripe; plus he is a birder—although I know it is a fallacy to think anyone can guess.

"You finding anything interesting?" Colin asks.

The birder smiles, eyes the two of us with what looks like suspicion.

(Maybe we look gay too?) "Some buffleheads and wigeons," he says. "They love the marshland. It's pretty deserted today. You here to go birding, gentlemen?"

My face is warm with embarrassment.

"Just an afternoon hike," Colin says, smiling mischievously, and we continue walking.

I am trying to think how I can tell Colin that I don't want to have sex in the forest, without hurting his feelings. But I have not come up with the right diplomatic tone because the fact is I do want to have sex, with him, somewhere, just not the forest. The forest is quiet and remote, but there are random hikers and sometimes runners and the occasional odd birder, and there are rangers who issue tickets to people who let their dogs wander off leash.

We descend to the bottoms, dense with cottonwoods. I can barely see the river through their branches. There is no one in sight. Colin takes my hand this time. Suddenly I understand that hybrid word: *tonguetied*. I grip firmly.

"Let's make a promise to each other," he says. "No matter what happens, we make sure the other guy honors his marriage. We don't let each other lose track of who we are. I don't want to leave Elise and you don't want to leave Eva and that will always be true, but we might forget because this stuff is uncharted territory. Let's be each other's reminder."

"I won't let you leave her," I agree. "You remind me, too, if I ever lose myself."

The next thing I know we have left the well-trodden path and I am following Colin as he cuts his way through the tall grass.

"Where are we going?"

We enter a remote meadow surrounded by cottonwoods. Colin takes a blanket out of his backpack and spreads it on the grass, then looks at me with determination.

"I don't think this is a good idea," I say, almost a whisper.

His hands slide under my shirt.

"We could get caught," I say, feeling dizzy. "There are the rangers."

"I didn't see any rangers," he says, running his nose along my neck. Then he kisses me, and kisses me again, and I kiss back, and I'm struggling to catch my breath, and my brain dissolves into incoherent bits. Sentences float like disconnected shards: *Someone will see us. We'll get caught.* We take off each other's shirts. My chest hair brushes his chest hair and our arms wrap around each other and his skin is warm and we are on the blanket lost in the rustling high grass. *He is my fellow traveler. He is my best friend.*

We are lying half-naked, intertwined, and Colin reaches down my pants.

"I don't think we should go this far," I say.

"You worry too much," he says, undoing my belt.

Maybe thirty feet away I hear voices on the path.

"People," I whisper.

"They won't come here," he says. "They can't see us." Now his hand grips my dick, which is hard, that traitor. It betrays my better judgment. *We'll get caught. He is my fellow traveler.* My body jumps at his touch. My mind isn't working. I am suppressing a sound in my throat.

Hands roving, Colin kisses my neck, then my chest. In some swift unconscious movement, my pants come off, and I notice that he's naked too. In the distance voices become clearer, seeming to encircle us. A young couple is having an argument. A baby whimpers. I cannot see them. They also think they are alone.

I recognize this age-old argument. It's "Who works harder at parenting?" He went out with his friend last night. She is angry he leaves so much kid work to her. She needed him to do a grocery store run. He works long hours and forgot.

Voices move around us like the merry-go-round of our own lives: baby crying; couple arguing; the suffocating blame of who is not doing enough. By now I have given up. My dick is in Colin's mouth and then his dick is in my mouth and we are so far beyond wariness and denials and protests and dejected fathers-in-exile and soul-crushing loneliness and I have failed in my effort to be a respectable dad who doesn't risk getting arrested for public indecency. The couple's voices and the murmuring baby recede and we are just ourselves, naked, wrapped in each other's bodies, lost in the blanket in the tall grass in the meadow in the forest.

We are filled up with the touch of each other. I have forgotten I was ever lonely. The prepared boy scout, ready for anything, Colin takes a towel out of his backpack and wipes off both of us. We put our clothes back on and put away the blanket. It is dusk.

As we come back onto the path, I don't see the couple with the baby anywhere. I worry we smell like sex. I worry that anyone can guess our mischief-making in our flushed faces. Our faces are scratched by the brush of each other's late-day whiskers. We ascend the zig zag to the parking lot. The old birder still looks though his binoculars. We try to pass him without any exchange.

He lowers his binoculars. "A good day to be in the forest," he interrupts, in a tone that seems bemused.

"Beautiful weather," says Colin. I can tell that my usually confident friend is hesitant to meet his gaze.

"*Lots* of colorful birds in the forest today," the man says, unable to suppress his grin.

Colin lowers his head. He is chuckling at the man's boldness, our private joke. "Good afternoon, sir."

"You gentlemen have a good day."

We ascend the path back to our cars. I am mulling over the forest romp, which I didn't want to have, both contented and confused. "He had binoculars," I whisper to Colin. "I think we were seen."

13
—

WE MET IN CHURCH

I am pacing the living room, glancing out the window at the space on the street where the car is supposed to be. The children are fed dinner and tucked in bed. A part of me wants the distraction of one of them having a difficult night: A bad dream? A sibling skirmish? Pining for mommy? (Everyone always wants mommy.) *Couldn't one of you fill this void?* But on this night when I need someone to give me a hard time, everyone sleeps. Even the two black cats, perched on the stairs—one of whom is usually hacking or vomiting or sputtering bubbly green goo—are stolid as Buddhas. Three school-age kids and two sickly rescue cats with attitudes: what are the odds that on the one night you want someone to act out or at least need an adrenalizing late-night ER visit, everyone is happy with life?

When will she get home from this thing?

Henry is a kind, intelligent man, Eva told me after meeting with him a few times. He is a college admissions counselor. He takes her to Shakespeare plays and concerts of Baroque music. He loves poetry. They pass volumes back and forth. (When she's not looking, I pick up a volume and read a poem. I like them. I wish I were part of that conversation too.) So far, he accepts that she lives with her children's father in a platonic, family-like friendship that is probably her and my dearest mooring in the world. He even told her he admired it: our "loving friendship" he called it.

Restlessness doesn't capture these scattered darts to my gut, although I am wandering. I look out the window again. There is a dry rectangle on the asphalt in front of the house where the car was parked, while the rest of the street is wet from a late summer storm. I need a new word for these feelings: Ripped with longing. Jealous burned. Jags of shattered nonsensical resentment. Shards of broken grief. Heart-cutting-chaos-then-hot-messy-feeling-bleeding. Maybe there are no words.

Whatever the feelings are, I am alone with them. I can't reach out to anyone. The situation is too odd. Even the kindest friends, like Naomi, might wrestle with judgment or at least their own discomfort. They would say the situation is untenable, unbearable. They would tell me to divorce. They might imply that we are pathologically attached to a marriage that is done. They might feel evaluated in their own relationship choices. I command myself: *You should not be feeling this way! It does not fit with your image of yourself as a more evolved, feminist man.* I hesitate to call or text Colin, my fellow traveler. Unless it's an emergency we shy away from contact when either one of us is at home; a kind of compartmentalization that preserves home tranquility, sometimes at a cost to ourselves. I don't want to pretend this is an emergency. But maybe it is.

Did she offer how late she'd be out? I was afraid to ask, reluctant to seem to limit her.

The night of her date—I can't recall how many there have been now—I continue to pace the dining room and living room, my core twisting. This arrangement makes sense for us, I remind myself. We are both committed to the course. And, ironically, I never cared about marriage. For most of my life I told myself that the institution didn't matter to me. Until I met Eva, I didn't even think it would ever apply to me. My mother was happier when she got divorced. My brothers Dean and Bruce and I were relieved it happened. And yet tonight, when Eva is out with a kind, intelligent man, a man who loves poetry and the arts, a self-aware man who knows his own feelings, I am wrung out, lost, humiliated, threatened, and rejected: a murder of nerve-jangling feelings that make no sense. *Can we really do this? How will I be able to endure it?*

What is that medieval word fossilized in our brain strata? *Cuckold.* Named for the cuckoo bird, whose mate lays her eggs in another bird's nest, where they are raised. There is no equivalent word for a woman who is betrayed, another blindness in the English language. A term of uniquely masculine humiliation since the days of Chaucer and Shakespeare; the reason Othello smothered Desdemona. It's as if I can feel the cruel weight of the centuries' old legacy of humiliation in my body, even though I think I should be immune, that I am better than this feeling. *Why is this so fucking hard?*

I pick up one of the cats, the one least likely to hiss at me, and stroke his head.

The other worrisome thing about this churn of emotion: My head feels like it could burst. I can't see any end in sight. I'm not sure I can stand the torture.

The cat struggles in my arms and bolts. *I'm not your damn therapist, you schmuck.*

I open the front door and step into the indigo stillness. The empty rectangle waits. *Don't look at it.* The moon burns yellow, constant. The streetlights, bluish white, make the sidewalks glow. The world silently awaits the interruption of her return.

I would gladly trade this pain for a case of planter's fasciitis. This—this jagged irrationality—is why couples don't do open marriages. No one can imagine this pain. No one can imagine surviving it. Looking at the scythe-like moon, I vow to the universe: *I will never proselytize this kind of arrangement to anyone.*

No matter how I think I should be dealing with the angst of Eva's date, one fact remains: from my earliest moment of awareness as a child, then daily, without conscious awareness, no matter how queer and immune I thought I was, I have absorbed pictures of what heterosexual marriage is supposed to look like. Marriage and divorce were everywhere, but everything I noticed pointed to the same ideal: an excruciating and narrow perfection; an inviolate promise. Even when it was an awareness of a neighbor's marriage that was floundering, an undercurrent of judgement, pity, even contempt reminded me: the standard of that ideal marriage on the distant golden hill was disappointed. I have absorbed the imperative of the monogamous pair-bond into the cells of who I am, and they are revolting.

By striking out on our own, the sense of violation is profound. But who have we offended? Now, it is as if my cells are in chaos, scrambling to rearrange themselves. There is an incoherence slapping around in my brain, infecting my body.

A pile of books sits on the nightstand, all of them recommended by Linné: *Sex at Dawn, Mating in Captivity, The Ethical Slut.* I haven't finished reading any of them. I'm skeptical of self-help. But I am trying to open my mind, to re-program myself, because this is the only way we will endure as partners: to shake loose from these unexamined, old-world shapes of domesticity. On a rational level, all this business about ethical non-monogamy makes sense to me. That one word from *The Ethical Slut*—*compersion*—bedevils me: "the feeling of joy that comes from seeing your partner sexually happy with someone else." Seriously?

People really feel that? The author talks about "unlearning jealousy," but how? And is that what I am: jealous?

Left out. Left alone. Left, left, left. So many deep, descending, dark degrees of leftness.

I don't want to know what time she comes home. I don't want her to come home to me fretting and pacing. I must do better. Most movies they could see would have been over an hour ago. But then dinner and dessert, right? (Then sex? Don't think about that.) Why do I have so little to fill up my night, other than thinking about her? Next time I will plan better.

I resolve to lie down, close my eyes, and let my body rest. I have no fantasies about sleep. But I don't want to be alone in the dark, listening for the sound of the car parking, the door slamming, the tumblers of the front door lock. I creep into my sons' bedroom. Philip sleeps on the top bunk, a single bed, his back to me, tousled blond head on a tattered stuffed black ape named "Little Gorilla." On the bottom queen-sized bunk, Louis sleeps, his face peaceful. He clutches a stuffed koala, its tan fur matted from slobber. Before I gave up the studio apartment and moved back into the house into a separate bedroom, on the occasional nights when Eva allowed me to stay, I slept beside him. Now, quietly I climb around his form, skirt to the other side of the bed, my back against the wall, where I can watch his body expand and release breath. I lay my head on an extra pillow.

In *The Ethical Slut*, they write that we can learn something from our jealousy and that that self-knowledge can drive deeper intimacy in the primary relationship. So, what is this pain? I wonder, looking at my son's sleeping body. The first image that comes up in my mind has nothing to do with marriage: It is that look in my father's face, baked in memory, more a feeling than a vision, a potent hit of his embarrassment, that I was "effeminate." (That was the word they used when I was a boy, as if it had a clinical truth.) It wasn't the familiar cliché that I always played with girls—yes, I wanted desperately to get to their glamorous, thin, long-haired Barbies—because all the neighbors with daughters, up and down the street, had already been forewarned about me. When I came to their door—*Can Alison come out to play?*—their daughters were never available, even though I suspected the girls were home, behind the door, playing in their toy kitchens. *No, Alison can't come out today.* The way I talked and walked and played was suspect. When boys on the playground, even in the classroom, targeted me with taunts and slaps, my father told me to fight back. He said it was the only way. That's what Shane would do. But I was too afraid of being clobbered.

Long before I realized I should be humiliated for being the kind of boy that I was, my father carried the feeling for me. Then, when I figured out that the humiliation belonged to me, he handed it off, a shame baton, so I could carry it alone.

Growing up I became quieter, willed myself to be invisible, moved with fearful stillness and disgrace.

Somehow the cruel, inked-in logic of childhood, the blue-green tattoo of not-enoughness, extends into this moment. Eva is out with another man and he is a better man, a preferable man, a straight-as-an-arrow heterosexual man, just like my father was a normal man, just like my brother Dean was the manlier son, the acceptable issue, the source of paternal pride.

I have lost the game.

Louis is nine years old. Under the blue flannel blanket his body is long and skinny and growing by the day. The koala is his cherished companion, by his side whether he is awake or asleep, at home or at school; his talisman against elementary school fears. In the classroom and on the playground, there are bullies, but these days vigilant adults identify and silence the little fuckers immediately. There is no tolerance. Louis shifts on his pillow, turns toward me, clutches his friend. I wonder if he has a koala in his dreams. His eyelashes are long and blond.

For a moment, gazing at him sleeping, I am lost in a consoling thought: He is perfect. It does not even occur to me to wonder whether he is masculine or feminine. The words have nothing to do with anything. That is the last thought I remember before, somehow, like a miracle, I fall asleep.

That night I have a dream about Linné.

Eva and I are sitting in her cramped office, in the early days when we first started, knees nearly touching. Linné bounces on the blue ball while we sit in our unmovable chairs, facing each other. Linné leans in, like always, her eyes sad, attending to every word. There is a seriousness in her gaze that compels a kind of heart honesty. Nothing else belongs in the space of her view.

In the dream, I drift inside and outside her head, the omniscient narrator seeing his character's secrets. She wants to tell us about an invisible disability that afflicts her, but part of the disability is that it can't be spoken. When she looks at us—we think it is compassionately—it is the scrambling of her brain to find a word that cannot be found: *Divorce*. She cannot pronounce it. In her mouth somehow the hard "d" is magnetically opposed to the harsh "v" sound. Her tongue refuses to budge into the word. She cannot say the words "mediation" or "custody" either. Her brain will not allow her mouth to form the words. In her line of work this is a serious hindrance. The disability is ruining her practice.

Unknown to us, her inability to speak the words keeps us stranded. Because the words to say otherwise do not come into the office—they are too bitter and final—we stay married perpetually, like it or not.

Maybe, I wonder, Eva prefers this sweet and searing uncertainty, where we are together in something that hasn't found its right words and its reality, to the pre-determined shape of divorce. But I cannot see into Eva's head, neither in the dream nor in life.

That explains it, I realize in the dream. Linné does not charge us a fee for her services because she cannot have the conversation. ("Couples counseling or mediation? $150 or $220?") She cannot articulate the word "divorce." And because we are in her office, struggling, we stay immobilized in her selective muteness, and we must figure out something else, something other than divorce, some other word she can pronounce.

Here's the other secret: I'm the one person in this dream office who could articulate that forbidden word—*divorce*—if I wanted. But I won't, ever.

The warm light comes through the shutters. Carefully I crawl around my son's sleeping form. At the window I check the street. The blue minivan is back in its spot. A wave of relaxation flows through my body. The long excruciating night of The Date is over.

I walk by Eva's room—the door is closed—and head downstairs. Already I am starting to breathe easier. Last night's pain seems like a fading memory, an embarrassment, a ridiculous crisis of masculine pride, something I can never admit to anyone. One cup of coffee and I will be a new man, a better, more evolved man, myself. Yes, coffee; the newspaper; my classical music station: they will restore me to my familiar self.

I click on the radio and put the kettle of water on the stove and then I notice it, on the back of the dining room chair, like a possessive marking: a worn brown leather bomber jacket. It is another man's jacket.

Fuck.

A surge of fury streams through my body. I walk to the window again, check the minivan, look for other unfamiliar vehicles. Doesn't Henry drive a motorcycle? Where the hell is it? The sun is rising. A neighbor is walking a dog, coffee in hand, yawning. The newspaper waits on the front porch in a blue plastic bag. How could she do this to me? What was she thinking? My heart thumps, a panicked snare drum, in my chest.

Fuck. Fuck. Fuck. Fuckfuckfuck.

We had an agreement.

If we are going to have this creative marital arrangement, we want to honor the space where we raise our family, not clutter it with the distraction of other people. We want to keep our dating lives and our domestic routines separate, at least in the early stages of this experiment. She has ruined the agreement. She has sabotaged trust. He is up there, in her bedroom. I can't imagine what I will say. How could she spring this on me? When and how will he exit? Do I say "hello," and what's the right tone? How will we explain this visitor to the kids? Will they interact with him? I am barely used to her dating, without the surprise of bringing men home to spend the night, without even forewarning me with a text or a call.

She is still pissed at me.

I sit at the dining room table and stew. The coffee grows warm in the brown mug. It has a picture of a yogi in a lotus pose, with the words "Let that shit go." Stupid. My morning routine is ruined. I am not returning to my normal, pre-date self. I am crazed again. I cannot think of anything else. I look at the bomber jacket: the worn brown leather still has a shine; there's a thick zipper up the middle; two sleek pockets. It is the kind of jacket that belongs to a different kind of man, maybe a man who has a motorcycle or even his own airplane, a man who goes on dates with pretty, married women living on the edge of respectability, not a worried, bleary-eyed guy in gray sweats who hauls kids around town in a dusty minivan strewn with rancid baby carrots and sticky, half-empty juice boxes. It is one thing for Henry to spend the night here, without even asking me, but add to that insult that he is a manlier man with hip clothes and sleek vehicles.

There is no etiquette for this situation. I don't remember any chapters about this kind of surprise encounter in *The Ethical Slut*. What would Linné say now? *That word* compersion *is a piece of shit.* I hope the kids stay asleep while we deal with this fiasco of poor judgment.

There is a movement on the stairs. My heart jumps. Do they know I'm up? What am I supposed to say? Should I pretend that there's no rule she broke? Do I look the other way? I don't want to argue in front of him. What would a cooler guy do in this situation? Should I have made more coffee? A quiche? My gut twists.

Eva comes down the stairs alone. She is wearing a cream-colored terrycloth bathrobe, worn gray slippers. Her hair is rumpled. "Hey," she says. "Good morning."

"Morning." I stare hard at the leather jacket. I want her to see me staring hard at the leather jacket, this monster violation, to intuit my crushed soul. I'll show her.

She puts her hand on my shoulder and kisses my head. "How were the kids last night?"

"No problems," I report. I am ready to start the argument. Can she not see that I'm enraged? "So, where's Henry?"

She pours herself hot coffee. My own coffee has grown cold. "I guess his place probably," she says. "Why?"

I can tell my face is burning red. "His jacket is here." I don't want to have this conflict, but I am glad that I am squarely in the right. I am rarely so certainly, so clearly, so beautifully, so unequivocally the right one. This morning it is she who has committed a domestic crime of extreme magnitude.

She sits down at the table, sips her coffee, rubs her eyes, casually glances at the jacket. "That's for you."

"Didn't he come back here last night?"

"No, that's against the rules," she says, looking puzzled. "He says the jacket doesn't fit him anymore. He wondered if you would like it."

"What?"

"That's what he said. It seems like an expensive thing to cast off, doesn't it? What do you think? Would you wear something like that?"

I look at the jacket again. Wait. I cannot shake this fury that has nothing to do with reality. That fucking cuckold humiliated me. Wait. He's giving me that leather jacket? I shake my head, try to reassemble the meaning. Wait. It's *not* a gargantuan symbol of domestic violation, of masculine possessiveness and superiority? *I just slept with your wife, you sniveling gay cuckolded weakling.*

I do really like the slant of those pockets. "I'm confused," I say. "He didn't spend the night?"

"I would never do that," she says and takes a sip of her coffee. "It's against the rules."

I see the jacket anew. Here's a secret, something I have never told anyone, not even Eva: I have always wanted a leather bomber jacket. Since I was in high school. But I would never entertain the thought because it seems so affected and false for a man like me. They are expensive and hip and macho, and I am broke and not and not. I didn't think I could pull off something so…manly. But could I?

"I've never even met him."

"Try it on," Eva says. "I wasn't sure it would fit. It's too small for Henry. I guess he's gained weight since he bought it."

I pick up the jacket. The leather is so soft. It does not look brand new. It looks like a jacket someone has worn for years, on motorcycle rides and hot dates. A shiny new jacket would really scream pretentiousness. To be cool, it must look like you've owned it forever. Could I really wear something like this? I put it on over my t-shirt. The weight feels solid on my shoulders, like a layer of muscle. The inner fabric against my skin is soft. It looks so tough on the outside, but inside it is warmly enveloping. By comparison my green rain jacket, a decade old, is flimsy, wrinkled and makes a loud, fussy rustling like the kerchiefs my grandmother tied around her hair. It doesn't even keep me very dry when it rains.

"Wow."

"Try zipping it."

"I don't know what to say." I zip the jacket. It does fit...perfectly.

I want this jacket. I cannot resist its charm. But I am supposed to dislike Henry, I think, maybe even hate him. How can I take something from someone who is supposed to disgust me? I walk over to the full-length mirror in the oak hall tree.

Eva is mixing granola, yoghurt, and fruit in a bowl. "It really looks good, honey," she says. That word makes me tremble: *honey*. She has no idea about my heart's manic thumping, the night of dark spiky misgivings. "You should keep it. Henry wanted you to have it. He was sincere. Should I make the kids blueberry pancakes?"

I see my face and my body and the leather bomber jacket and it all comes together, as if maybe I could convince myself it belongs on me. The jacket really does fit.

My heart is beating wildly at the same time I am becoming this other man, this man more like Henry, the acceptable issue, this man who maybe even feels a wisp of compersion, and even though I still feel breathless, I try to steady my voice. "Yeah, blueberry pancakes sound great, sweetheart."

"I don't want to go to church," Louis whines, tying his shoelaces.

Rosie pulls on her orange kangaroo socks. "I don't really want to go either, Dad."

"It's boring," says Philip, the six-year-old who always agrees with the older two. He is doing nothing to get ready.

"We're going to church," I say. I put Philip's arms into his sweat jacket that says "The University of Chicago, Class of 2024" in maroon letters. "Everyone in the van!"

The three children trudge grumbling out to the minivan.

"I'm honestly not in love with this church either," Eva says low in my ear as I lock the front door.

"We're going!" I insist. This routine of whiny rebellion happens every Sunday since we signed the children up for the Sunday School program. In the beginning Eva supported it—we feel inexplicable pressure to raise children in a faith community, even though it's nothing we have sought out in our pre-child adult lives—but she has begun to find the sermons dry. The three children are united in their complaint: Sunday School is boring. On a weekend morning they would rather be lounging at home reading comics in the newspaper. "They're expected in their class. We're going to see this through. Today could be different."

It is a warm day, but I am wearing the leather bomber jacket because I can. I am a badass Unitarian.

We drive across the Steel Bridge, high and black and sharp-angled above the slate-colored Willamette River, to downtown Portland. The children are singing quietly along with Raffi. *Oh Mr. Sun, Sun, Mr. Golden Sun, please shine down on me.* We have been playing the same CD for seven years. The brick church with the pointy green steeple comes into view.

"Is that Linné?" Eva asks, alarmed, as we get closer to the church, gesturing out the window. "Look there."

Two women, maybe together, are crossing the street. The long thick white-gray hair, the kind expression, the soft slant of her eyes, the efficient walk: Linné is one of them. She looks the same as she does in her therapy office, maybe more resolute and focused, and she's toting two daughters, the same age as our oldest children, who straggle in a line behind her. Another woman follows, lips pursed, eyes set in what looks like a glare that could be her normal expression or could be rage.

"I didn't know she went to this church," Eva says. It has a very large congregation, with two Sunday services.

"Me neither. Maybe they just started? Or they usually go to the later service?"

They look like a family where an argument is happening.

"What's the rule for seeing your therapist in public? Do we say hello?"

"There's no one rule," I say. It is odd to see Linné with a family. Who is the angry woman walking behind her? She was walking close enough, she looked like she was part of the family, but that enraged expression?

We enter the church with throngs hurrying to find their seats, take the children to their classrooms, and then rush up two flights of stairs to the balcony seats where parents of clingy children who might become unmanageable are asked to settle themselves. I am wondering if we will bump into Linné and the mysterious woman. What will I say? How would we be introduced? What is the etiquette? "Hello, I had a dream about your selective mutism last night."

On the stage a pianist is playing Gershwin's "Summertime"— spare, unaccompanied, no words but we all know the words. It is the pure sweet sound of nostalgia, a dirge about the passing season, and I am thinking about the way in the forest the sunshine bathes the ferns a yellow light like happiness. The feeling is religious but not religious. I love the worship of the secular. Whole services can pass in this religious space without a mention of Jesus or Mary or any religion, without mind-numbing repetitions of "Hallelujah" and "Amen." I can feel my body slow down and move out of high transition mode and settle into just being myself with the music and the order of service to browse and morning sunlight streaming through the tall, arched windows which are cut into geometric shapes of red and blue and yellow and green.

I watch the congregation assemble in their seats. My favorite part of church is listening to the music or the words on the stage and scanning the rows and rows of people staring, rapt. I am wondering when Colin and Elise will arrive. They are often late. We never say hello when we see them across the pews. I know what he and I are to each other—fellow travelers, *Blutsbrüder,* who see each other weekly—but I don't know what they are to us.

Furtively I am wondering where Linné and the woman will sit and if we will acknowledge each other. We are not friends; we are not family; we are not even acquaintances because she knows us so intimately, but we don't really know her at all, except what we read in the nuance of her gestures, the inflection of her voice, the way she appears in dream stories.

Today one of the parishioners rises and goes to the pine pulpit on the stage. Each service begins with a poem.

> *i carry your heart with me(i carry it in*
> *my heart)i am never without it(anywhere*
> *i go you go, my dear;*

It is an e.e. cummings poem. I can follow it on the page of the service. Words and punctuation slosh together, without spaces, an urgent jumble of meaning, a puzzle trying to assemble itself, a feeling trying to emerge from the frustrating constraints of human grammar.

> *and whatever is done*
> *by only me is your doing, my darling)*
>   *i fear*
> *no fate (for you are my fate, my sweet)*

In the row of chairs that run in the balcony perpendicular to ours,

Colin and Elise sneak to their front row seats, mid-poem. He is wearing khakis and a white-striped maroon pullover shirt that shows off his chest. Elise has long brown hair and kind brown eyes and she wears a forest green fleece over a cream-colored turtleneck. They look like the fit Northwest couple that they are. He does not notice me yet, so I can watch him, unselfconscious, in his natural environment.

i want
no world (for beautiful you are my world,my true)

The printed words break all the rules. Some truths emerge more clearly from the body than the page. When the reader recites the poem, the words make a jubilant sense, like the rush of a heartbeat. I hear the right meaning when the poem is spoken. The "you" is me, it is Eva beside me; and it is Colin, it is Elise beside him. You is all of us. *for beautiful you are my world,my true*

I do not often see Colin looking so peaceful and contemplative and settled in one place. With me he is always moving and striving and pushing—hill after hill after root-tangled hill. He and Elise sit together and hold hands. They are beautiful, I think. They look right. This is a moment when they are together, and Eva and I are together, and it is good. I move my hand toward Eva's, and she takes it.

and it's you are whatever a moon has always meant
and whatever a sun will always sing is you

Then Colin notices me noticing him and he grins, and I smile back. He makes a gesture with his hands, pointing at his chest: *What's up with that boss leather jacket?* And I wink back at him. There is a story to tell.

here is the deepest secret nobody knows
(here is the root of the root and the bud of the bud
and the sky of the sky of a tree called life;which grows

higher than the soul can hope or mind can hide)

My eyes move through the seated congregation as I listen to the e.e. cummings poem that bursts out of the logic of grammar into its own kind of buoyant rule-less truth, and then I notice Linné and the woman who is probably her partner sitting side by side but pulled away from each other, four rows behind Colin and Elise, almost hiding in a corner of the section, where the light from the window does not reach. The woman is shorter than Linné, stocky, her brows crunching down on her eyes. There is a kind of melancholy in Linné's expression that seems to communicate that—I am sure of it, in the same way, in my dream, that I was sure she couldn't pronounce "divorce"—something is ending.

The puzzle slowly assembles in my head, although of course I don't know if it is true, but all the pieces point to it. I know that look of estrangement in a couple that is together but moving apart from each other, unable to fix an unbudgeable brokenness. Now I know, I think I know, why Linné can't say the word "divorce" to us. I know why it's too painful. She doesn't want it to happen to us, to her and the angry woman, to anyone. But maybe she also knows that sometimes it happens, even when you don't say the words.

and this is the wonder that's keeping the stars apart

i carry your heart(I carry it in my heart)

Maybe this is why, in this moment in time, Linné didn't charge us, couldn't bring herself to offer the plaintive, business-like question: mediation or couples counseling? If she had raised the issue of the fee, had used the word "mediation," it would have recast our purpose, forced us by pride and wordless compulsion down a societally acceptable path of divorce, the accepted grooves of language with its exacting unimaginative polarities. Maybe she wanted to save someone's marriage, if she couldn't save her own.

A heart-breaking truth: there is no Linné for Linné.

My heart swells with sad love for her.

The service ends and it is time to fetch the children. The congregation rustles, readying to return to the outside world. On the other side of the balcony, Linné and the woman make a quick exit. Colin and Elise are putting on their coats. Until now Eva and I have never ventured into the awkwardness of an encounter, unsure of who we would be meeting and who we would be when we meet them. Although Colin has wondered about connecting in church—"Shouldn't we be...friends?" he asked—he hasn't pushed it because of the uncertain terrain.

I am guessing that Eva is as aware of their presence, sitting catty-corner to us. Once she told me she wasn't ready to meet him. "Let's wait and see," she said testily. "What if it's not serious? What if you break it off? Then I'll have gone through all that anxiety for nothing." "Of course, it's serious!" I said, hurt. I was mad at her for a few days and we hadn't spoken about it again.

Today something shifts. Maybe this badass leather jacket has given me new boldness. Suddenly it all seems silly. She has known about him for months now, I tell myself. Despite occasional flare-ups of uneasiness, we feel stronger, resolved about our situation. "Would it be OK if we say hello to Colin and Elise today?" I whisper to Eva. I don't think she will agree, but maybe I'm looking for an argument. "They're right there. It won't take long. Just hello."

She puts on her windbreaker and looks up. "Sure," she says.

I don't understand what changed.

I wave to Colin, gesture for them to come. I see him whisper something in Elise's ear, her soft brown hair conceals his face, and I know they are having some version of the same conversation: Are we ready for this? And what is "this"? They make their way through the congregants along the front of the balcony. He holds her hand and leads, the married couple moving into the next adventure.

We met in church.

I catch Elise's eye first and I can sense the trepidation.

"Hi, I'm Wayne." I offer my hand.

"Elise," she says with an awkward smile. "I've heard nice things about you, Wayne."

I cannot suppress my smile. From anyone else it might just be a piece of mindless flattery, but I know that when she heard about me, the "nice things," the stakes must have felt high. "The same," I offer, and it is true.

"I'm Eva." She offers her hand to Colin, then Elise. Miraculously we—who already know so much about each other because we have key roles in the endurance of each other's marriages—are finally introduced; in the same conversational space; humans standing together in breathless awe of the myriad shapes of love, outside any commonly accepted grammar. For a moment, no one recalls any pleasantries beyond hello.

It is Eva who remembers that this isn't hard. We do know who we are. Moving out of the pew, she asks Elise, "What did you think of the sermon?" They walk side by side. I walk with Colin. We merge into the stream of exiting congregants.

"I liked it," Elise answers. "And no kids needed me today. That was the best part."

"Us too," says Eva. "No interruptions."

They move two steps ahead of Colin and me, descending the stairs, their heads leaning into each other. They are also fellow travelers.

Something clicks about who we are when the four of us are together. "That wasn't as hard as I thought," I tell Colin.

"We built it up to be so big," he says. "It's just friends meeting in church."

We are Wayne and Eva. They are Colin and Elise. During the service he held her hand. I held Eva's. He and I do not hold each other's. They are fetching their two children after the service and we are gathering our three. Clear, unequivocal roles. He and I are friends who run together, talk about our complicated lives in the forest, and have occasional sex in untoward places. It does not seem so far-fetched or impossible that these two identities, these pieces of who we are, exist side by side.

"Pretty simple," he says.

I watch them talking ahead of us. Their conversation seems as innocuous as what happens on the sidelines of the soccer field.

As we follow the crowd down the stairs, he leans in. "I've never seen you wear anything like that jacket."

"Henry gave it to me. Do you think I can pull it off?"

"Are you kidding?" Neither of us know what the wife's boyfriend is supposed to do when it comes to the wife's husband. "Looks good on you, dude."

"Does this mean I have to like him?"

"Hmm." He puts his hand on my shoulder, touches the worn leather. "You might have to be his best friend now."

"Where you headed?"

"We're going to brunch, like we always do. You?"

We pause in front of the Sunday School classrooms. Eva and Elise are still talking about the program, and the tone is sour. I can see Rosie and Louis waiting impatiently by the door and I can tell the reviews will be dismal. I am losing the battle about church. "We ate already," I say. "We're driving up to the mountain for a hike."

"Three kids on a hike," he says. "Good luck with that."

We say goodbye and head to our respective frowning children.

14
—

CALL YOUR DEADBEAT DAD

There is a popular bike path that zigzags from Portland's eastside down to the Willamette River, where it runs along the austere, black geometry of the Steel Bridge, crossing onto the grassy esplanade that borders downtown. Several times a week, I catch a glimpse of graffiti spray-painted in large, purple, blocky letters onto the white pavement:

CALL YOUR DEADBEAT DAD HE STILL LOVES YOU

As I pedal across the bridge and along the esplanade, I think about this strange message and I wonder how to make sense of it. I imagine a father coming to this deserted path at midnight with his spray paint and scrawling this message to his estranged son, hoping for reconciliation. I imagine a mother, maybe someone like Grace, writing this plea because she wants peace in the family and knows that her husband wants it too, even though he's too full of masculine pride to admit it.

This is not a stretch of sidewalk visible to everyone who travels the highway, or a huge billboard over the city, or a sign by a busy train stop. This is a very particular path, unique to a small cadre of bikers who commute via the riverbank esplanade. Is there a biker who sees it, day after day, and stubbornly refuses to call home, too hurt or too proud or too mad to connect? Or is this message for all of us who suffer in the wake of our fathers' disappointments?

CALL YOUR DEADBEAT DAD

I am superstitious. Without admitting it to anyone, I do believe the message is for me. Even though I wrote and published an essay about my troubled relationship with my father—it ends, tragically, when he declares that the pull of alcohol is more powerful that any love for me—I wonder if the universe is sending me this judgment. That story didn't end in the right place, Wayne. You still haven't made the right sense of it. There is a wisdom that eludes you.

But how is that possible if my father is dead? The story of his life is over.

With Eva, I am rebuilding a partnership, free of the strong scaffolding that defined our beginnings, in a new way that fits us. In my mind, I am turning over, recreating, definitions of important words: husband, father, brother, man. However fitfully, I still struggle to free myself from deep feelings of inadequacy, wrongness, failure, and shame that saturates my bones. Inescapable and damning.

Day after day, the wheels of my bike slice through the plea.

HE STILL LOVES YOU

At nearly forty-five years old, I believe I have forgiven my father. But maybe I've just made an uneasy peace with the fact that very little good came from him. Then his death ended the story, made any other ending impossible. Perhaps I am still mad.

The specter of the deadbeat hangs like a backdrop behind everything. The word is emblazoned on a brightly lit fabric that hangs in the back of the stage set where all the characters in my life perform their roles around me. I have not made my peace with this drum-thump of a word: deadbeat. But how do you write a story about a character who never showed up? A man who took his secrets to the grave?

And then, a stranger sends me a message me on Facebook one day. "I'm looking for Wayne Scott from the Baltimore area. A Navy veteran about 72 or 73. A relative by any chance?"

"You don't know what branch of the service your own dad was in?" Colin asks, shocked, when I tell him. Colin is too normal to understand me sometimes. "How can that be?"

A phone call to Grace—"What branch of the service was Dad in?"—confirms what I thought: Scotty, who was so close-lipped about his life, had dropped out of high school and joined the Navy when he was seventeen.

"Yes, that's my dad," I write back to the stranger. "I'm the oldest of his three sons. He came home from the service and married my mother." Then, a reluctant confession: "I wasn't close to him, but I am curious. I'm interested in any recollections you care to share."

The stranger, Ken, is a friend of my father. He is an extraordinary keeper of the network, the one who keeps tabs on everyone, convening reunions of men who have been friends since their service days. He's sorry to hear that Scotty is gone. "Wayne, your dad and I were good friends and I'm sorry to hear about his death," he writes. "I'll pass the word along that he's gone."

It's been fifteen years since he died. These days I rarely think about him. For years, during my teenage years and young adulthood, I was enraged at him and thought about him constantly: the demeaning ways he treated my mother before and after their divorce; his secrecy and disappearances; his refusals to pay child support and alimony and tuition that kept Grace going back and forth to court throughout my high school and college years; and the never-ending forgetting of details of my life, of me. I was an obligation he didn't like to think about, or so I felt growing up. When Eva and I separated, I worried that I had become like him: the alley cat, the fidelity-failure.

Ken has warmer memories. "Scotty fancied himself as a lady's man," he writes. "Whenever we walked into a bar, he would pause in the doorway to make sure everyone saw his entrance. Then he would pick out a girl at the bar and start buying her drinks. We all got a big kick out of it."

Ken scans old black and white photographs of Scotty and his Navy buddies and sends them to me. In one shot, during a night on the town in Okinawa, Ken, Scotty, Jim, and Will are crowded together, arms around each other, grasping cigarettes and beers, flushed, their shirts unbuttoned. Everyone has a broad grin. In another, the sailors wear their black uniforms with white stripes, still holding cigarettes and beers. They exude youthful bravado, an almost aggressive joy and belonging. I study the picture of Scotty as a man-boy: perched above the others, fresh-faced with dimples, clearly still a kid.

I tell Ken that I have written two stories about Scotty, if he's interested in seeing them. The first story, "Separation Ritual," seems safer to share. It tells about a failed intervention when I was nearly thirty years old. I send Ken a copy of the essay. Though the tone of the essay is compassionate, it portrays Scotty in the harsh light of addiction and parental abandonment. I worry it violates the code of silence that predominates among men of Scotty's generation. Anticipating that my correspondence with Ken will end once he reads it, I send it anyway.

Within a few days, a message comes back. "Wayne, I have to admit, your article brought a tear to my eye," he writes, "partly because it so closely resembles the relationship I had with my own dad."

Here I am, a man who told himself he didn't need to think about his dead father anymore—didn't need to dwell in the tensions of all that exasperated distance, our bond—because I know how the story ends, and suddenly I feel compelled to revisit old grudges and hurts, to return to the puzzle of it all, just one more time, to study it again, in case there was something I missed. Maybe I don't know where the story ends.

"Wayne, is it ok if I pass along your article?" Ken asks. "There are three or four friends of Scotty that would love to read what you have written."

A Midwesterner, Ken is retired, in his mid-seventies, the same age my dad would have been if he had lived. On his Facebook page, the cover photo shows an idealized sketch of an anonymous man with a chiseled jaw and a determined expression, cowboy-like and cool, looking into the distance, an American flag rippling in the background. In photos Ken is a vigorous, trim man with a sheepish grin, his arm around a grandchild or camping by a river with his wife. He and I exchange occasional emails, a mix of memories and anecdotes about our lives: his retirement activities and vacations; my domestic routines with an old, ridiculously drafty house, two asthmatic cats riddled with neuroses, three loud, tow-headed children. He warns me about being his Facebook friend. "I'm pretty conservative. You probably won't like it." I struggle to reconcile the kind soul who reached out to his friend's son in an almost fatherly way and the venom he articulates on social media: contempt for the Democratic president and healthcare reform; pro-gun and anti-immigrant rhetoric; words like "freaks" and "fags;" a sharp decibel of contempt. I never comment, but I marvel at the irony of his warmth toward me, an artsy west coast social worker. "I don't even have a fucking sense of humor anymore," he posts, reflecting on the Democratic president. "It's literally just sarcasm and a general hate for the majority of the human population."

Everything I share about Scotty, Ken forwards to his network of Navy buddies. Their common friend Eli makes a comment about "Separation Ritual" that Ken shares:

*When Scotty and I were out drinking he would talk about
his father not caring for him. As a matter of fact, his dad
called him while he was in Japan and wanted to see him.
Scotty told me that he didn't care anything about seeing his
dad.*

The legacy of fatherly estrangement goes deep. The glimpse of
Scotty refusing to see his own father reminded me of the time that I, at
the same age, had refused to see Scotty. The second story I wrote about
him, ten years after he died, is titled "Scotty." At the end of the story, I
recall a time when I was twenty, preparing for a trip back to college in
Chicago. Scotty had insisted over the phone on coming to the airport
to see me off, but I was mad at him. It had been three years since I had
seen him sober. I told him to stay away. What I didn't tell him was that
at the airport I would be saying goodbye to Cass, with whom I was living
for the past year, who had relocated to Baltimore. I had no intention
of coming out to my father. Scotty showed up anyway, catching me in
a long embrace with my boyfriend. Cass quickly retreated. I glared at
Scotty. He didn't know what to say, garbled his words. "I just wanted
to say goodbye" was all I could understand. Later, when I was back in
Chicago, he called. "It's OK," he told me. "It was nice to meet Cass. He
seems like a good man."

I send Ken the link to *The Sun's* webpage, which only shows the
first few paragraphs of the story before the paywall. It doesn't include
anything about being gay or the ending about Scotty seeing me with a
boyfriend.

"Wayne, can you send a copy of the whole article? We all want to
read how the story ends."

Oh my god.

Right before I send off a copy of the magazine in the mail, I think:
This is it. He's going to read the part about me having a boyfriend in

college and not want anything more to do with me. I'm never going to hear from Ken again. Though it's been a short acquaintance, I will miss him.

The next week he writes back: "Scotty was a good and loyal friend and it's bothersome to learn of the way he lived his life. He had everything going for him, looks, personality, family, success, but he chose the comfort of the bottle. It's a sad but common story. When we reminisce, he will always be part of the conversation. Thanks for these articles, Wayne." He passes on another essay to the Navy buddies.

Several times since Scotty died, I have tried to re-watch *Shane*, the 1953 Western that obsessed him, thinking it might contain a clue to who he was, but I would lose interest or fall asleep. After I connect with Ken, I renew my determination. I draw deep on my dormant manliness and force myself to watch the whole thing, awake. Then I understand. Alan Ladd, the actor who portrays the gentleman cowboy, looks like the idealized figure on Ken's Facebook cover. The story of *Shane* offers a logical scaffold for Scotty's life: romanticizing the cool, rugged individualist who doesn't need anyone, who prides himself on avoiding the frilly charms of the domestic front, who brawls and wins, drinks and boasts, then brawls and wins again. Eight-year-old Joey gazes admiringly. His real father, an ordinary rancher in dirt-covered overalls, is so scared in this lawless world.

Who wants an ordinary father, anyway, when you could have a cowboy?

Scotty liked acting out scenes with his friends while they all drank. Scotty knew how to do all the voices, all the intonations, all the gestures. He knew when to pull for an imaginary gun, when to throw a pretend punch. I can still hear it in his voice: Joey's last line, as Shane leaves, riding toward distant purple mountains, "Shane! Come back!"

He was the father. He was the son. He was the cowboy who wouldn't admit he was either.

I wonder if Ken also remembers these acted-out scenes.

Ken and his Navy buddies plan their next reunion in Portland, where coincidentally one of them lives only two miles from my home. Ken writes and asks me to join the three of them. He promises they will regale me with stories of Scotty. Because of the distance and the brevity of the men's visit, my east-coast brothers will not be able to attend, but I promise to share stories.

"What a gift," Eva says at the stove. She is flipping quesadillas for dinner. The kids are watching *Zoboomafoo*. We hear the lemur puppet talking with the two sexy Kratt brothers, grown men, like favorite uncles, who are always dousing water on their tight T-shirts, to titillate all the moms and dads watching with their offspring.

Meet them in person? I am in a panic. I am not sure what to do. I must be different than who I am. I must be manlier. I must blend.

"Of course you have to go," she says when I waffle, stacking the quesadillas on a plate. "Can you give the kids a five-minute warning?"

"I don't know," I say walking into the living room. I try to see myself in that picture of the four of them as young sailors, out drinking on the town, holding cigarettes and bottles of beer, all shit-eating grins and looks of wild masculine abandon in their eyes, and I don't fit. I am the one in front of the camera, in fact, the one at whom they're jeering and laughing.

"You're not eight years old anymore," Grace reminds me when I share my worries. "You can do this."

There is a moment recalled in "Scotty," where one of many therapists I consulted told me that the problem with my father and me was me: my rigidity and judgment. *Go drinking with him*, she admonished.

Meet him where he's at.

The problem was, I didn't drink. I didn't like Coors Light, my father's favorite form of alcohol. I didn't like any beer. After a few sips of any alcohol, I garbled my words. I hated the feeling of incoherence. But I resolved to try.

Scotty took me to his favorite dark bar outside Baltimore, where he introduced me to everyone. "This is my son," he said. "He goes to graduate school in Chicago." When the bartender asked me what I wanted, I said, "Just seltzer water." My father scowled and told me to have a beer. This was the familiar tussle between us: *Pick up the damn bat and get out there on the field and hit the ball. Eyes open.*

To save face, I ordered a white Russian. It has alcohol in it, I rationalized. Vodka even. It was Grace's favorite cocktail. Scotty knew this and eyed me skeptically.

"I'll see if I can find some cream," the bartender offered, raising his eyebrows.

Twenty years later, I still gravitate toward what my friends teasingly call "girlie drinks": margaritas with lime wedges, daiquiris with umbrellas, pink Cosmopolitans, lemon drops in sugar-crusted martini glasses. But if I'm going to join this merry band of brothers, I need to find an alcoholic drink that is respectably masculine. Girlie drinks will not suffice.

Colin takes me around to bars in some of Portland's older hotels to sample different cocktails. He introduces me to Manhattans. He has strong opinions: about premium bourbons, the splash of vermouth, the special drunken cherry that rests in the cone of a perfectly chilled glass. Maybe this could be my manly order? I wonder. Or is the Manhattan now a gay drink? I don't want to drink a gay drink in front of Scotty's friends, I tell him.

"It's a vintage drink," he corrects. He has never worried about how he appears to other men. The high school jock, he has never been bullied. "Maybe it's just a little gay because gay men like antiques."

I quiz my other friends. "Is the Manhattan a gay drink?"

"It's not gay at all," says Scott, and Fred agrees. My straight friends confirm: "It's something from the *Mad Men* era. Something John O'Hara would drink."

I decide on the Manhattan. I have my drink, I will join the party, and I will blend, I announce to Eva.

"Thank God," Eva says, exasperated, relieved again to be a woman. She does not understand the depth of my panic, I know it's ridiculous too, but she also knows I am still stuck in a story with an abrupt ending that doesn't feel right.

Even though Ken invited me for the whole night, I decide to drop by for a short visit after dinner. I don't want to intrude on the intimacy of men who have been friends for over fifty years. I ride my bike to the address—a modest brick 1940's corner house—then circle the block, not quite ready to go in. Oh God. What if I can't keep up with the drinking? What if they're already drunk? What if they think I'm a freaky fag imposter, an offense to all the good fathers and grandfathers and other decent cowboys of the world?

Finally, I knock on the door. No answer. I bang harder. Still nothing. The windows look dark. Is it supposed to be this hard to gain entry to a party? I check the time, then call Ken on his phone.

"Where the hell are you?" he asks, shouting above men's voices.

Did he just yell at me? My heart pounds. "I'm outside," I tell him, voice shaking despite my resolve. "No one's coming to the door."

"Well, the TV's on," he barks. "We can't hear anything."

He lets me in, and I finally shake hands with this friend of my father. He has a strong build, a powerful grip that almost hurts. His face has deep creases. Inside, the two other men from the picture—Jim and Will—are sitting at the dining room table, talking loudly, interrupting each other, while Jim's wife, at the foot of the table, listens and endures. Fox News is blaring in the living room, but no one is watching it. The men interrupt each other so frequently that I strain to decipher what anyone is saying. At one point Will, bald and pale with a faint voice, pushes a manila envelope across the dining room table toward me. "These are for you," he says with a shy smile. His eyeglasses are thick and magnify his weary eyes. Inside are black-and-white photos of the four friends as young men. My presence inspires a series of stories about Scotty: how hard he worked during his Navy days, his bright smile, his charm, his bravado and humor. They do recall playacting scenes from *Shane*. One of them howls in a high-pitched voice, "Shane! Come back!" and I feel a chill in my spine and a weird impulse like I might tear up. "He could make friends with the whole bar," Jim says, voice booming. He is stout like a bear.

I am quietly astounded that these men are so kind to me. They know everything about me, that I'm married and artsy and a therapist and queer and that my father, their friend, and I didn't get along. I wonder what they've said privately about my oddness, our family situation. But the warmth is undeniable.

Mostly this evening I provide an audience for their boisterous reminiscing. Sitting there, just hearing them talk, my body slowly relaxing into my role as witness, I can see Scotty through their eyes. It might have been fun to hang out with him, I think, a radical thought, if I were his friend and not his disappointed son.

They ask me about his last years. Jim wipes away a tear when I share how quickly Scotty died after he was diagnosed with lung cancer. They ask me about my job and my family and whether Scotty ever met his grandchildren. Their clear-sighted, genuine curiosity touches me. Scotty only asked questions because, inebriated, he couldn't recall what I had just told him. I show them photos of Rosie, Louis, and Philip on my phone.

"Beautiful children," Ken says proudly.

"The boys have Scotty's nose," adds Will.

They are grandfathers by proxy, as if a split-off piece of Scotty is lodged inside each of them, feeling the love vicariously. And some of their love of Scotty is rubbing off on me. Of course he would have loved his grandchildren.

The generational divide between us doesn't seem that vast. A monstrous chasm separates an eight-year-old boy and a thirty-three-year-old man, but not so much forty-five-year-old and seventy-year-old men. We all have aging bodies. We all have complaints. There is an underlying melancholy that unifies us: the sense of having made big choices and closed off other possibilities. I catch myself feeling young in their presence, then recognize how laughable that is.

I did not get to know my father at this autumnal stage of life. Suddenly I can imagine that maybe things might have evolved beyond where they were stuck. Maybe there would have been wisdom awaiting him, a different ending, if he had lived. And maybe I can still reach that wisdom, a belated forgiveness, or at least a grace that he and I were both doing our best. When I get home, I will cry with relief. But now, still his well-trained son, I need to hold it together.

Before I know it, it's nine o'clock, and Ken and Will rise from the table. "Well, we'll be getting back to our hotel," Ken announces.

"Already?" I ask.

"We aren't young men anymore," he says with a wink.

But I'm ready to have my Manhattan! I look at the dining room table covered with dessert plates and forks and crumpled napkins and realize: No one is drinking. No one has been drinking all evening.

(When I get home, I will look up all of Ken's old emails. Early on he told me that everyone had had a drinking problem. Everyone, except Scotty, eventually got sober. Somehow, lost in my father's story, I had forgotten.)

Ken and Will put on their coats. They tell me they will walk me to my bike, which is locked to a stop sign beside Jim's house. "Wayne, if Scotty were in a position to see how you turned out," Ken says, smiling broadly, "he'd be beaming with pride."

Jim's wife takes a photograph of the four of us with everyone in the same position as when the guys were out on the town in Okinawa in 1958. Everyone is grinning. And I am in my father's place.

15
—

LOVE SCRABBLE

We are going to play a game of Scrabble: me, Eva, her boyfriend Henry, and Naomi, who is visiting from Chicago, who brought us together so many years ago.

While we are chopping crudité in the kitchen, Naomi asks, "You're sure you want to do this, Wayne? This seems really big."

Why hadn't I met him yet?

At this point Eva has been seeing Henry for almost a year. We had decided to embark on a journey in which our marriage's fate was not certain, casting off the husk of convention, the old rules, rather than abandoning each other. Eva sees Henry one night a week and usually spends the night with him once on the weekend. After the leather bomber jacket made such a splash, he continued to send home gifts with her: an oatmeal-gray Henley shirt, almost new, that didn't fit him anymore; a red wool scarf with tassels at the ends which wasn't to his taste (and wasn't to mine either, but the gesture was sweet); and pricey tickets for both of us to go to the theater when he was out of town. Enough gifts had followed her dates that I often wondered with anticipation, like a child waiting for a parent to return from a business trip: What will he give me next?

What kind of man would be interested in a woman who still lives with her husband?

Henry is ten years older than us. He loves that she has children she adores. Because he has two college-age sons, they talk about the travails of parenting. They enjoy readings at bookstores and nights at the theater, the same activities she and I pursue. He lives with one overweight, standoffish cat in a spotless thirteenth floor condominium downtown. A committed bachelor, he thrives in stretches of quiet and stillness, but he still wants the occasional companionship of a beautiful and intelligent woman. He likes to dote. Just not to live with anyone.

There was a tipping point when I decided I was being ridiculous not meeting him. I had asked Eva, "What made you decide to meet Colin and Elise when we were in church that day? I didn't think you were ready."

"I didn't think I was either," she said sheepishly. "But when I told Henry I was hesitant to meet Colin, he said I wasn't being fair to you."

It cannot be denied: not only is Henry good for her, but he is good for the two of us. I am not going to be a perfect husband, ever. But as we two humans travel alongside each other, I want to try harder, to be embracing, to push against ego. A marital courtesy: I didn't think we would be friends, but it seemed right not to be strangers.

I need to make sure he stays with her.

I am scraping a carrot. Naomi is pulverizing chick peas in the Cuisinart to make hummus. She interrupts my reverie. "Are you going to answer me, Wayne?"

"You bet I can do it," I respond. We pile cut celery, carrots, and cauliflower on the indigo glazed plate that Eva and I got at our ceremony so many years ago. I don't remember who gave it to us.

"You really *aren't* nervous?" Naomi whispers when Eva goes to the door to meet Henry. "I'm nervous and she's not even my wife!"

A small voice inside me wants to shout: *Stop the train! Call off this madness!* But I smile and say: "Yeah, of course. A little."

Naomi hugs me. "It's going to be OK." She has been our friend for over two decades. Over the years we've raised our children together and weathered each other's infidelities and marital crises. Her divorce three years ago—like most crumbling relationships I've witnessed—was splintered by raw emotions, polarities of blame and criticism, an absolute inability to tolerate each other. She and her ex-husband barely talk and still fight over children and parenting and money and how they live their separate lives. I had seen the same thing happen to so many others. I was glad it hadn't happened to us.

Ordinarily I love having new people visit our home. I love the vicarious pleasure of re-seeing it from a newcomer's perspective. Our house is made entirely of clinker bricks. At the turn of the century during the firing process the brick molds placed closest to the fire often cracked, split, or exploded, or became discolored or misshapen. Turn-of-the-century bricklayers layered these imperfect shapes—red, purple, yellow and brown—in even, geometric rows, occasionally interrupting the careful pattern with a broken brick jutting outward. The wooden swing sways in the evening air under the golden glow of the porch light. On the back panel, there is a bronze plate with a quote from Goethe, in German, to honor Eva's father:

> *Was du ererbt von deinen Vätern hast,*
> *Erwirb es, um es zu besitzen.*
> *(What we inherit from our fathers,*
> *To make it ours truly, we must earn.)*

Inside, oak mission-style furniture fills every room: heavy lines, predictable patterns, solidity. Children's fantasy books, Legos, and toppled

Tinker Toy constructions litter the hand-knotted sepia and gold rug. Though we have guests coming to visit tonight, despite our best efforts, it is an unapologetic mess. It does not look like the home of a couple who have an "open relationship." I can't imagine what that couple's home looks like.

The first thing I notice? Henry is bald. He has a stocky football player's build and carries about twenty extra pounds. While he is, I must admit, a good-looking guy—warm brown eyes, an easy smile, a sporty, blue-and-white striped cotton pullover—in terms of looks, he is no rival for me.

"It's good to meet you," he says, grinning, confidently extending his hand, but neither of us grips firmly. Eva and Naomi stand off to the side to witness this encounter between the husband and the boyfriend. It feels illegal. "I hear you like Scrabble," he says.

"Love scrabble," I correct him. About most things, I like to tell myself, I am not competitive. "Really?" Eva once asked, eyebrows raised. Except words, I say. I want to spell and use them flawlessly. In my home office, near my desk, I keep a fifteen-pound Oxford English Dictionary, on permanent loan from Scott, who has no room for it. I love the detailed definitions, fancy pronunciation keys, elaborate etymologies, obsessive nuance. I love the magnifying glass.

"So how long have you lived in Portland?" Henry asks. He has a jolly quality, an effusiveness that makes me think either that this is going to be OK, that I will be able to like him, or that he is a big phony. We open the tattered Scrabble box and turn over tiles. We make what sounds like small talk but to me each statement feels like a feat. Eva is in the kitchen, pouring wine. Paul Simon's "You're the One" plays in the background: *You're the one/You broke my heart.*

"We moved to Oregon twelve years ago," I say. "We wanted to live someplace beautiful." Immediately I think that I have violated the terms of some new etiquette, that my language is odd. Eva comes into the dining room with two glasses of red wine—we're drinking Côtes du Rhône these days—hands one to Henry, then one to me. Then she sits beside him on the opposite side of the table. Naomi, the loyal ally, sits beside me. Suddenly, I am looking at Henry and Eva. They look good together. They are the *we* at this moment. Theirs is the common story evolving over time. *The night we played Scrabble with Eva's husband.* My *we* statement sounds disjointed, possessive, out of place.

So I vow for tonight: No more *we* statements.

Two other words floating in my mind right now, as I spy Eva touching Henry's back, as he says something in a low voice that only she can hear: *husband* and *wife*. Which technically, legally, still apply to us. From the time she and I were married, neither of us liked those words. They smacked of associations that never fit us. *Wife* sounded like Donna Reed in *It's a Wonderful Life*. *Husband* sounded like any one of a parade of television heroes: deep-voiced, unflappable men in narrow suits, brown or navy blue or gray, arriving home at the end of the day with pronouncements; handy men with toolboxes, dirty overalls, and a fountain of top-down advice.

For years we insisted on saying "partner" or "spouse," but everyone always called us "husband" and "wife." It was tiresome always to be correcting people. "When you said 'partner,' I just thought you were gay," one colleague, an older woman, told me. I wasn't sure how to respond.

Everyone chooses seven tiles and begins to study.

"Jesus," Henry mutters. His broad shoulders hunch over the wooden tray of alphabet letters with intense focus. "Look at all these u's."

"Am I allowed to put these back," Naomi asks, "if I have four vowels?"

"But that's not a real rule," Eva mumbles, not looking up.

"I think it's a Midwest rule, though," Naomi replies, "and I'm from the Midwest."

"Oh, please, Naomi," I say, pulling out the dog-eared directions to prove she is wrong. For a moment I am grateful for a game with rules so clear, they are almost etched in my unconscious.

Henry plays Scrabble with zeal. He is a rigorous, strategic player, always thinking several moves into the future. I wonder if he has read one of those books on competitive Scrabble-playing that I am always intending to read but they look so boring. Before long he seems to be stealing every double word score. *Christ, how did he get the Z and the Q? Is zedonk really a word? Honestly? Where's the dictionary?* A secret thought surfaces in my mind, the first of two clear, strong truths that will occur to me this evening:

I must win this damn game.

While I wait for Henry to lay his tiles, I steal glances at the two of them. I see her through his eyes. I see her fresh. Like me, she is now forty-five. She still has those high cheekbones, that tilted nose that fits her face perfectly. Sometimes, when I am bored at a party, I compare Eva to the other middle-aged women in the room and I usually think she is the most beautiful. I'm not idealizing her. I know she has aged. But somehow, when I see her, she is many people layered onto one; young and old selves all at once: the blond undergraduate, tanned, just returned from back-packing in Europe, in a polka dot black and pink tank-top; the graduate student in the library, fretting over *Rules for Radicals*; the advocate rushing out after midnight to the emergency room to help a teenager whose date ended terribly.

I make jokes. I tease Eva about putting down measly two-letter words. She never cares about winning. I'm not sure she even likes Scrabble, but she's played it for years because I like it. I lean over and help Naomi spell *sinew*, which scores well and gets a sarcastic howl from the onlookers. I gawk when Henry uses six letters at one turn.

Shit.

For better or worse, the habit of being a psychotherapist has given me this gift, which is sometimes a curse, of putting dark feelings and petty, irrational jealousies at a distance. Of putting my best self forward at all costs. I take a deep breath and repeat the secret mantra.

I must win this damn game.

Maybe because I'm not putting out any awkward vibes, maybe because I'm seeming so casual with the situation, Henry puts his arms around Eva's shoulders. He rubs her back with encouragement when she complains she has nothing but t's. *OK, this is hard. I don't think I want to watch this guy.* After each turn, he is winning the game by just a few points. *How the hell is this happening to me?*

I imagine I see a bead of sweat on his bald head.

An amazing construction of chance, our Scrabble board crowds up with words, building its own dense contingencies, tight squeezes, inconveniences, and traps. We study it, looking for openings and clever ways to adapt. Someone inevitably mentions the elusive dream of "opening up the board." Suddenly it hits me, something I've always known, because less enthusiastic players complained, a fact which has never bothered me before tonight:

THIS. GAME. GOES. ON. FOREVER.

Henry's been in the house for two long hours now. Everyone at the table is laughing. I imagine Naomi, the skeptic, thinking, *What a surprisingly successful social event!* Although my emotional reserves are running low, my façade remains strong. Or so I think. He and I are playing neck-and-neck, clearly the only players interested in winning. I am five points behind him when I take the last tile. The end is in sight.

I get a W. An auspicious letter; the first letter of my name. I am feeling golden, jostling my seven tiles, scanning the board for a high points opening. Everything is salvageable if I can win this game. And then, I see it: an unbelievable, once-in-a-lifetime, eleventh-hour word; a word that just reaches a *triple word score* to take me over Henry's lead.

WHORE

I stare at it in giddy amazement mixed with shock. *Triple fucking word score. This never happens.* All I can hear is the patient clicking of tiles on the other players' wooden racks. I know Henry has his eye on the same triple word score spot. *There's no fucking way you're going to get it, buddy.*

Staring at my prize word, I lie. "God, it's hard to find *anything* at this stage of the game." I wonder how much I want to win.

How will everyone react? Clearly, WHORE is just the luck of the draw. Certainly it's no message I'm intending to send anyone. And, even though it's ugly, it's a valid word that'll score a whopping fifty-four points. *Fifty-four points!* In games with other players I've laid down FUCKER and ASSHOLE and CUNT without thinking twice, if it racked up a superior score. Who cared what anyone thought then?

And yet...

Naomi is losing terribly and doesn't like Scrabble anyway. She yawns. "Do you need help?" she says sarcastically, leaning over. I jerk the tiles away from her gaze.

"I'm OK."

"Do you want to pass?" Eva offers, not caring who wins or loses at this point in the night. I remember that she's on the same sensitive foreign ground as I am.

His brow furrowed in deep concentration, Henry studies his seven tiles. He's not done with me yet.

The ticking of the clock gets louder, more insistent on bedtime. I'm using up the good graces of my fellow players. Is it timidity or a sudden surfeit of niceness? Is it the worry that someone might make an awkward joke? Or my alertness, on this odd, untrodden path we've taken, to the potential for hurt? (Henry defends the lady's honor and yells, *What the hell do you mean by* that *word, Wayne?!* Eva bolts from the room. *I should have known you couldn't handle it! It's* your *fault we're in this situation!* Naomi of course follows her. *I can't believe you would imply something so coarse!*) All evening no one has talked about the strangeness of this troupe of game-players. This word seems to violate an unspoken rule. We can all play a civilized game of Scrabble as long as no one calls attention to one fact: Eva is married to Wayne but dating Henry.

Staring at the tiles, I shake my head, rattling all the words I've absorbed over my life, and have a different thought: Maybe I'm reluctant to put down this word because it has no place here. It's obsolete. We can cast it out of the dictionary, a legacy that has nothing to do with us.

"All right," I say, laying down four tiles.

WORE. Past tense. Like *worn down*. Like a costume I put on in another life.

The word just misses the triple word score and puts me a mere seven points ahead of Henry. The game moves to Eva who lays three letters. Then at the end Henry, the competitive cuss, pulls out the punches with a twenty-five-pointer, and I lose by five. The Scrabble game is over.

It is almost midnight. I clean up the Scrabble board—it's a West Coast rule that the loser cleans up the board—then stand like I'm going to leave. We still have the same rule: no romantic partner spends the night in the family home. Before Henry even arrived, I had decided that the proper etiquette for a husband in my situation was to exit first and let them say a private goodbye.

"I need to turn in now."

"It was good to meet you, Wayne," Henry says, getting up, shaking my hand. This time it's a sincere, strong grip. Eva stands beside him.

I look him in the eye, the Scrabble loss fading. "Thank you for all the generous gifts," I say. "I forgot to say that earlier."

"You're very welcome, sir." He adds, "Tonight was special for me."

"It was good to meet you too," I say, nodding. "I really mean it." He not only met the guy she lives with; he spent three hours with him, something I imagine few good men would do. Inside I feel a glimmer of confidence, on this path that is forming, that Eva and I are not lost, that we have in fact achieved something.

"I'm heading to bed." I say it to everyone but looking just at Eva, who smiles. When I take a last glance of her, I see her tonight and at other ages: the weeping thirty-year-old, cursing a pregnancy test yet again; the laughing crying mother being handed baby Rosie in a hospital room; Eva at my side, two toddlers in hand and baby in a backpack, on the long ascent to Mirror Lake; that last dance at Breitenbush, when we danced together to Earth, Wind, and Fire, and I did not think I could tell her that I did not want to leave, ever. She moves toward me and gives me a hug and whispers in my ear, "You were great. Thank you."

Another thought comes to mind, the second clear, strong truth of this evening:

I am devoted to her.

"It was fun everyone." I smile back at Eva. "Good night."

I hear clinking in the kitchen as Naomi puts dishes in the dish-washer. Without looking back, I walk up the stairs. I kiss each of our sleeping children—*good night, Rosie, good night, Louis, good night, Philip*—pass Eva's dark room, the door slightly parted, then head to my bedroom, where a new book awaits, and softly close my door.

EPILOGUE

—

THE HIKE TO MIRROR LAKE

Once upon a time, there was a father, a mother, and three children who went together on a long walk in a dark forest.

"Is this a good idea?"

Church is over. The complaining has subsided. The children are buckled in the minivan, holding granola bars and orange juice boxes, munching and sipping. The plan is to listen to Jim Dale read *Harry Potter and the Deathly Hallows*. The whole family has been nervous all summer, waiting for the final book to come out. At this point we have been living in Harry Potter's world for the entirety of their little lives.

We will take Highway 26 toward Mount Hood, headed for the Mirror Lake trailhead. It is a simple ascent on a well-marked trail through dark firs and maples, a good hike for children.

"Dad, I think she's going to let Harry die," Rosie, the worrier, states, voice trembling. We have been having this conversation, with mounting consternation, all summer. "I don't think he's going to make it."

"We have to listen and find out," insists Louis, the not-worrier, impatient.

"I hate Voldemort," pipes up Philip.

I whisper to Eva, "Kassel said it wasn't too awful, right?" Kassel is our fifteen-year-old neighbor, a brilliant student, the babysitter who knows everything about Harry Potter and *The Lord of the Rings* and hobbits and elves and shape shifters. The night *Harry Potter and the Deathly Hallows* was released, she purchased it at Broadway Books, the neighborhood bookstore, at a midnight release and read it, all 750 pages, straight through until dawn. We waited for the Jim Dale CD. Now we are near the end of the epic, the final bloody confrontation between seventeen-year-old Harry and ancient, hissing Voldemort.

We cruise through the outskirts of Portland, through Wood Village and Gresham, the snowy peak of Mount Hood in the distance. Then we are in a wide, fir-lined expanse of valley. As we ascend the winding highway, the view of the mountain disappears. We cannot see the mountain anymore because we are on it.

The Deatheaters have invaded Hogwarts, our hero's beloved School of Witchcraft and Wizardry. Wounded students and bleeding teachers lie in the blasted ruins. Suddenly, the villain, hissing like a sick tenor snake, can be heard by all, like the voice of a contemptuous God:

> *'...I shall wait for one hour in the Forbidden Forest. If, at the end of that hour, you have not come to me, have not given yourself up, then battle recommences. This time, I shall enter the fray myself, Harry Potter, and I shall find you...'*

The terror of Harry Potter's story—above and beyond the fantastic beasts and hideous monsters he encounters—is the burgeoning aloneness of this orphan, the way his journey narrows into a solitary quest.

"Oh no!" Rosie cries. "They're losing the fight."

Eva pauses the CD for a moment. Philip is dozing in his car seat.

"Harry's never gone into the Forbidden Forest by himself," Louis observes.

"I think we should stop listening," Rosie says. In addition to debating the likelihood of a happy ending all summer, she has reported several nightmares.

"Rosie, get a hold of yourself!" Louis commands. "Mom, put the CD back on. I need to know how this thing ends. I've been waiting my whole damn life."

"Language!"

"Do you want me to tell you what Kassel said about the ending?" Eva asks Rosie. They do not realize that we would not let them listen to the story unless we had some reassurance about the ending. *I shall wait one hour in the Forbidden Forest...* "Would that help?"

"No!" they both yell in unison.

We are snaking along the side of the mountain. "We're almost at the trailhead, anyway," I say. "Let's take a break for a little while and come back to the story on our way back to town, after everyone relaxes for a bit."

Eva plugs in another CD—the familiar voice of James Taylor—and the mood in the van relaxes with his reassurances. *I'll come running, to see you again.*

At the trailhead, the two awake children leap out of the van and run to the narrow wooden bridge over the rushing water of a creek. Eva follows. I unhook Philip from his car seat and try to rouse him. "We're at the trailhead," I say. "Will you walk with us, little guy?" And he puts his arms out, like he did as a toddler, and I pick him up and carry him across the bridge. His head perks up at the sound of the rushing water, the feel of the crisp air, the clean sharp green smell of pine. After I enter the forest, he squirms in my arms, I put him down, and he runs behind his brother and sister. There is only one path to Mirror Lake and they enjoy the freedom to run ahead of us, knowing we follow behind them.

"Should we just tell them that Harry lives?" Eva asks.

"Louis doesn't want to know before he hears the story," I say. "He likes the suspense. Rosie might calm down after she's had a break."

(Later that day, when we return to the minivan, we will listen to the last chapter of Harry Potter on the way home and learn, of course, that he survives. He grows up. He marries his sweetheart Ginnie. In the last scene Harry and Ginnie, now parents themselves, take Albus, their son, to the train station to begin his Hogwarts adventure. Though the words on the page will stop, we will have this illusion that the characters continue in some universe that hasn't yet been written down. This is the way that stories unfurl, finite concoctions within a world of painfully infinite possibilities. Exquisite anticipation. Always the question hovering over the last pages: will it satisfy? And, within the shapes set up by the writer, what will it be like to lose the story, to experience its end?)

But now Eva and I walk side-by-side on the same dusty path. Within fifty feet of the trailhead, the forest grows shadowy and dark. Stray threads of yellow sunlight slice through the canopy of firs. Switchbacks keep us zigzagging up the side of the steep hill. We are mulling over the church service, the strange glimpse of Linné's life, the surprise meeting with Colin and Elise, our fellow travelers.

"I think Linné's relationship is breaking up," Eva says. "I don't think we're supposed to know that about our therapist."

"No," I agree. "That woman looked furious."

"I'm sad for Linné," Eva says.

"She really helped us."

"We still haven't paid her!"

"How would we calculate the cost?" I wonder aloud. "I'm not even sure what we were doing. Was it magic?"

The zigzags feel never-ending and steep. The path is littered with a carpet of brown needles. Throughout the forest we see fallen trees at different angles: some flat on the ground, others slanted, caught in the branches of the living, some chain-sawed into pieces. Our bodies move through the cool shadowy space, breath quickening, sweat rising on our skin. Our conversation is outside the children's hearing.

"So it's interesting to meet Colin," Eva says. "I couldn't imagine what he'd be like. Up close he looks like you."

"No, he doesn't."

"Same height, or nearly; same sandy hair color; both blue-eyed. Similar build."

I bristle, then shrug. "He's more muscular."

"Hmmm," she says, which means she doesn't agree.

"I'm glad I met him with Elise," she says. "I think it was easier to see them together."

"I'm glad too, now that it's happened," I say.

In the distance, Rosie, Louis, and Philip cross a section of the path without any tree covering. On a sheer hillside, there is a cascade of white-gray boulders, a narrow gravel path cut through them. The sun reflects hot on the stones. The sky is even blue. In the distance there is a view of wavy fir-lined hills.

"You actually don't want to be in a full-time romantic relationship with him, do you?"

"No," I say. "Neither of us is available that way."

She looks puzzled. My mind runs in such endless irrational circles, wondering about the threat Henry poses. I forget that there's probably a similar cycle threading through hers. "What do you think you do want?" she asks.

I don't want a husband or a lover. Even as a young man, when I had had boyfriends, I hadn't wanted them in any conventional way. There is no word in the English language to explain my desire—even D. H. Lawrence had to borrow an ancient word from another language—which is to have a kind of body-friendship with another man, a forbidden-ness of tenderness between this-close almost-brother fellow travelers. This is not a feeling that leads to marriage. It is its own thing.

"I want to be with you," I say. "But not I guess like we thought we'd be married. Not anymore. I don't want my commitment to you to be measured by sexual fidelity. What do you want? Do you want this?"

Eva pauses. "I guess...yes."

"Why did you hesitate?"

"It's still hard," she says. "I mean, I still struggle when you go out with Colin. It's hard to be different from other people, from family and friends, from other marriages. We're outsiders."

"I know." This is one of those times I know the expression on my face looks hurt, because I feel hurt, but I am trying desperately to look a different way, which just compounds the obviousness of hurt. There is a part of me, deep in the cells that make me, even after everything that has happened, that still wants to be the perfect husband.

I will never be the perfect husband.

"What I can say is this," she says. "I do adore you." She offers her hand to me and I take it.

We are not alone in the dark forest. We are on separate journeys streaming together, side by side. We follow our children, who know the path, who love that it leads to only one bright place they are sure to find without our guidance. In the distance they run and call out to each other: "It's here, Mommy!" "We made it!" "You can see the mountain-top, Dad!"

"It really isn't a surprise that we've ended up like this."

"I couldn't imagine this possibility when we got married," I say.

The end of the trail opens to a wide meadow. Mount Hood rises magisterially in the background, so close we can feel the chill of its snowy surface on our faces. Its image ripples on the surface of a lake.

Philip and Louis are skimming stones across the clear still water, trying to make them skip. Rosie is studying a tadpole in the shallow edge.

Eva and I rest on a warm boulder. Why is it, every time we burst onto this view, which we've seen so many times, in so many seasons, it surprises us? The world formed this mountain and its rippling image through the happenstance of geologic forces: shifting tectonic plates, moving glaciers, avalanches, volcanic explosions; a rumble of terror leading to this serenity. It has gathered all accidents into this beautiful almost-symmetry: the real thing and its trembling visual echo, shifting, imperfect, in the sky-painted lake.

ACKNOWLEDGMENTS

—

It is a dubious thing for a man to tell a story about a marriage gone awry. When I was writing through the dark days of the pandemic, my friends in an eighteen-month workshop offered through Corporeal Writing in Portland, Oregon sustained me: Amy Bond, Kristin Brown, Maraya Karena, Kimberly Knutsen, Sarah Leamy, and Emma Pattee. These extraordinary women helped me to be my best, most compassionate self when writing about marital struggles. Our brilliant teacher, Lidia Yuknavitch, mind and heart without end, inspired us with humor and authenticity and her oceans-deep faith that art saves lives. She transformed my thinking about story-telling and the role of writers in the world.

With grace and equanimity, Diane Goettel at Black Lawrence Press was the perfect hands-on editor for a jittery debut author. Deep gratitude to Mitchell Waters, Rayhané Sanders, and Brian Benson for sensitive editorial insights. Jay Ponteri of Literary Arts was generous to a fault, reading the manuscript at an early stage and helping me articulate the questions at the heart of the narrative. Martha Gies was direct with me in ways that were both astute and sometimes frighteningly to-the-point, for which I am thankful. Editors Andrew Snee, Laura Demanski, Livia Kent, William O'Sullivan, and Pam Wells helped shepherd chapters that appeared in journals. From the beginning Mary Ruth has offered steadfast support building smart-looking Word documents.

Lance Cleland and Jeannie Vanasco offered warm encouragement during a winter retreat on the Oregon coast with Tin House, where I also befriended Christie Tate, inspiring role model.

All the way back to my kindergarten teacher Mrs. Morris at Toby Farms Elementary School, who really understood separation anxiety, I owe a heartfelt debt to the many humans who devote their lives to teaching, especially the English teachers. Two in particular transformed the ways I think about literature and queerness and identity: Lauren Berlant, my professor in a life-changing class, "Feminist Theory and Practice," at The University of Chicago, and Richard McCann, my mentor in the MFA program at The American University. Both died, too young, in 2021.

I am grateful to the University of Chicago Class of 1986 for sharing nostalgia about the Hyde Park years through our social media forum.

The setting of "Once More to Breitenbush" no longer exists. While I was writing, the Lionshead Fire devastated the old growth forest by the river, causing ripples of grief to many for whom Breitenbush was a treasured touchstone. Although I have never met them, I am grateful to the brave firefighters—Neil Clasen, Hollywood Dan, Tim McDevitt, Jordan Pollack, and Erik Wennstrom—who, at great peril, protected the land so that it could be rebuilt and remain a healing place for future generations.

I cannot think of anything I have written in the last thirty years that Benjamin Chambers, friend since my undergraduate days, hasn't graced with his sharp intellect, wit, exceptional taste, and sensitivity.

Deep love from the bottom of my beating heart to: Coleen Alexander, Mary Jo Barrett, Jim Bogue, Hipolito Rafael Chacon, Lynn Collins, Tim Collins, Stephen Correll, Rob Cowie, Ken Crowley, Darcy Daniels, Kassel Galaty, Jonathan Hutchison, Michael Kohler, Tori Lopez, Lauren Mac Neill, Al Marks, Jack Mitchell, Sam Portaro,

Kathy Ruberg, Grace Scott, Michael Scott, Rick Scott, Carolyn Shapiro, Joan Stewart, Elizabeth Thielman, Julian Thielman, Miles Thielman, Miriam Thielman, Bob Nystrom, Pete Wilson, Will Woods, and Harry Zweben.

Over the years my three children have figured in much of my writing, remaining loving and tolerant and good natured while also cueing me to their boundaries. To them I want to say: I had the challenge of growing up with a father constrained by his secrets. You don't have that problem. I don't know for sure if this is preferable. I hope it is. I love the three of you very much.

In critique groups, when discussing memoir, writers refer to the author's character in the third person, which prevents a craft discussion from descending into group therapy. During the writing of this memoir, my partner, for whom we chose the name Eva, often rocked with me on our porch swing while I talked in the third person about difficult times in our marriage as if we were characters in a book we'd read together. (That must have been weird. I'm sorry.) There would be no story to tell, at least not a very interesting one, if she had not made imaginative choices with me about our life together. Although this story, our story, reflects the limits of my perspective, without her patience, fearlessness, expansive love, and big beautiful soul I could not have written it.

CREDITS

—

1. Baldwin, James. *Giovanni's Room*. Vintage Books. Copyright © 1956 and renewed 1984 by James Baldwin. Reprinted with the permission of The Permissions Company LLC on behalf of the James Baldwin Estate.

2. Brightman, Sarah. "Time To Say Goodbye" from *Hymm*. Village Studios (Los Angeles), 2018. (Original lyrics of "Con te partirò" by Lucio Quarantotto, translated by Sophia Alexandra Hall for ClassicFM.com: https://www.classicfm.com/artists/andrea-bocelli/time-to-say-goodbye-lyrics-meaning/)

3. The Communards. "Don't Leave Me This Way" (lyrics by Kenneth Gamble, Leon Huff and Cary Gilbert) from *The Communards*. Sigma Sound (New York City), 1986.

4. cummings, e.e. "i carry your heart with me (i carry it in" from *Complete Poems: 1904-1962*, edited by George J. Firmage. Copyright 1952, (c) 1980, 1991 by the Trustees for the E. E. Cummings Trust. Used by permission of Liveright Publishing Corporation.

5. Ellman, Richard. *Oscar Wilde*. Alfred A. Knopf, 1988.

6. Etheridge, Melissa. "Come to My Window." Words and Music by Melissa Etheridge. Copyright © 1993 MLE Music All Rights. Administered by BMG Rights. Management (US) LLC. All Rights Reserved. Used by Permission. Reprinted by Permission of Hal Leonard LLC

7. Forster, E.M. *Aspects of the Novel*. Harcourt Brace & Company, 1955.

8. Lawrence, D. H. *Women in Love*. Penguin Books, 1976.

9. Lorde, Audre. *The Cancer Journals*. Penguin Books, 1980.

10. Lorde, Audre. *Zami: A New Spelling of My Name*. The Crossing Press, 1982.

11. Loving, Jerome. *Walt Whitman: The Song of Himself*. University of California Press, 1999.

12. Moffat, Wendy. *A Great Unrecorded History: A New Life of E. M. Forster*. Farrar, Straus and Giroux, 2010.

13. Paley, Grace. "Debts," "A Conversation with my Father," and "Living" in *Grace Paley: The Collected Stories*. Farrar, Straus and Giroux, 1994.

14. Paley, Grace. "My Father Addresses Me on the Facts of Old Age" from *Here and Somewhere Else: Stories and Poems*. The Feminist Press, 2007.

15. Rich, Adrienne. "Twenty-One Love Poems" from *The Dream of a Common Language: Poems 1974-1977* by Adrienne Rich. Copyright © 1978 by W. W. Norton & Company, Inc. Used by permission of W. W. Norton & Company, Inc.

16. Rowling, J.K. *Harry Potter and the Deathly Hallows*. Bloomsbury, 2014.

17. Schaefer, Jack. *Shane*. Clarion Books, 1976.

18. Simon, Paul. "You're the One." *You're the One*. The Hit Factory (New York City), 2000.

19. Taylor, James. "You've Got a Friend." *Mud Slide Slim and the Blue Horizon*. Crystal Studios (Los Angeles) 1971. Original lyrics by Carole King.

20. White, E.B. "Once More to the Lake" in *Essays of E.B. White*. Harper Perennial, 1999.

21. Whitman, Walt. *Leaves of Grass*. Penguin Books, 1984.
22. Wilde, Oscar. "Ballad of Reading Gaol" (1898) from *The Complete Works of Oscar Wilde: Volume 1: Poems and Poems in Prose*. Oxford University Press, 2019.
23. Several chapters of this memoir appeared, in altered form, in journals: "Ghost Triangle" (*The Sun*, 1998); "Call Your Deadbeat Dad" (*The Sun,* 2010); "Botching the Wedding" (*The University of Chicago Magazine*, 2015); "Once More to Breitenbush" (*Timberline Review*, 2016); "Scotty" (*The Sun*, 2017); and "Love Scrabble" (*The Psychotherapy Networker*, 2021).

©Teresa Dalsager

WAYNE SCOTT'S writing has appeared in *The Sun*, *Poets & Writers*, *Huffington Post*, and *The Oregonian*, among others. His *New York Times* essay, "Two Open Marriages in One Small Room" was adapted for the Modern Love podcast. He writes frequently for *The Psychotherapy Networker*. He is a writer, psychotherapist, and teacher and lives with his partner in Portland, Oregon.